The Comprehension of Jokes

The Comprehension of Jokes consolidates and develops the tradition of analysing jokes, by defining a framework of concepts which are suited to capturing what happens when someone understands a joke. The collection of concepts presented improves upon past work on joke analysis, outlining a simple model of text comprehension which supports all the assumptions necessary for a model of joke-understanding. This proposed framework encompasses and integrates a relatively wide range of disparate factors, including incongruity, superiority, and impropriety. Written by an expert in the field of humour, it provides a conceptual basis which will help to map out the landscape of joke comprehension.

The book draws on past suggestions in many areas, primarily philosophy, psychology, linguistics, and artificial intelligence. Current theories of how people understand non-humorous texts offer some important ideas, such as the need for representations of differing beliefs about the world, or the way that predictions may occur during the understanding of a text. The framework improves the clarity and coherence of some existing theoretical proposals and combines these ideas into a well-defined way of describing how a person understands a newly-encountered joke. All this is illustrated using typical textual jokes, some analysed in considerable detail. The book enables hypotheses about why jokes are funny to be stated more precisely and compared more easily, and should contribute to the development of a fuller cognitive model of joke comprehension.

The Comprehension of Jokes will be of great interest to academics and postgraduate students in humour research, as well as those in disciplines like linguistics, psychology, and cognitive science who wish to explore the field of jokes and humour.

Graeme Ritchie began his academic career in artificial intelligence in the 1970s, and for the past twenty-five years has increasingly concentrated on research into humour.

The Comprehension of Jokes

A Cognitive Science Framework

Graeme Ritchie

Routledge
Taylor & Francis Group
LONDON AND NEW YORK

First published 2018
by Routledge

2 Park Square, Milton Park, Abingdon, Oxfordshire OX14 4RN
52 Vanderbilt Avenue, New York, NY 10017

Routledge is an imprint of the Taylor & Francis Group, an informa business

First issued in paperback 2020

British Library Cataloguing-in-Publication Data
A catalogue record for this book is available from the British Library

Library of Congress Cataloging-in-Publication Data
Names: Ritchie, Graeme D., author.
Title: The comprehension of jokes : a cognitive science framework / Graeme Ritchie.
Description: Abingdon, Oxon ; New York : Routledge, 2018.
Identifiers: LCCN 2018005961 (print) | LCCN 2018016766 (ebook) |
ISBN 9781351232753 (E-book) | ISBN 9780815378280 (hardback) |
ISBN 9781351232753 (ebk)
Subjects: LCSH: Wit and humor–Philosophy. | Wit and humor–Psychological aspects.
Classification: LCC PN6149.P5 (ebook) | LCC PN6149.P5 R57 (print) | DDC 801/.957–dc23
LC record available at https://lccn.loc.gov/2018005961

ISBN: 978-0-8153-7828-0 (hbk)
ISBN: 978-0-367-48883-3 (pbk)

Typeset in Bembo
by Out of House Publishing

Contents

Preface

This book brings together themes that I have been developing over several years, principally in a small number of published works (Ritchie, 1999, 2000, 2002, 2004, 2006, 2009, 2014). In order to make this new text as self-contained as possible, it has been necessary to repeat some material from these previous publications, but this has been kept to a minimum, resulting in frequent self-citations to places where the fuller arguments may be found. The current book shares much of the motivation and assumptions of Ritchie (2004), but it is not essential to have read the earlier book prior to tackling this one. Those who have read the older book will find some of the topics in the current volume familiar.

The topics discussed in the book are illustrated with short example texts. Most of these are jokes which have been taken from various sources, primarily joke books and academic publications on humour (not necessarily where the jokes were first created). These sources are acknowledged either in the surrounding text or in citations directly attached to the items. A very small number of the jokes have no attribution, as they have been reconstructed by memory from long-past publications or conversations. A few of the example texts are labelled as 'constructed', as they have been created here to illustrate particular points.

I would like to thank Kees van Deemter and Chris Venour for providing helpful comments on drafts of this book. The diagrams were prepared by Illugraphics.co.uk.

Chapter 1

The programme of work

1.1 What this book is about

This book starts from the following assumptions:

- The quest to find an empirically accurate theory of humour is still in progress.
- Jokes, and in particular verbally expressed jokes, are a very useful testing ground for developing and testing ideas about how humour works.
- It would be extremely helpful to have a detailed account of joke comprehension (the process of 'getting' a joke).
- To be able to describe joke comprehension properly, we need a set of concepts which are pertinent to that process but which also connect to more general models in related areas such as text understanding.

The central task we will pursue, over the course of a dozen or so chapters, is the fulfilment of the need indicated in that final point. Our goal is to develop a repertoire of related constructs which are suitable for giving a theoretically sound and precisely specified description of what goes on as someone understands a textual joke.

We will not, however, offer a full theory of jokes, or of humour more generally. Although we will examine the process by which someone can make sense of a joke, we will not attempt to give precise answers to the questions 'what makes a text a joke?' or 'what makes a joke funny?' Instead, our aim is to make steps towards answering these two questions by consolidating existing ideas about joke mechanisms into a overall framework for talking about joke comprehension, which may in the longer term contribute to a cognitive model of how jokes are understood.

1.2 Cognitive science and humour

This volume can be seen as based in cognitive science (not to be confused with cognitive psychology), a field that is inherently interdisciplinary, and that is summed up well in this passage:

> Cognitive science, the interdisciplinary study of cognitive phenomena, has its origins in philosophy and can be viewed as the empirical pursuit of age-old questions in the philosophy of mind. ... Cognitive scientists study a broad range of cognitive phenomena, including attention, perception, memory, language, learning, and reasoning. ... The field draws from a number of disciplines including philosophy, linguistics, psychology, computer science, anthropology, sociology, and the neurosciences.
>
> (Coulson & Matlock, 2003)

(Interestingly, much the same could be said about quests to devise a theory of humour.)

This means that we will be drawing on ideas from a number of fields, particularly psychology, linguistics, philosophy and artificial intelligence, but we do not aim to deliver what some of those disciplines might regard as customary. There will be no new experiments, no detailed linguistic descriptions, no novel philosophical insights and no algorithms. Instead, the aim is to integrate our various borrowings into a conceptual whole that better underpins a central area of humour research.

1.3 Towards a theory of humour

Over recent decades, research on humour has grown considerably. Much of this work has been directed towards what might be called 'theories *about* humour', in that it aims to characterise the role and function of humour in some wider context, such as the cultural, social or political setting. For example, these studies have cast light on questions such as 'what is humour used for?', 'what are the broader consequences of particular types of humour?', or 'which social groups use which kinds of humour?' (Davies, 1990; Krikmann & Laineste, 2009; Kuipers, 2006; Ruch, Hofmann, & Platt, 2015). The expansion of this type of investigation may be partly because of the strengthening, in the late twentieth century, of the social sciences, which provided well-tested methods for examining these wider questions, along with an increasing community of scholars interested in such issues.

In comparison, there has been less work on constructing 'theories *of* humour'; that is, descriptions of the internal workings of humorous situations and artefacts, aimed at explaining why these entities lead to amusement. This is not to say that there has been no work on the mechanisms of humour, as will become apparent in later chapters when we review, adopt, build upon or criticise various strands of research. Nevertheless, attempts to elucidate the underlying causes of humour have been, by comparison with the more social and cultural studies, less abundant. A cursory inspection of articles appearing in the *Humor* journal and of presentations at the annual conference of the

International Society for Humor Studies gives the clear impression that not every humour researcher is focused on the construction of detailed, precise, abstract models of the causal mechanisms of humour.

Although 'theories about humour' are important and provide real insights into the use of humour, they are not the context for this book. Instead, we focus on the road towards a 'theory of humour': the development of descriptive or explanatory accounts of what gives rise to humorous effects. The plan is to show how some existing ideas from the research literature on humour can be combined in a consistent fashion to create an integrated account of one important type of humorous artefact – the textual joke – in a way that provides a foundation for further systematic investigation.

1.4 Joke comprehension and joke analysis

In building our framework for describing joke comprehension, we will draw upon two kinds of previous work: research into text comprehension with no particular emphasis on humour, and past work on the mechanisms of jokes. The former will guide the development of a general processing apparatus, and the latter will indicate which facilities might need to be included to handle jokes.

The previous work on jokes largely belongs to a long tradition which we will call *joke analysis*. Although no methodological guidelines have been explicitly agreed for this activity, there is a common pattern to such work. The joke analyst considers a relatively small number of jokes, taken from suitable sources such as joke books, and argues that the humorous effect of a joke is caused by its having certain abstract properties. That is, some theoretical entities, which may not be directly observable, are posited as underlying the joke and as being critical to the way in which the joke results in amusement. Such hypotheses are typically substantiated by argument, as is commonplace in philosophy or traditional linguistics, rather than by experimental procedures.

There is a sense in which an analysis of a joke is an informal and abbreviated description of joke comprehension. Published analyses usually do not give a full commentary on the comprehension process, instead merely highlighting one or two aspects which the authors see as crucial to the humour. Nevertheless, these analyses make certain assumptions about the underlying text comprehension process, either tacitly or by remarks in passing, allusions or hints.

In pursuing our goal of a more detailed description of joke comprehension, one of our main strategies will be to develop ideas from existing joke analyses. We will attempt to fill in the implicit assumptions of past work on jokes, guided as much as possible by theoretical proposals for general, non-humorous, text comprehension. We will also try as far as possible to integrate disparate proposals in a relatively coherent manner. This means that the framework set out in this book could be seen as a more detailed and explicit version of an approach which has existed in a less precise state for centuries.

The rationale for our approach is that it is not possible to test any hypotheses about the causes of humour without some empirical findings about what does and does not result in humour. The study of jokes can lead to such findings (subject to certain working assumptions that we will expand upon in Chapter 2), but only if we have some clear concepts, at an appropriate level of detail, with which to state precise hypotheses about how jokes work. That is what this book aims to deliver: *a theoretical vocabulary which allows the formulation of commentaries on how jokes are understood, in a way which is more precise and more detailed than previous accounts.* This vocabulary should be sufficiently broad that it allows for various factors which might contribute to the humorous effect, rather than narrowly adopting one particular proto-theory of jokes. That does not mean that we have to allow for absolutely any future theory of humour whatsoever – we will cater only for those ideas which have already received attention within the field, or minor variations of those ideas. This reflects one of our assumptions: that any factor which might affect the way that a joke creates humour has already been put forward somewhere within the field of humour research, but we do not yet know which of these ideas, or which combination of ideas, most accurately reflects reality.

1.5 The plan of action

Humour research is known to be multi-disciplinary, with the result that the methods of one subarea of research may seem puzzling or even misguided to those who work within a different discipline. It is therefore worth explicitly setting out the premises and goals of this book, in order to clear the ground for more detailed material; this we will do in Chapter 2. (Some of this was covered in Ritchie (2004, Chapter 2), but it is worth emphasising these points again.) Further basic issues will be explored in Chapter 3, which considers the process of joke comprehension in very general terms. Topics covered include the context of joke comprehension, and the distinction between recognising that a text is a joke and being amused by a joke. All this is part of the laying down of foundations and terminology for later chapters.

In Chapter 4, we present the model of text processing that we will adopt for our integrated joke description framework. This model is relatively abstract and general, for reasons which we will explain, and is not intended as a novel contribution to theories of text comprehension. Instead, it is an indication of the assumptions we need to make in order to give a more adequate account of joke comprehension.

Chapter 5 briefly considers some aspects of joke comprehension which crucially depend on the temporal sequence of events during the understanding of a joke.

The next four chapters examine the more conceptually oriented (or 'logical') aspects of jokes. Chapter 6 deals with the role of logic, and Chapter 7 looks in some detail at what might be regarded as the current cognitive theory of humour, 'incongruity-resolution', which has had a strong influence on the design of our framework. Chapter 8 examines the idea of surprise, how this might connect to the concepts explored in Chapters 6 and 7, and what a 'surprise theory of jokes' might look like. In Chapter 9, we indicate, very briefly, how linguistic knowledge should be located in our framework.

Chapters 10 and 11 review some ideas that go beyond the aspects of the framework dealing with reasoning: ideas of impropriety and feelings of superiority, respectively. These are included because of their prominence within past work on humour, and are formulated here in a way that is compatible with the constructs from the earlier chapters.

We then review the various factors we have considered (Chapter 12) and go on to illustrate how these can be applied to describing the mechanisms of jokes (Chapter 13).

Finally, we reflect on our descriptive framework, including some remarks on the next steps in moving towards a theory of jokes and perhaps even a theory of humour generally (Chapter 14).

Although each chapter has its own focus, as summarised above, the chapters are not designed to be read in isolation, since they attempt to integrate disparate ideas.

Chapter 2

Towards a theory of jokes

2.1 Getting down to details

This book contributes towards a number of related goals in humour research, to varying extents. The first of these goals, ambitious but unoriginal, is the creation of a full theory of humour. A full theory would describe all types of humour, and would relate the mechanisms of humour in an explanatory fashion to more basic human faculties such as perception and cognition, as well as providing a convincing account of the evolution of the phenomenon of humour. It would also connect outwards to theories *about* humour (in the terminology of Chapter 1), in the sense that there should be a consistent relationship between what the theory of humour says about cognitive or affective aspects of humour and what the social and cultural frameworks have to say.

The fulfilment of this goal is not likely within the next few decades. Here, this grand and unreachable target serves merely to influence the setting of guidelines for the tackling of closer and more tractable goals, which can be viewed as subgoals on the way to this notional destination.

The field of humour research might appear to be well supplied with theories of humour, to judge by phrases of the form '*X* theory of humour' which are encountered, where *X* ranges over terms such as 'incongruity', 'incongruity-resolution', 'superiority', 'relief', 'Freudian', 'aggression', 'benign violation', 'reversal', etc. However, these are competing visions of humour, with no consensus (which may be what leads Raskin (1998) to lament the lack of a 'major theory' of humour). Although these 'theories' contain useful insights, none of them are wholly adequate, as may become clearer when we examine them in the coming chapters.

Most of these proposals have insufficient detail to allow full empirical testing. Some might argue that such lack of connection with potential evidence undermines any claim that these are true scientific theories. However, there is a more relaxed way of looking at this work. As a first step towards a complete theory, it can sometimes be useful to sketch what we will call a *broad brush* theory. This would map out, with very few details, the major components of the humour theory and their interrelations, leaving the details to be filled in by further research. We would argue that most currently available 'theories of humour' are best seen as 'broad brush' drafts, awaiting further development. What are typically referred to as 'theories' of humour could instead be viewed as preliminary outlines of ideas (or clusters of ideas) which, if considerably developed, might become full theories of humour.

Such early designs can be extremely valuable. Developing a theory can be a long and untidy process, in which early drafts are proposed, refined or discarded, and later versions evolve. This, we would argue, is the current state of research into theories of humour: there are plenty of interesting ideas around, some of which may well become part of, or even act as the foundation of, an eventual full theory of humour. If we apply the yardstick of being a total theory, it is highly likely that most of these preliminary versions will fail, but this is not a reason to discard them. Instead, we have to assess the many theoretical suggestions on their merits, developing them where possible, and borrowing insights where we find them.

A broad brush theory is not only a rough draft of an eventual theory. It offers some abstract concepts (e.g. 'incongruity', 'pseudo-logic'), and possibly some indication of how these concepts fit together. Even if rather underspecified, these concepts and their interrelations offer an initial map of the landscape, to guide further exploration. Research can be focused on subproblems which are defined, usually implicitly, by the theory. Under these circumstances, the most obvious type of subproblem is the provision of more detailed definitions for the broad concepts in which the theory has been stated. This quest to increase the level of detail is one of the motivations of the current work. Although our resulting framework is still relatively 'broad brush', it is intended to add more detail to some of the ideas currently available.

Another intermediate subgoal on the route to a fuller theory is to aim for more accurate descriptions of humour phenomena. In studying jokes, it is desirable to develop descriptions which, at a suitable level of detail, accurately state what goes on as a joke is understood. This is a central concern of our work: to have a framework in which a clear and relatively detailed description of the workings of a joke (as reflected in the comprehension process) can be stated, in a way that could lead, in the longer term, to empirical testing.

There are a few methodological desiderata which cluster naturally along with the need for detail, perhaps best labelled as 'precision', 'formality' and 'operationalisation'. It is hard to draw the line between these various criteria, as they are all facets of the same perspective on the building of a theory of humour (see Ritchie (2004, Section 2.5) for more discussion). It is virtually impossible for a theory to meet all these requirements as it develops. Nevertheless, these ideals provide a direction and some guidelines as we make steps along the long road to a theory of humour.

One reason for mentioning the desirability of detail, precision, and related matters, is that these aspirations can sometimes be seen, within humour research, as in conflict with the quest for theoretical generalities. If there is a claim that all humour is caused by the resolution of incongruity (see Chapter 7), then this has a pleasing simplicity and generality. To then attempt to flesh out the concepts of 'resolution' or 'incongruity' (i.e. to add precision and detail) might be criticised as unnecessary (because we already have the theory), or even as casting doubt upon the validity of the elegant generalisation (by implying that the simple statement is insufficient or even incorrect). Such critiques would be, in the long term, counter-productive, as only by working out the details (precisely and in objective terms) can we connect theoretical statements to actual data, and hence test the theories.

2.2 Describing jokes

Why examine jokes?

Ritchie (2004, Section 2.9) makes the distinction between *jokehood* (being a joke) and *funniness* (being funny), and puts forward (pp. 15–16) four arguments for narrowing the research focus to jokes: there are plenty of attested examples of jokes; jokes are relatively portable, in that they are less tied to a specific context; jokes are manageably small; jokehood is a more tractable concept to study than funniness. To these we could add a further advantage: since jokes are crafted to be humorous, they contain relatively concentrated effects, with few extraneous factors beyond those needed to create the humour (but see the discussion of 'enhancers' in Section 3.5). Strictly speaking, these advantages apply to what are usually referred to as 'canned' jokes: '... short humorous stories or riddles ending in a punch line ... easily transferable from one context to another' (Kuipers, 2002, p. 451). Unless otherwise stated, when we use the term 'joke', we mean 'canned joke'.

In this book we confine our attention to jokes. There is nothing novel about this approach – research into humour has for many decades included the study of jokes as a central component, with Freud (1966 [1912]) possibly starting this trend in modern times. This emphasis is widespread amongst prominent and influential works (Attardo & Raskin, 1991; Oring, 2003b; Raskin, 1985; Suls, 1972), and is reflected in the presence of 'joke(s)' in the titles of many books (Chiaro, 1992; Cohen, 1999; Hurley, Dennett, & Adams, 2011; Legman, 1972; Oring, 1992d; Wilson, 1979).

Our study focuses not only on jokes, but specifically jokes conveyed in language – 'verbally expressed'. The restriction to verbally expressed jokes is simply to make the investigation more manageable. This allows us to be specific about the medium being processed (language, either written or spoken), and the operations which can be performed upon it. There is a wealth of work in linguistics and psycholinguistics on the comprehension of text from which we can borrow. The hope is that any interesting regularities discovered in the comprehension of textual jokes can, with further work, be generalised into patterns of non-textual jokes, and to non-joke humour.

Jokes and humour

Jokes are a highly specific form of artefact, and humour is, as many authors have pointed out, a much wider and more complex phenomenon. A study of jokes could potentially be misleading about the general mystery of humour, in various ways. (See Morreall (2009, pp. 83–89) for some of the limitations of putting an emphasis on jokes.)

A joke is a culturally defined and carefully crafted artefact, designed to create particular effects in the audience. To this end, it relies on human propensities in a few areas, including perception, cognition and emotions. Some of these human tendencies are culturally defined, and some of them may be more deep-rooted instincts which have evolved over hundreds of thousands of years. Almost all of them are part of human behaviour for reasons that have nothing to do with humour (with some exceptions, such as cultural knowledge about joke-telling). The successful operation of a joke depends upon its constructed characteristics triggering these human reactions, usually without the audience being aware of the machinery. Hurley et al. (2011) offer an analogy between the human fondness for sweet-tasting food and the liking for humorous experiences. The taste for sweetness came about through evolution, and its utility can be clearly seen in that context, just as the human desire for sexual activity can be understood. Hurley et al. argue that humour had, in its original form, a evolutionarily helpful purpose, but in the cultures of recent centuries it has become a commodity to be manufactured and exploited, just as confectionery manipulates our sweet tooth. They draw a parallel, in this respect, between comedians and confectioners (or pornographers). Hurley et al.'s analogy could be taken slightly further, to ask whether the highly crafted and conventionalised jokes of modern comedy could be comparable to an artificial sweetener, in that both are artificially constructed items which exercise the original tendency in a way that may be qualitatively different from the operation of the stimuli that led to the evolution of the preference. It might then be the case that trying to understand humour by studying joke mechanisms is comparable to trying to understand the human reaction to sweetness by analysing the content of an artificial sweetener (as opposed to analysing a piece of fruit). This does not mean that the exercise is pointless, merely that one has to take care in extracting generalisations or insights about humour from the details of jokes. Also, rather than looking entirely at the interior structure of the artefact of study (the joke or the sweetener), we should examine how particular characteristics of the artefact will affect certain human faculties.

Another possible risk is that the particular techniques used in jokes may be so prominent that they are assigned excessive importance. Although we have argued (Section 2.1) that it is important to correctly describe the details of jokes, this is simply to ensure that any claims about jokes are anchored in reality: without detail, empirical validation is difficult. However, this does not mean that every detail must be carried upwards to a general theory of humour. Here we introduce a second loose analogy: a joke is like a trap, as used by hunters. A joke can be seen as luring the audience into a position in which something unexpected or unusual happens, albeit only at some conceptual level. This luring is dependent on the audience's perceptual and cognitive reactions, which have typically been developed to deal with the vast array of non-joke circumstances that humans encounter every day. This is comparable to the way that the bait in a mousetrap, for example, relies on the mouse's natural impulse to try to eat any available food. A trap, at the level of working mechanisms, can be implemented in a wide variety of ways. (A vivid, if slightly flippant, illustrative reference is provided by the wonderfully inventive contraptions deployed by the character Wile E. Coyote in the Warner Brothers animated cartoon shorts.) Consequently, a superficial review of traps would tend to record this variety, rather than discerning that many traps have, at some level of abstraction, a common purpose, and that many of them share a dependence upon particular inclinations of the intended prey. Similarly, jokes can operate in several very different ways, but this should not disguise underlying commonalities, nor should we jump to the conclusion that any particular techniques are essential to the notion of a joke. Judgements in this area may not be straightforward.

Descriptive work on jokes should aim, eventually, to cover all types of joke. We do not claim to have achieved this, but the goal does seem relatively realistic, and it could be achieved within a few decades. Whether it would, as we hope, act as a stepping-stone to a full theory of humour should then be clearer.

The simplicity of descriptions

We have already discussed the issue of detail and precision in a theory (see Section 2.1). There is also the question of how much detail should appear in the analysis of an individual joke.

Typically, past analyses of jokes have involved examining a few selected jokes and proposing various abstract entities or properties which underlie either the meanings or the processing of these jokes. This is largely an informal methodology, and echoes practice in the linguistic analysis of grammatical or other aspects of languages, in which data (texts of various kinds) are described in quite brief terms by a single analyst making an intuitive inspection (see Ritchie (2004, Chapter 3)). This practice in joke analysis has meant that a description of a joke is usually very brief and does little more than observe that the working of the joke can be viewed in terms of the author's preferred broad brush theory. Although this style of description is very readable and can be helpful in conveying the central points, it may not fully engage with the complexities of joke comprehension, which may involve many factors interacting in ways which are not simple to describe, even for an individual example joke. Joke descriptions which are short, simple and able to be devised relatively easily may have limitations if the long-term goal is the development of a cognitive theory of joke comprehension. The activity of constructing relatively brief descriptions based on very simple labels should be seen not as an end in itself, but as a useful first step towards these more intricate and messy accounts. This is, to some extent, a distinction between informal description in the linguistic tradition and the building of detailed process models in the style of cognitive science. In later chapters, our commentaries on specific jokes will, owing to considerations of space and readability, still be quite brief outlines. However, these accounts will be stated in terms of our relatively detailed framework for joke comprehension, developed across several chapters. For this reason, we hope that these sketches can serve as high-level summaries of fuller descriptions in terms of cognitive processing, as well as being interim versions until more details can be worked out. We will touch on this topic again in Section 13.1.

2.3 The route to a theory

Description and characterisation

Our theoretical aims can be clarified by considering three possible objectives in analysing joke mechanisms. The first is *description*, which specifies the structures and processes which are involved in the comprehension of a joke. A step beyond that is *characterisation*, which states the conditions (in terms of structures and processes) which are essential to the status of a text as a joke (or as funny). (We have adopted the term 'characterisation' in order to avoid the term 'prediction', because that word will be heavily used in another sense in later chapters.) Finally, *explanation* involves showing how the humorous effects follow from more general theories or principles in other areas, such as psychology, where those other theories are independently motivated and/or better understood.

The main focus of this book is the first of these functions, 'description'. The aim is to provide a theoretical vocabulary in which a relatively detailed commentary can be provided for joke comprehension, recording all factors which could be pertinent to the text being a joke; that is, an integrated descriptive framework. The second function, 'characterisation', requires (or constitutes) a theory of jokes (or perhaps a theory of humour) and hence is a more ambitious aim.

Expressing in non-humorous terms

Despite the disclaimer stated immediately above, there is one aim of scientific explanation which we will endeavour to pursue. We noted above that in an 'explanation', humour would be characterised in terms of concepts which either are already well understood or are in some sense more general. In the long term, humour research should show how humorous effects arise from theories – in areas such as perception, cognition and emotion – which are derived from considerations unrelated to humour; that is, not relying on constructs invented solely to capture patterns of humour. Ritchie (2004, pp. 24–25) states that constructs which are 'theory-internal' (i.e. not provided by non-humour external theories) should eventually be eliminated by explaining them in other terms, rendering them 'theory-external'. Arguably, one of the problems with past theorising about joke mechanisms is that it has sometimes relied on theory-internal concepts such as 'incongruity' and 'resolution' (see Chapter 7), without spelling out what these terms mean in other terms, whether psychological, semantic or socio-cultural.

The need to connect to non-humour has been noted by others:

> The necessary and sufficient criteria for humor... are all relational. In other words: humor arises from the combination of otherwise ordinary, non-humor specific 'materials'...
>
> (Hempelmann & Attardo, 2011, p. 126)

With our narrowly focused goals, we will comply with this metatheoretical guideline by attempting to state our generalisations about joke mechanisms in terms which either are, or could plausibly be, abstract concepts from models of other activities, such as logical inference, storytelling or text comprehension. Our particular choice of such concepts will be outlined (mainly in Chapter 4) in a manner explained in the next subsection.

The abstract view of other models

As noted above, it is theoretically desirable to frame theories of humour in non-humorous terms. In fact, it is virtually impossible to avoid some connection to other activities and phenomena, since even simple textual jokes are inextricably linked to other aspects of human behaviour. Consequently, any account of joke comprehension inevitably strays into areas such as formal reasoning, text comprehension, linguistic structure, narrative, etc. It is therefore essential to be systematic about the connection between the description of humour and any models of these other areas. This seems to offer the humour theorist two options. For all these neighbouring areas of research, there might already be complete and accepted theories, which the humour scholar could adopt wholesale. Alternatively, we could try to construct such theories at the same time as building our description of jokes and humour, which would be an overwhelming challenge.

The compromise solution suggested briefly by Ritchie (2004, p. 29) and Ritchie (2006, p. 259), and adopted in this book, is 'data abstraction between theories'. The term 'data abstraction' (distinct from plain ordinary 'abstraction') is borrowed from computer science, where it refers to an approach in which interfaces between different computer programs are defined in such a way that each program does not need complete information about the internal details of the other – each program knows only about certain well-specified aspects of the other. For theorising about humour, the plan is that where some aspect of a non-humour phenomenon (e.g. text comprehension) is required in order to describe some joke mechanism, there should be a statement of the assumptions which must be made about that other phenomenon in order for the description of jokes to make sense. In this way, we build up a partial, and probably rather minimal, specification of the kind of model of the neighbouring area that we need for the support of our humour description. This has some methodological advantages: it avoids over-commitment to irrelevant details of the other phenomenon (as might happen if we arbitrarily selected some model that covered many aspects about which we had no interest), and it also means our humour description is compatible with any theory of the related area just in case that theory meets our partial requirements. (This seems to be similar in spirit to the approach adopted by Hurley et al. (2011): '...we want to specify the *functional* requirements of such a computational system so that one day a more technical approach ... can provide detailed working blueprints based on the outline we have sketched' (p. 4).)

Although such assumed interfaces to related theories are, in some sense, logically prior to the theory of jokes, in practice they are constructed as the descriptions of jokes are developed. This is because of their 'need to know' nature: we do not know what we require from the nearby theories until we have some ideas about how jokes work. In this way, these inter-theory interfaces are part of the outcome of the descriptive work on jokes: we are not just describing the joke mechanisms, we are specifying the theoretical environment which those mechanisms require.

There is, in principle, a risk in this approach. We are allowing ourselves licence to posit whatever support we require from the other theories, driven only by our need to capture the generalisations about jokes (or humour). This freedom could lead us to demand completely impossible requirements from the other theories, or to adopt superficially plausible hypotheses which research in the other area has already shown empirically to be incorrect. This is a risk we are prepared to take. If we genuinely reach a stage where humour theorising can be conclusively proven wrong by (for example) psychology, then we have reached a highly desirable level of empirical verification. A disproof of this sort would provide hard evidence that part of the draft theory of jokes needs to be revised, and this should lead to progress. Ideally, a theory would develop by a cycle of conjectures which, if refuted by evidence, are replaced by improved hypotheses. This can happen only if, as argued in Section 2.1, we can create testable claims. Hence, if we make explicit the necessary assumptions about supporting areas, this may help to connect the humour investigation to empirical evaluation.

In some sense, this strategy differs from past practice only in making the inter-theory assumptions explicit. Past analysts of joke mechanisms have often assumed that the environment of joke comprehension works in a particular way, thereby implicitly relying on notions of cognitive processing or discourse structure, but have not spelled these assumptions out explicitly. Hence, if it seems, particularly in Chapter 4, that our list of assumed interfaces is worryingly lengthy, this does not necessarily mean that we are putting forward greater demands than previous scholars. It may just mean that we are making our assumptions explicit, instead of hoping that tacit assumptions cost less.

Is this a theory?

It might appear from the discussion so far in this chapter that we believe we can make progress in describing joke mechanisms while avoiding any form of theory or theoretical claims. This is not the case. Any analysis of a joke implicitly makes theoretical statements of some kind, simply by assuming the availability of certain abstract concepts (see discussion above), and hence adopting a particular theoretical perspective. The concepts in our repertoire have been derived, broadly, in two ways: there are assumptions about non-humour mechanisms (e.g. text comprehension, inference) and there are various concepts which have been proposed in the past as pertinent to humour (e.g. faulty logic, superiority). The purpose of Chapter 4 is to spell out many of the underlying non-humor-related assumptions that we need to describe joke comprehension. Chapters 6 to 11 review other components which we will use, based on work by past authors. From all these, we attempt to formulate coherent commentaries on what takes place during joke comprehension, or at least an idealised model of that process. As argued earlier, we see this as moving along a lengthy road towards a full theory of jokes, but it is not based on such a theory at the start.

We cannot claim to be offering a theory of jokes, since we make no testable hypotheses about what constitutes a joke, for the simple reason that we do not yet know where the boundary between humour and non-humour lies. However, the ideas that we present could be argued to form a theory of joke comprehension, since it puts forward an account of what goes on as a joke text is processed. This would be at best a 'broad brush' theory (Section 2.1), since it certainly requires much further development. In particular, some work would be needed to extract firm, testable hypotheses. Nevertheless, the work here is not devoid of theoretical content, even if it is far from being a complete theory of jokes. (It could be seen as limiting the range of factors which could determine if a text is a joke.)

2.4 Summary

We can summarise the aims and assumptions outlined in this chapter as follows:

- Constructing a theory of jokes is a useful subgoal on the way to an eventual theory of humour.

- In tackling such a subgoal, it is realistic to aim initially for a 'broad brush' account, which can be used as a map upon which further details should be filled in as much as possible.
- In order to reduce the problem of humour to a manageable size, we are narrowing our focus with a number of simplifications; in particular, we study only verbally expressed jokes.
- In working towards a theory of jokes, it is helpful to develop detailed and precise descriptions of the workings of a variety of jokes, even if an over-arching general theory is not yet available.
- We aim to express regularities within joke comprehension in terms of independent, non-humour mechanisms, by developing a minimal abstract specification of what facilities would be needed from other theoretical areas.
- All this means that although we are not aiming to produce a theory of jokes, we will be making theoretical statements which narrow down the range of possibilities for such a theory.

Chapter 3

The process of joke comprehension

3.1 Joke understanding as a process

It seems obvious that joke comprehension is a process, in the sense of being a sequence of events (perceptual, cognitive, emotional) occurring over a short period of time. The order in which information is released to the audience often affects the humorous effect, and the humorous impact on the recipient is something which happens during time.

Borrowing a convention from Sperber and Wilson (1986), our accounts of comprehension, both in this chapter and later, will use the pronouns '*she/her*' to indicate a speaker or writer, and '*he/him/his*' to refer to a listener or reader.

Although previous work on joke analysis typically assumes this sequential perspective, the prominence given to process aspects varies greatly between authors. Perhaps the most influential work which emphasises the processing perspective is that of Suls (1972, 1983), in which joke comprehension is defined using a computer-style flowchart, and little is said about the nature of the joke texts which might give rise to the process. Most of the articles which, following Suls, discuss the incongruity-resolution account of humour (see Chapter 7) also assume, to some extent, some form of temporal sequencing. More recently, Hurley et al. (2011) develop a detailed processing model as part of their account of humour comprehension, and Wyer and Collins (1992) explicitly discuss the comprehension process. Some other commentaries on joke mechanisms may mention the temporal order of certain eventualities, or they may allude to something happening when the end of the joke is encountered (Attardo, 1997; Oring, 1992b). Freud (1966 [1912]) can be seen as positing a process involving 'psychic energy'. Most, perhaps all, of these earlier analyses are not really about the text as a static item, but concern the underlying comprehension process. In effect, these analysts are considering an idealised comprehension process, brought about by the joke text in a relatively predictable manner, and about which the various claims or comments can be made. That is, these descriptions assume a sequence of (cognitive or perceptual) events which take place as the joke is processed by the (idealised) audience.

Despite this widespread apparent assumption, theoretical proposals sometimes include few or no explicit details of processing as part of the critical conditions for humour (Oring, 1992a; Raskin, 1985), even if it is clear that the conditions they describe (typically, the perception of incongruity) are assumed to be embedded within a process of joke comprehension (see Section 7.7).

From a theoretical point of view, there are two subtly different questions to be considered. Firstly, should we adopt a sequential processing perspective in building a model of joke comprehension? Secondly, should particular aspects of that processing be treated as key components in the humorous experience?

The above discussion indicates that the consensus within joke analysts is to answer positively to the first question, sometimes implicitly, and we will also take that position: we will definitely aim to describe not the static internal structure of a (textual) joke, but a sequence of events that occur when a joke is comprehended. We will also reply in the affirmative to the second question, by including constructs which depend crucially on time sequencing.

There is one property of jokes which we will assume throughout this book: the main humorous effect of a joke is experienced as, or shortly after, the end of the text is perceived. This assumption is the basis of a traditional segmentation of a joke into an initial *set-up* and a final (usually quite short) *punch line*. The principle here is that the set-up provides most of the necessary information for the joke, but not enough to create the humour, and the punch line supplies that final essential instalment. We will adopt this segmentation and terminology.

It could be argued that some jokes do not naturally have this segmentation. These could include certain 'double entendres' in which there is no specific final segment of text which triggers further inference (see Section 7.6); in such cases, the entire text is the set-up and the punch line is empty. Also, for some jokes it can be argued that it is hard to ascertain the exact boundary between set-up and punch line (Ritchie, 2004, Sect. 8.6.3); for these, we would take the position that there is a boundary, but its location is unclear.

We also highlight four stages in the comprehension process which are useful points of reference in describing the flow of information:

(i) *Initial*: At the start, before any of the text has been perceived.
(ii) *Post-set-up*: After the set-up has been fully processed, but before the punch line is perceived.
(iii) *Post-text*: After all the text, including any punch line, has been perceived, but before it has been fully processed.
(iv) *Final*: After the text, including any punch line, has been fully processed.

The distinctions between these stages should become clearer in the course of later chapters, and we will make particular use of them in Chapter 8. As each stage in comprehension will be associated with a particular state of knowledge for the comprehending agent, we will occasionally use the term '*X* state' to refer to the overall state of knowledge at the *X* stage; for example, the 'final state' is the knowledge state in the final stage.

3.2 Texts and input sequences

The process of joke comprehension can be seen as an activity that is within the mind of the joke's audience (an instance of a 'mental behaviour' (Hurley et al., 2011, p. 121)). We need to have some indication of what that process acts upon, or starts from, but we do not need much detail about how that input came into being.

The input is, at some level of abstraction, the text of the joke, or, more precisely, the text as perceived on some particular occasion. A joke can be treated as having an identity separately from any instance of comprehending it or any occasion upon which it is told, and hence its text can be seen as a representation which may be presented, and encountered, many times in very different settings. For example, when someone refers to 'that joke about the two old men in deck chairs', they are alluding to an abstract joke text rather than a particular use of that text. We will not make any significant distinction between the use of a joke in print and the same joke delivered orally. We will focus on the audience's view of the particular encounter with the joke. (This could be seen as a 'type/token' distinction (Cherry, 1970), in the sense that the abstract text is a 'type' and individual encounters with it are 'tokens' (Ritchie, 2004, p. 30).)

The text, as a convenient representation of a joke across all encounters with it, will also provide the basis of the input to the comprehension process: we will regard the input as a sequence of phonetic or orthographic elements. Both of these media (spoken and written) are included, because some jokes work properly only in a particular medium. (Some jokes also require visual elements such as hand gestures or facial expressions, but we will ignore these, as our task is already complicated enough.) Also, we will assume that a joke is a grammatically well-formed text in whatever language is used. (See Ritchie (2004, Sections 3.2–3.5) for fuller discussion of these assumptions.)

Thus there are a number of routes from abstract joke representation to something which the audience can perceive. The idea of a joke may be invented long before the joke is told to an audience, and may be stored either as an idea (remembered) or may be explicitly recorded in written or audio form. Alternatively, the joke idea may be created immediately before the telling, as spontaneous humour, with no intermediate recorded version nor need for long term memory. The actual instance of the joke may involve the teller generating, from some remembered idea, an audio sequence or (for example in an internet chat) an orthographic sequence. The teller could also recite verbatim a remembered textual form, although this seems less common in everyday joke-telling. Yet another variant is that the audience directly experiences the recorded form without the intervention, at that time, of a human teller, for example by reading a joke book or listening to an audio recording. We have nothing to say about how common each of these routes might be, or what others might be possible. Nor will we consider creation of jokes or texts. This is not to imply that there is nothing of interest involved in joke creation, but we do not want to widen this investigation to consider how aspects of the creation of a joke affect the way that the recipient of the joke comprehends it.

For our purposes, all that matters is that the audience somehow encounters the text as a sequence of linguistic elements, either phonetic or orthographic. This might seem to be exactly the same kind of data as would be examined if we were to analyse the text of the joke in isolation. However, there is a slight shift of perspective: instead of seeking an abstract linguistic description of a static piece of text (for example, documenting ambiguities or choice of vocabulary), we will view the linguistic items as a temporally ordered sequence that is the starting point for a process which involves not only linguistic computation but also inference of various sorts (of which more details will follow in later chapters). Perhaps more importantly, focusing on the concrete instance of encountering a joke allows the inclusion of factors not present in the abstract text (joke type), such as the context of telling, or the knowledge, beliefs and mood of the audience.

We will say more about our assumed processing model in Chapter 4.

3.3 Security and playfulness

One aspect of joke usage which has been remarked upon is the need for a suitable setting, in the sense that joke-telling will be successful only if there is a favourable combination of the social context, the audience's mood and the audience's beliefs about what is taking place. In particular, the audience must feel reasonably secure, and must be prepared to accept some degree of unreality or play. 'Playful readiness in addition to surprise is another necessary (but still insufficient) condition of humor' (Ziv, 1984, p. 90). Morreall (1983, p. 53) talks of the audience needing '... to be without urgent practical needs...', in an overall state which is 'relatively secure' and even in control of circumstances. He points out that an incongruity which involved genuine danger (such as the sudden appearance of a ferocious tiger) would not appear amusing at the time of experience. Morreall also mentions the playful aspect: the audience must be '...enjoying it for its own sake' (p. 91). (See also Morreall (2009, pp. 70–72).)

The notion of playfulness is part of a wider agreement that the telling of a joke is in some sense outside the normal conventions of verbal exchanges. Raskin (1985) suggests that normal, non-joke, verbal interactions generally involve 'bona-fide communication' (BFC), but joke comprehension operates within 'non-bona-fide communication' (NBFC). The main characteristics of NBFC are that certain conventions of sincere communication (Grice, 1975, 1978, 1981) are flouted. Raskin suggests that joke comprehension may involve the detection of such violations of BFC, triggering a switch by the audience to NBFC which then allows the joke to be understood.

Perhaps the most developed proposal is within the 'reversal theory' account of humour (Apter, 1982, 1989). Reversal theory treats humans as moving between different 'metamotivational states', which condition their responses to events around them. These states are characterised by the values of certain two-valued variables, sometimes called 'modes', one of which varies between 'telic' and 'paratelic'. The telic mode is serious, using planning to achieve definite goals, with an avoidance of risk and anxiety. In contrast, the paratelic mode is playful, enjoying an activity for its own sake, happy to contemplate risks. In telic mode, high psychological arousal produces unpleasant feelings such as anxiety, whereas someone in paratelic mode enjoys high arousal. For a joke to be successful, the audience must be in paratelic mode. This can come about in two ways. Either the audience is in paratelic mode before the joke encounter (and remains so throughout the encounter), or the audience moves into paratelic mode as a result of detecting certain humour-related aspects of the joke. (This is reminiscent of Raskin's idea that the audience adopts a different mode during joke comprehension on the basis of evidence that a joke is being perceived).

The idea that the playful mood is not required as a prior state of mind, but can be adopted as a result of detecting the characteristics of a joke, tends to complicate attempts to substantiate the need for a paratelic mode, as the claim becomes harder to falsify. If someone appears to appreciate a joke despite showing all the signs of being in a telic (serious) mode just beforehand, we have to conclude that the audience flipped into a paratelic mode during the telling because they experienced the (joke-creating) attributes.

McGraw and Warren (2010) say that a 'a broad review of the literature' shows that '... humor occurs in contexts perceived to be safe, playful, nonserious, or, in other words, benign ...' (p. 1142). They develop this notion of 'benign', offering three specific forms, two of which echo the earlier ideas of non-serious activity: the audience is only 'weakly committed' to the central 'violation' in the stimulus, or regards it as 'psychologically distant'. (See Sections 7.11 and 10.8 for more on this theory.)

There seems to be a general consensus: jokes, like tickling and certain other activities, function best when within a secure and playful setting, and these circumstances are preconditions for a joke to provoke amusement.

3.4 Detection, recognition, and appreciation

Joke detection

A distinction has sometimes been drawn between 'humour comprehension' and 'humour appreciation' (Suls, 1983, pp. 52–53). There is no precise or accepted definition of these terms, but their existence draws attention to the need to clarify some distinct aspects of joke comprehension.

We will use the term *joke detection* to refer to the judgement which was alluded to in Section 3.3, when the audience realises that a text being read or heard is to be treated as a joke. This does not mean that the text has been completely delivered, nor that it has been fully understood. This is simply a judgement that the audience makes about the status of the text: that it is playful, and is intended to amuse. Although we refer here to the intentions of the joke teller, joke detection is about the audience's perception of that intention, not about the true nature of the joke teller's motivation. Joke detection could occur before the text has commenced, if the environment has firmly established that a joke is about to be heard or read, for example if the audience is reading items in a joke book. Alternatively, it might occur only at the end of the joke-telling, as the audience belatedly realises that the text is not intended seriously.

In our investigation of joke comprehension, we will take joke detection for granted, in the sense that we will not try to incorporate any mechanisms for this decision into our descriptive framework. This is because joke detection is a wholly general requirement for the successful telling and comprehension of any joke, and does not (apparently) vary between jokes. Hence, it has little effect on what must be specified in our model of joke comprehension, unless we find a need for some particular parameter which interacts in some way with joke detection. As noted in Section 3.3, some authors suggest that joke detection may occur late in the processing of a joke, but these authors give no evidence to show that this late judgement affects the perception of the joke. That is, no accounts of the workings of joke comprehension have shown that changes in the moment of joke detection affect the outcome of joke comprehension.

Joke recognition

The next concept we require is *joke recognition.* This is a judgement by the audience, on the basis of comprehending all the pertinent aspects of the text, that the text is indeed a well-formed joke. This is essentially what is known colloquially as 'getting the joke'. Joke recognition, like joke detection, is usually an all-or-nothing step: either the audience gets the joke, or he does not. However, understanding a joke is not the same as being amused by a joke.

(Being a joke – what we called 'jokehood' in Section 2.2 – might not be a simple binary classification into jokes and non-jokes. Some texts, such as comic songs, amusing verses, metaphors and epigrams, might be borderline cases. It might be more accurate to adopt some form of categorisation based on typical prototypes (Rosch, 1973; Rosch & Mervis, 1975). However, we will not pursue these subtleties here.)

To sharpen up the notion of joke recognition (and the concept introduced in the next subsection), we can consider some of the different ways in which a joke text may be encountered (attaching mnemonic but arbitrary labels to each for ease of reference):

Natural: The recipient encounters the joke for the first time, succeeds in grasping the full information content of the joke, including inferred material, but does not anticipate the content of the final segment of the text, and so does not form a full interpretation of the text until after the text has concluded.

Remembering: The recipient encounters the joke, but not for the first time, and grasps the full information content of the joke, partly or fully from memory, including anticipating the content of the end of the joke.

Reencounter: The recipient encounters the joke, but not for the first time, and grasps the full information content of the joke, partly or fully from memory, but does not remember the content of the end of the joke until it is delivered.

Anticipating: The recipient encounters the joke for the first time, and succeeds in grasping the full information content of the joke, including guessing the content of the end of the joke before that part is delivered.

Analysing: The recipient has previously encountered the joke and is now examining it for the purpose of research or a similar activity.

Intuitively, joke recognition could occur in any of these settings, but genuine amusement might be highly unlikely in some of them (see next subsection).

Although we have defined joke recognition as a judgement, such an outcome is the result of a process that goes on during joke comprehension. Sometimes, for convenience, we will use the term 'joke recognition' as if it denoted that process, rather than simply the resulting verdict. This deliberate ambiguity will normally be resolved by the context.

Joke appreciation

The third reaction to a joke that we consider is *joke appreciation*. This is where joke recognition occurs and in addition the audience experiences a subjective feeling of amusement as a result. Joke appreciation is a matter of degree, ranging from nothing at all (that is, amusement does not occur) to some extreme level of hilarity. We have stipulated that joke recognition is essential to joke appreciation. This means that we are defining joke appreciation narrowly, to include only amusement resulting from aspects of the joke, leaving aside any feelings of amusement that might coincidentally occur when the joke is being told, for example as a result of a bucket of slime being poured over the teller of the joke.

If we consider the five ways in which a joke might be encountered, as listed in the previous subsection, the chance of amusement occurring varies considerably across the scenarios. Plausibly, only the Natural case seems to have a good chance of causing amusement in the recipient, with some amount of joke appreciation less likely in the other four conditions. This is not to argue that a non-trivial degree of amusement would necessarily follow joke recognition in the Natural scenario – there are, as we will explore over the coming chapters, additional conditions which affect joke appreciation.

One noticeable difference between the Natural case and the others is that only in the Natural sequence can the ending of the text cause the audience to experience temporary puzzlement (see Section 7.3) or to be surprised by the ending (see Chapter 8).

The question of what contributes to joke appreciation is potentially very open-ended, shading off into many emotional, social and cultural factors, perhaps even overlapping with the concerns of 'theories about humour' in the sense of Chapter 1. We will explain in Section 3.6 how we intend to keep this potential explosion of factors under control.

Just as we may sometimes use 'joke recognition' as denoting a process, we will often use 'joke appreciation' to refer to whatever process leads to that outcome (in this case, some degree of amusement).

Another look at 'paratelic' mode

In Section 3.3, we briefly reviewed some formulations of the idea that joke comprehension depended on some sort of 'non-serious' attitude. It is not entirely clear how these ideas are related to the distinction between the recognition and the appreciation of a joke. In the cases both of Raskin and of McGraw and Warren, their particular mechanisms affect the audience's identification of something as being a joke – that is, joke recognition. In the case of Apter's reversal theory, this is less clear. Apter gives detailed conditions for a stimulus to be humorous, none of which seem to crucially depend on the paratelic mode; that is, the need for paratelic mode is a further, independent stipulation from the theory. However, given the characterisation of telic and paratelic modes, it seems highly plausible that this difference would have considerable effect on joke appreciation. A similar remark could be made about McGraw and Warren's 'benign' condition.

3.5 Devices and enhancers

The variety of devices

Various authors have proposed collections of devices which are implicated in the creation of humour, and which describe particular facets of the joke comprehension process. A parallel can be drawn with a similar practice in the wider area of storytelling in literature, theatre and film, where it has long been observed that there are various established techniques which are used to create particular effects (Aristotle, 1920; Forster, 1927; McKee, 1999). There are very low-level phonetically based devices such as 'assonance', more semantically based techniques such as 'metaphor', and strategies involving narrative development, such as 'mistaken identity'. Generally, these are seen as a collection of devices from which the writer (typically, a poet or storyteller) can select and put together in various ways to achieve specific (usually deeper) outcomes of emotion or insight.

Like literary texts, jokes make use of a variety of techniques to achieve their effects, and many devices have been proposed over the years as being components of jokes. These cover the full range from a strong form of assonance, used in puns and word play, to misunderstanding (where a character completely misinterprets some situation). Others commonly deployed are ambiguity, vagueness, repetition and exaggeration.

A typical example of this, which also illustrates that such devices are abundant and widely varied, is the list offered by Berger (1998, Chapter 1), which contains forty-five 'techniques' of humour, such as 'Allusions', 'Caricature', 'Accident' and 'Slapstick'. Although Berger says that these are '... the building blocks of all humor and are found, in varying combinations, in all genres of humor' (p. 58), they are in effect a catalogue of devices which are sometimes used in literary or dramatic comedy. Berger presents no real argument that these constitute a theoretical description of essential humour mechanisms. Many of these 'techniques' seem to deal with the content of the overall interpretation of the joke, while other techniques appear to concern the development of the interpretation during comprehension, the cultural function of the joke, the narrative structure, properties of the linguistic form, or the supposed origin of the text.

A joke may manifest more than one of these devices. For example, (1) could be seen as displaying, from the Berger catalogue, 'Insult', 'Repartee/Outwitting', 'Sarcasm', 'Repetition/Pattern', and 'Embarrassment'.

(1) Two grand Southern ladies are taking the air on the veranda of a fine mansion. One says, 'You see that there Rolls-Royce? Well, my husband gave that to me on our fifth wedding anniversary.' Her friend says, 'Well, isn't that fine.' The woman points to some horses in a paddock. 'And on our tenth wedding anniversary he bought me a string of race horses.' Her friend says, 'Well, isn't that fine.' The woman points to huge swimming pool at the side of the house. 'And for our fifteenth anniversary, he built me this beautiful pool and spa, all for me.' Her friend says, 'Well, isn't that fine.' 'So tell me,' says the woman. 'Does your husband buy you nice things?' 'Why, yes,' says the friend. 'Only last year he sent me to a charm school to improve my vocabulary.' 'Your vocabulary?' says the woman. 'Yes,' says the friend. 'I used to say "I don't give a rat's ass". But now I say "Well, isn't that fine."'

(Haskins & Arnott, 2017, p. 292)

For most of the devices suggested in past work, there exists at least one joke in which the device could plausibly be argued to be prominent, in the sense of being very noticeable when inspecting the workings of the joke. However, being obviously present is different from being necessary and/or sufficient for the status of the text as a joke – a text might clearly involve, for example, 'exaggeration' without this being the key to the humour in the joke.

Nevertheless, some previous authors state, either explicitly or indirectly, that they see their proposed devices as holding the key to humour.

Many, perhaps all, of the patterns which authors have previously listed as 'techniques' or 'devices' of humour are valid observations about some specific aspect of the comprehension process or the knowledge structures involved in that process. If any device is to be taken up as part of a theory, then it is necessary to specify that device more precisely: what structures or processes does it describe, and what is its function (if any) within the overall creation of humour? This latter point is very important. Joke comprehension is complex, with many different functions being fulfilled by a variety of mechanisms. For any potential device of interest, we need to have clarity about the components on which it is dependent, and what outcomes it has. Describing how jokes work involves the teasing apart of devices which are noticeable but peripheral to the humorous effect from those which are crucial but perhaps less obvious.

Ritchie (2004, Section 3.8) argues that, in describing a joke, a distinction has to be made between 'effects' which the text creates (semantically, pragmatically, etc.) and which may lead to humour, and 'methods' which may be employed (e.g. linguistic constructions) to achieve those effects. The idea is that a theory of jokes should concentrate on determining which effects are humour-generating, but not be distracted into potentially laborious itemisation of a multiplicity of linguistic (or other) techniques for achieving those effects. For example, even if a theory of jokes/humour relies directly on the concept of ambiguity, a list of the many different ways in which linguistic ambiguity can occur is not really a substantive part of the theory of jokes.

Although this is an important conceptual distinction, and should help to reduce unnecessary effort on the part of joke analysts, it does not mean that it is easy to discern the exact role played (in humour) by each aspect of a text, even a prominent aspect. A superficially obvious aspect might be completely irrelevant to the humour creation, or it could, with other components of the text, lead to a combination of circumstances which together form a critical humour-engendering configuration. As we will illustrate in Section 7.6, ambiguity can lead to multiple interpretations, which in turn lead to misinterpretation, thence to puzzlement, cognitive effort, the discovery of a revised interpretation, and the revelation of some hitherto obscured absurdity or impropriety. The question is: if this scenario leads to humour, which of these stages are essential to the humour, and which are merely preparatory stages, which could in principle have been achieved in some other way? This can be hard to answer in some cases.

Enhancing the effect

The previous subsection argued that text comprehension takes account of many aspects of the text, and that the exact function of each device may not always be obvious. One function which has been remarked upon (Apter & Desselles,

2012; Hurley et al., 2011; O'Shannon, 2012; Ritchie, 2004; Triezenberg, 2004) is *enhancement*. That is, jokes contain, along with core components that ensure the text is a joke, further embellishments that increase the effect upon the audience. Ritchie (2004, Section 12.3) refers to these as 'supplements', and lists twelve possible types. Triezenberg (2004) calls such factors 'enhancers', listing five types, two of which are similar but not identical to items in Ritchie's list. O'Shannon (2012) similarly talks of 'enhancers' (of which he gives five illustrative examples), and also observes that there can be similar negative factors, 'inhibitors', which reduce the humorous effect. Toplyn (2014) lists twelve 'joke maximisers' ranging from phonetic aspects to 'use the rule of three'.

Some illustrative examples of these additional (positive) factors are:

Funny words/diction: (Ritchie, Triezenberg, O'Shannon, Toplyn): The vocabulary chosen can make a text seem more amusing.

Repetition: (Ritchie, Triezenberg, Toplyn): A cycle of repeated occurrences can build up tension in a narrative.

Admiration: (Ritchie, O'Shannon): If the audience is impressed either with the cleverness of the joke or the skill of its telling, this may increase the effect.

Apter and Desselles list just three 'enhancers': heightened arousal (which can happen in various ways, including sexual content or surprise), social cues (such as laughter), and cognitive effort (the latter dubbed 'engagement'). Hurley et al. mention several topics that boost the effect of humour, including sex, violence, death, excrement, racial perception, empathy, and a delight in transgression.

O'Shannon suggests that Hobbes's idea about superiority (see Chapter 11) is an example of an enhancer being miscategorised as a key factor, remarking of enhancers:

> Some are so powerful that they become dominant factors in the laugh, far surpassing the impact of the raw information [in the joke]. Over the years, this has fooled people into thinking that the enhancer is the joke, or that certain common enhancers are the basis for all comedy.
>
> (O'Shannon, 2012, p. 239)

Hurley et al. tend to agree, mentioning aspects such as 'Schadenfreude and recognition of superiority' (p. 214) or 'disparagement of an outgroup member' (p. 248) as non-crucial components of humour. Ritchie's list of twelve potential supplements includes 'puzzle-solving', 'thwarted expectations', 'disparagement', and 'superiority', all of which are possible candidates to be core components of joke comprehension (as we will discuss in later chapters). All this underlines the fact that it is not always evident which factors are essential to the humorous effect, and which are enhancers.

In the next section, we will set out in more detail how we intend to approach the distinction between core component and enhancer.

3.6 Joke comprehension and joke analysis

The hypothetical comprehension process

It was mentioned in Section 3.1 that past work on joke analysis often makes observations or assumptions that are not, strictly speaking, about the text as such (viewed as a static structure of words and punctuation), but are about some imagined comprehension process. This process seems to lead to some degree of joke appreciation (except perhaps in the case of the SSTH – see Section 7.7), which means that it must involve joke recognition, by our definitions in Section 3.4.

The hypothetical joke comprehension process appears to fall into the category of a Natural encounter, in the terminology we used in Section 3.4. That is, the joke analyst is hypothesising that a Natural encounter with the given text would proceed in a way which manifests the proposed features.

(Something similar could be the case in some of the other encounter scenarios, such as Remembering. It is possible that in these scenarios, joke recognition is achieved by imagining the outcome if a Natural encounter with the text were to occur.)

In the remainder of this section, we will try to be more precise about the roles played, within the comprehension process, by joke recognition and joke appreciation.

Appreciation and enhancement

Although we have defined joke appreciation as requiring joke recognition as a precondition, at least in a logical sense, this does not mean that these are two separate processes which follow each other in sequence. It may be that joke appreciation operates in parallel with joke recognition. Or it may be that, although we are separating these two processes for the purposes of our research, they are really two facets of a single process, rather than two phases. In any case, this logical relationship means that anything which contributes to joke recognition also facilitates joke appreciation. However, there may also be aspects of comprehension which are not essential for joke recognition, but which contribute to joke appreciation. We remarked that, of our five ways in which a joke can be encountered (Section 3.4), it was very plausible that some of the scenarios, such as Remembering or Analysing, could lead to joke recognition but no joke appreciation. This suggests that any features which are relevant only to joke appreciation but do not affect joke recognition may occur only in the Natural case. As we will see in later chapters, these could include certain variations in cognitive effort during comprehension, or the occurrence of some form of surprise.

The idea that joke appreciation does not follow strictly after joke recognition is supported by the varied nature of enhancers (Section 3.5), which – by definition – influence joke appreciation, but which can involve factors that arise at all stages of joke comprehension, such as the presence of particular words or variations in cognitive effort required. If some condition is solely an enhancer, then it cannot be essential for joke appreciation. In fact, the reverse is the case, since enhancement of appreciation can occur only if there is some appreciation.

To sum this up, when describing the comprehension of a specific joke, any aspect of the description can fall into one or more of three classes: essential for joke recognition, essential for joke appreciation, enhancer.

The distinction between a factor essential to appreciation and an enhancer is about the function of some content or process, not about any absolute qualities of that entity in isolation. In principle, any given property of the comprehension process could operate in either role.

The question of whether a particular aspect of a joke is an enhancer or something more central is not a peripheral issue. It is at the heart of characterising which ingredients determine the jokehood and funniness of a text, since categorising something as a mere enhancer is equivalent to saying that it is neither necessary for joke recognition nor a pre-requisite for joke appreciation. This means that any analysis which aspires to characterisation of jokehood (as opposed to mere description – see Section 2.3) must, even if only implicitly, indicate which factors are more than just enhancers. A well-defined theory of jokes would provide criteria which will guide the decision about which aspects are or are not enhancers for a particular joke, but we do not have such a resource for guidance. Rather than offering a firm decision about which factors are solely enhancers, we are aiming for a less demanding goal. In the chapters which follow, we will investigate the various factors which can contribute to joke recognition and those which allow the possibility of some amusement; that is, we will consider conditions which might enable the occurrence of joke appreciation, however minimal. The term 'joke comprehension' will be taken to refer to a process, largely the same as ordinary text comprehension, which may result in joke recognition and potentially joke appreciation.

Delineating the audience

It should be clear from earlier sections of this chapter that we will be considering a sequence of cognitive and/or affective events which occur while an idealised audience comprehends the joke. It is uncontroversial to observe that different audiences can react completely differently to a particular presentation of a joke or to different encounters with the same joke.

In particular, a joke can be understood (as a joke) only if the audience has certain knowledge, without which the text is either unhumorous or incomprehensible (Ritchie, 2004, Section 3.6). Strictly speaking, the required 'knowledge' may not be factually correct, so it is more accurate to talk of the comprehension requiring particular beliefs. This means that a text is not a joke in isolation, but is a joke relative to certain pre-requisite beliefs. This will be assumed in later chapters, and it will only occasionally be necessary to draw attention to the effect of the audience's beliefs on joke comprehension.

We do not intend to compare individual differences, but our focus on a single idealised audience means that when we offer an analysis of a joke, we are offering a description of one particular, potentially idiosyncratic, comprehension of that joke, and hence we are adopting one specific model of the audience. Another reaction (e.g. a difference in joke appreciation) would mean that the audience model was different in some way.

This means that a detailed account of the comprehension of a specific joke implicitly delineates the assumed audience in more detail, by specifying, often indirectly, attributes that this audience must have (beliefs, preferences, etc.) in order for the events within the comprehension to proceed as described. For example, if the analyst proposes that successful comprehension depends upon a particular interpretation of the text being more salient (see Section 4.7), then that sets a constraint on the set of possible audiences which would appreciate the joke: that analysis will apply only where the audience's beliefs/knowledge lead to that assessment of salience. Thus an analysis is not saying 'this will always happen during the comprehension of this joke'. Instead, it is saying 'if the audience has these attributes, then comprehension will proceed in this way'. Hence, the joke analysis provides a sketch of the class of audiences for whom this comprehension will occur. (The possible structures for an idealised audience will be further explored in later chapters, particularly Chapter 4.)

Hence, a full analysis of a joke deals with three kinds of information:

(i) a sequence of events (which can be thought of as 'in the mind' of the audience);
(ii) a sequence of interpretations of the text, which are the outcomes of these events;
(iii) a set of knowledge structures which characterise any beliefs, emotions, etc. which are necessary (as part of the audience) for the events and interpretations to occur as described.

The last of these delineates the type of audience who will comprehend the joke. Details of all of these will be developed in later chapters.

3.7 Summary

We can summarise what we have argued about joke comprehension in this chapter as follows:

- Our description will explicitly treat joke comprehension as a process in which a single idealised audience makes sense of sequential text.

- We accept the consensus that a joke will be successful only in under certain conditions of security and playfulness, but this will have little effect on the details of our framework because there is no evidence that these environmental aspects interact with the mechanisms of joke comprehension.
- We distinguish joke detection, joke recognition and joke appreciation, and will treat joke comprehension as covering the last two of these.
- Jokes involve a wide variety of devices and effects, and it is sometimes not wholly obvious how important a particular mechanism is to the overall humorous outcome. A particularly notable class of device is the 'enhancer', which affects joke appreciation.
- We are interested in those constructs which could influence joke recognition or joke appreciation, particularly if they might be essential to the latter, rather than being merely enhancers.
- A detailed analysis of the comprehension of a particular joke indirectly specifies a class of possible audiences for whom that analysis applies.

Chapter 4

Text comprehension

4.1 The plan

As we argued in Section 2.3, any mechanisms invoked to explain the workings of jokes must be expressible in terms of constructs which are generic; that is, they should not be proposed solely for humorous effects. This raises a question: what would be a suitable non-humorous basis for describing the mechanisms of joke comprehension? The current chapter offers a possible set of answers, in the form of a relatively abstract outline of various text comprehension mechanisms that would be needed in order to state the generalisations which humour researchers have made about the workings of jokes.

In this chapter, we will consider only what might be called the 'conceptual' mechanisms of text comprehension. This term covers anything that is instrumental in extracting from a text its full meaning and any implications: linguistic processing, including syntax, semantics and pragmatics; logical matters, including consequence, inference, and probability; and the content of, and relationships between, states of knowledge and belief. Having sketched these mechanisms in the current chapter, we will discuss their use in joke comprehension in the course of Chapters 5 to 9.

On the other hand, the 'attitudinal' mechanisms of joke comprehension involve particular valuations, by the supposed perceiver of the joke, about social or cultural importance, propriety, desirability, etc. This could include, for example, an estimation of what is proper to mention in polite company, or a dislike of a particular individual. We will look at attitudinal aspects of joke comprehension in Chapters 10 and 11. (The distinction between conceptual and attitudinal is made here largely for expository purposes, and is not proposed as having any significant theoretical import.)

We take the position – which we believe reflects a widespread if tacitly adopted consensus – that both conceptual mechanisms and attitudinal aspects can affect whether a person will recognise a text as being a joke and also whether this results in amusement. (These judgements are discussed further in Chapter 3.)

The aim in this chapter is not to present a complete, detailed, and novel model of text comprehension. Instead, we are setting out what we believe are the minimum requirements for a comprehension model that would allow adequate descriptions of typical joke mechanisms (as discussed by many authors in the past and as analysed in later chapters of this book). This is in keeping with the points made earlier (Section 2.3) about the benefits of specifying an abstract interface between the area of concern (joke mechanisms) and some other area where there is no definitive accepted theory but many theoretical suggestions.

In this chapter, we will not attempt to analyse any jokes, nor to propose joke-creating mechanisms. Instead, we will explore a more general problem than joke comprehension, namely the comprehension of text (particularly fictional text).

We will describe what we believe is needed, but with no formalisation and no attempt at innovation. This is because we are aiming to sketch only those facilities that are required for our later commentaries on joke comprehension. We will also give some brief indications of the extent to which the proposed characteristics are derived from other relevant areas of study, such as psycholinguistics and narratology, to show that we are adopting a reasonable approximation to what is known or theorised about these aspects of cognition.

We will start by outlining (Section 4.2) the overall arrangement that we have adopted, and then consider the following principal aspects:

- the construction by the audience of some form of 'mental model' of the world of the story, the need for multiple belief spaces, and the relation between real and fictional knowledge (Section 4.3);
- the distinction between the system of logical relations within a fictional world and the reasoning process by which the audience makes sense of that world (Section 4.4);
- the nature of the logical system that connects beliefs within a fictional world (Section 4.5);
- the ways in which the audience's reasoning involves supplying information left implicit by the text (Section 4.6);
- the processing that goes on during the construction by the audience of a basic meaning from the text (Section 4.7);
- the extent to which we include various aspects of storytelling (Section 4.8).

We have tried to be clear and precise about those properties which will be helpful, in our later analyses, in providing a good account of joke mechanisms, but we have deliberately omitted any details which we regard as being of no import for joke comprehension, thereby avoiding excessive arbitrary detail (this may be what Genette (1988, p. 26) refers to as '... the excess of precision as an epistemological obstacle.') As a result of this abstraction away from particulars, we should, by the end of this chapter, have characterised a very broad family of comprehension models, comprising any account which includes the facilities we have summarised.

4.2 The overall arrangement

Context is all in the mind

It is a truism that texts make sense and have effects only relative to some context. Context can be taken to include any or all of a number of influences: general knowledge about the world, the specific beliefs of the listener/reader, the immediate physical surroundings, the current state of a dialogue or other social setting, cultural conventions, and knowledge of society and politics. We are considering the comprehension of a single joke by a single (idealised) person, the *audience*, and therefore we will adopt the assumption that the audience's knowledge and beliefs constitute the entire context for comprehension. That is, any factor (social, cultural, physical, etc.) can potentially influence the comprehension process if and only if it affects the audience's knowledge/belief in some way. This is not to claim that a potential contextual influence requires conscious awareness on the part of the audience, since various kinds of priming or subtle effects can happen without the individual being aware of them (Lupker, 1984; Maldonado, Chemla, & Spector, 2017; Meyer & Schvaneveldt, 1971; Reder, 1983; Swinney & Hakes, 1976). We will say more about audience knowledge and belief in Section 4.3, but the main point here is that, for an individual cognitive agent, no aspect of the context is relevant unless it somehow affects that agent's beliefs. Here we interpret the term 'beliefs' very broadly, to include, for example, the audience's mood, or the relative salience to the audience of various concepts (see Section 4.7 below).

Hence, the starting point for the comprehension of a particular joke is the audience's state of beliefs, in this broad sense, before the first part of the text is perceived.

This does not mean that we cannot make observations or hypotheses about the utilisation of different types of belief that the audience may possess, and contextual effects of particular kinds may show up as particular kinds of concept within the audience's store of knowledge.

From text to meaning

Because some jokes are heavily dependent on the details of the language used, we need to take some account of the mechanisms of language processing. In particular, our model must allow for formal rules which operate upon input text, and some form of lexicon with information about specific words. We will say more about these in later chapters, especially Chapter 9, as particular aspects become relevant.

Following many traditional linguistic theories, we will assume that it is possible to associate a 'meaning' with a segment of text, where this meaning does not take account of any further inferences that might be triggered (see Section 4.5), but captures only the semantic content of the linguistic material of the text, which we take to consist of lexical meanings combined into larger semantic or conceptual structures. This is sometimes referred to as the 'literal meaning' of a text (Carston, 2012; Foss & Hakes, 1978, pp. 100–101; Levinson, 1983, p. 14, p. 17).

One much-discussed way in which language goes beyond literal meaning is the use of figures of speech such as metaphors. These can be regarded as being in two broad types: 'dead' or 'frozen' devices which have become conventionally accepted as having a particular (originally figurative) meaning, and novel figurative expressions, for which the audience will have to determine the underlying meaning using reasoning. Here, we view the former category (dead) as merely being part of the text-to-meaning mapping, in much the same way that idioms are, while the latter category (novel) are treated as first being mapped to their 'literal' meaning, with the figurative import determined by a subsequent reasoning phase.

For many joke analyses, it would probably be possible to omit explicit mention of the conversion from text to literal meaning, and to assume that texts directly cause deeper changes to an audience's view of the world. Nevertheless, we have included a separate stage in order to allow for jokes in which the language phase is central to the humorous effect; we will return to this in more detail in Chapter 9.

Where a concept forms part of the literal meaning of a segment of text, we will say that this text *directly mentions* that concept. If a concept is part of the result of some inference which non-trivially involves the literal meaning of a segment of text, then we will say that this text *indirectly mentions* that concept. If a concept is either directly or indirectly mentioned by some text, it will be said to be *mentioned* by that text. In general, if a concept forms part of some large proposition, then when a proposition is mentioned (directly or indirectly), so is the concept. (These constructs will be useful in Chapter 10.)

4.3 Worlds and beliefs

Mental models and storyworlds

For a few decades, there has been a commonly held view within psychology that text comprehension should be viewed as the construction and maintenance, by the audience (reader/listener) of some form of 'mental model' (Johnson-Laird, 1983); that is, an image of the situation(s) being described by the text. For some psychologists, the internal representation is known as a 'situation model'. The following quotations capture the essential idea:

> When people comprehend language, such as narrative texts, they create mental representations that capture the circumstances and events being described. These mental representations are situation models ... which serve as mental simulations of what is being heard or read.
>
> (McNerney, Goodwin, & Radvansky, 2011, p. 454)

> The assumption that readers construct a situation model as a referential representation of the state of affairs described in a text ... is now a commonplace assumption in the psychology of language ...
>
> (Schroeder, Richter, & Hoever, 2008, p. 237)

(See also Zwaan, Langston, and Graesser (1995, p. 292), Zwaan and Radvansky (1998, p. 162)). When Nieuwland and Berkum (2008, pp. 604–605) outline a similar idea, they use the term 'narrative text comprehension', but the idea of mental models is usually taken as applying equally to texts which are not really narrative in the sense that any scholar of storytelling would recognise, since little happens in the storyworld and there is no real temporal change. That is, the construction of mental models is seen as applying very generally to any text which describes relationships between objects, not just narratives in a narrower sense.

In studies of genuine narrative, many of which predate modern psycholinguistics, it has been more or less assumed that a story will describe some fictional 'storyworld' (e.g. Walton, 1978). In comparison to these older literary ideas, the more modern psychologically motivated proposals put more emphasis on cognitive mechanisms and on empirical testing of such conjectures. Text world theory (Gavins, 2007; Werth, 1999) provides a complex development of this central idea.

In many cases, a joke is in essence a very short story, involving a relatively straightforward description of some very limited world in which there are a small number of objects which are related in various ways, and which are involved in some short sequence of situations. (There are many jokes which are clearly not narratives, such as punning riddles – see Chapter 9 – and some jokes may even involve metanarrative tricks at the expense of the audience, but the quintessential 'funny story' is a basic narrative.)

The idea of storyworlds and mental models has been tacitly assumed within the tradition of joke analysis that we are building upon here. When a joke analyst indicates that some character in a joke has suffered an indignity, or has revealed some sexual desire, there is an implicit assumption that there is a world inhabited by these characters, in which situations arise and characters can have attributes such as emotions. We are simply underlining and making explicit this fundamental assumption.

Since joking may occur spontaneously during normal conversation, the creation of some sort of storyworld may occur 'on the fly', in the sense that the audience may need to consider, often unconsciously, some abstract space of possibilities within which joking conventions apply. (Similarly, it has been suggested that a joke may itself conjure up a playful context that it requires – see Section 3.3).

Gavins (2007, Chapter 1) gives a good review of the various strands of thought that have contributed to the general idea of abstract worlds as representations of discourse meaning. We will not attempt to draw fine distinctions between the psycholinguists' mental or situation models and the narratologists' storyworlds, as these appear to embody the same intuitive idea. In fact, the two lines of research have moved closer with the development not only of text world theory, but of 'cognitive narratology' (Herman, 2009). We will take a storyworld to be a particular kind of mental/situation model in which the content is treated as fictional.

Separate belief spaces

One key aspect of the audience's management of a fictional world is that statements about the fictional entities must be treated differently, and distinguished from, statements about the real world. For example, joke analysts sometimes posit a particular emotional reaction, by an audience, to situations depicted within a joke, but these are not feelings about the real world (see the discussion by Walton (1978) of emotional reactions to stories). Even where a joke involves a non-fictional character (e.g. President George W. Bush, the Pope), the audience knows that what is taken as true within the storyworld is not necessarily true of the real-world character.

The above remarks might be regarded as too obvious to mention, but we are attempting to make explicit even basic assumptions like this, and it would be desirable to delineate more clearly how this separation works. If we are to move towards a detailed cognitive model of joke comprehension, there will need to be some examination of the real world/storyworld boundary. The exact relationship between these two worlds is not usually mentioned in analyses of jokes, which often assume the deployment of real-world knowledge within the storyworld without indicating that some conventions are needed (a topic we will return to in more detail shortly). We will borrow from Emmott (1997) the term *text-specific* to describe information that is acquired by the audience from the text rather than from real-world knowledge.

We have already noted (Sections 3.2 and 4.2) that we are examining a process of joke comprehension that takes place within the mind of the audience. In view of this, what we are focusing on here is not the distinction between the fictional world and the real world in all its physical, concrete solidity, but the relationship between the fictional world and the audience's knowledge and/or beliefs about the actual real world. (Hurley et al. (2011) refer to the contents of a person's long-term memory as 'a sort of surrogate world' (p. 105).) In our approach to text comprehension, everything is relative to the audience, and so even the 'real' world has this degree of unreality.

Certain stories and jokes also need a distinction between the information states of different fictional minds. That is, when a narrative involves one or more characters, there needs to be a mechanism for each character to have distinct beliefs. Some stories and jokes rely on characters imposing different interpretations upon occurrences in the narrative, or having different beliefs about how the world works. There are also stories (and a few jokes) which depend on one character having particular beliefs about the knowledge or belief of another character; this could be regarded as a small fictional manifestation of the 'theory of mind' (Leslie, 1987; Premack & Woodruff, 1978).

Thus there are two motivations for having several distinct views of the possible facts about the world: to separate the storyworld from the real world and to distinguish the perspectives of different characters within the storyworld.

The idea of 'mental spaces' (Fauconnier, 1994) has been suggested as a possible way of representing separate but related sets of belief such as these, as have the 'viewpoints' of Ballim and Wilks (1991). Ritchie (2006) discusses some ways in which such abstract structures could be used to describe certain typical joke mechanisms. The joke comprehension model of Hurley et al. (2011) relies centrally on using mental spaces to organise sets of beliefs. We will adopt such a scheme as a central part of our framework, where we will use the term *viewpoints* for these spaces.

Relating the knowledge between worlds

Perhaps the main function of viewpoints is to organise the way that information can flow between closely related spaces. When an audience first encounters the start of a story, he will have no explicit information about the storyworld, in terms of what entities exist in that imaginary world and what norms or conventions apply within that world. Although it is clear that fictional 'facts' are often not true in the real world, there is a widespread convention that a fictional world is like the real world except for differences indicated within, or inferrable from, the narrative:

> ...both counterfactuals and fiction are subject to what I have called above the 'principle of minimal departure'. This principle states that we reconstrue the world of a fiction and of a counterfactual as being the closest possible to the reality we know. This means that we will project upon the world of the statement everything we know about the real world, and that we will make only those adjustments which we cannot avoid.
>
> (Ryan, 1980, p. 406)

The inheritance of knowledge from the real to the fictional world covers not only simple facts about specific objects, but more general knowledge:

> Typically, fictional worlds are a mixture of what is false in that world but asserted as true in the fictional world, and what is true in the real world.... we would still assume that there was an Eiffel Tower in Paris unless told explicitly that there was not, and would be able to use our real-world knowledge to infer that sharp knives still cut, and that aubergines are edible.
>
> (Sanford & Emmott, 2012, p. 47)

In particular, potential logical relationships (see Sections 4.4 and 4.5 and Chapter 6 for more discussion of logic) are inherited into the fictional world, until information to the contrary is encountered. Thus any real-world generalisations about normality, likelihood, logical consequence or cause and effect are taken to hold in the storyworld by default. This is the case whether the logic is a classical truth-valued logic or a system based on some notion of 'normality' or 'likelihood'; see Section 4.5.

We will not delve into the precise formalisation of the interworld relationship, but merely note that this issue has been dealt with in much more detail within philosophy (Heintz, 1979; Howell, 1979; Lewis, 1978), where the systematic similarity between the real and fictional worlds has been likened to a comparable arrangement underlying the meaning of counterfactual statements (Lewis, 1973).

As noted earlier, jokes sometimes depend on each story-character having a distinct view of the storyworld. However, there is again a general principle of inheritance, in that the audience can initially assume, until conflicting information appears, that each character has an accurate view of the storyworld, in the sense that the character's view matches the audience's current view of the storyworld. As before, this inheritance covers not only simple statements about the current state of affairs, but general statements (rules) about relationships between possible situations.

To describe the inheritance relationships between the different world views, we can arrange the viewpoints into a hierarchy; that is, a tree-shaped network with the root corresponding to the audience's knowledge and/or beliefs about the real world. At one level down from the root space is the storyworld, which is subordinate to the (audience's) real world, as in Figure 4.1.

(Surprisingly, the model sketched by Hurley et al. (2011) includes no belief space for the storyworld, using mental spaces only for the audience's view of the real world and for the beliefs of real or fictional characters, although those authors make occasional remarks which seem to assume the presence of some sort of story space.)

To represent the various viewpoints in a story (or joke) in which there are characters who could potentially have idiosyncratic sets of beliefs, these

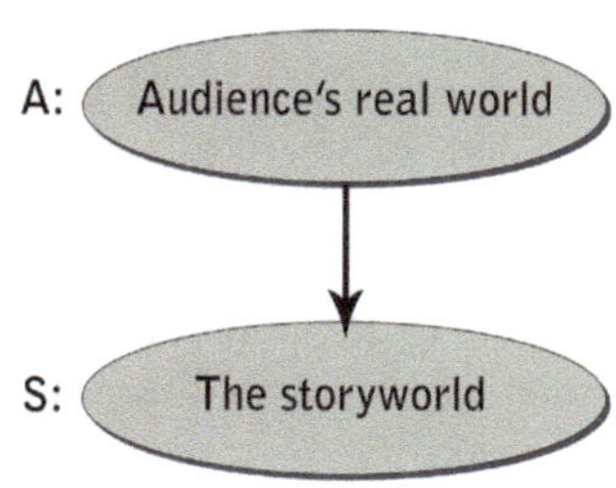

Figure 4.1 Audience and storyworld viewpoints

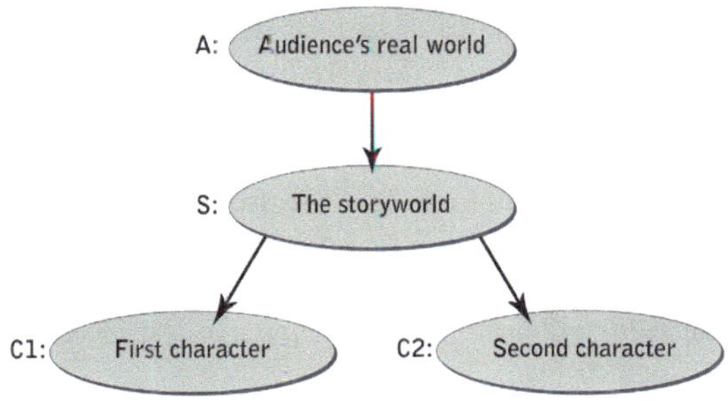

Figure 4.2 Audience, storyworld, and character viewpoints

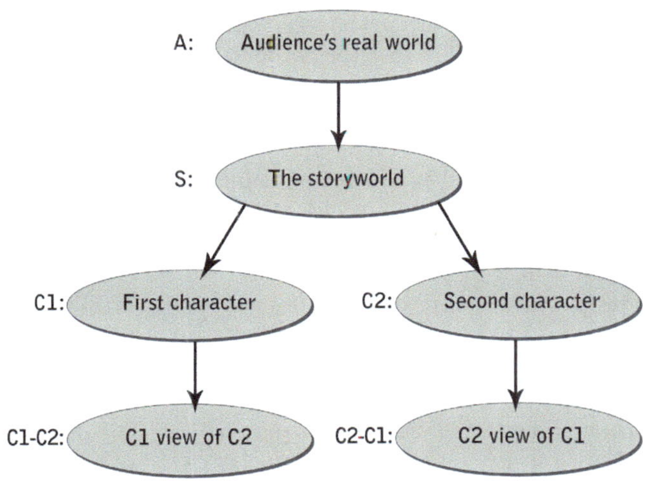

Figure 4.3 Audience, storyworld, and nested character viewpoints

viewpoints would be subordinate (linked below) the storyworld, as in Figure 4.2.

Should we need to represent the view that one character C_1 has of the beliefs of another, C_2, then there would be a version of C_2's space linked below that of C_1, as in Figure 4.3.

These hierarchical configurations reflect the flow of inherited information: a node in the tree (a viewpoint) *inherits* from its immediate parent node all knowledge, except where discrepancies are explicitly indicated by the interpretation of the text. The hierarchy also emphasises the nesting of the knowledge: the storyworld is really the audience's view of the storyworld, and the beliefs of a fictional character are the audience's view of the storyworld's view of the character.

Information inherited in this way has a 'default' status, in the sense that, however certain it is in the higher viewpoint, in the lower viewpoint it is merely an assumption, albeit a very strong one. Hence, as mentioned above, inherited information can be overridden by more specific content supplied by the text, either directly or using inference.

Many structures inside a particular viewpoint will be there as a result of the inheritance mechanism, in the sense that the structure in the lower viewpoint is notionally a replica of an identical structure in the higher viewpoint. In this case, we will refer to these two structures as *counterparts* of each other. Any item that has been inherited will have a counterpart in the viewpoint from which the inheritance occurred.

This makes possible a reverse flow of information, from lower viewpoint to higher viewpoint, in the following way. If new information has been inferred about a particular item *S* in the lower viewpoint (e.g. the storyworld), and *S* has a counterpart S' in the upper viewpoint (e.g. the audience's view of the real world), then it is possible that the audience may *export* this information to the upper viewpoint, treating it as being about S'. This could happen, for example, if a fiction about a real-world person attributed certain characteristics (e.g. mendacity) to the fictional counterpart of that person, and the audience derived the idea that the real-world person had those characteristics.

The viewpoints of Ballim and Wilks represent exactly the beliefs of one person, and Fauconnier's mental spaces can be quite fine-grained and represent a wide variety of semantic possibilities, as can Werth's text worlds. However, for our limited purposes, we need to distinguish only certain kinds of belief sets:

- the beliefs of an individual, real or fictional (in fiction, this can include non-humans);
- a hypothetical state of affairs;
- the world of a story (which could be seen as a kind of hypothetical state).

It would probably be possible to formulate our 'viewpoints' as a special case of any one of the theoretical approaches cited above. As ever, we are not presenting a detailed all-purpose mechanism, but are merely outlining those aspects which seem to be needed in describing joke comprehension.

4.4 Knowledge and reasoning

Internal logic

Each viewpoint has to represent, at a suitable level of abstraction, a state of knowledge. We will do this by regarding each viewpoint as containing a *belief base*, which embodies the information about the world as seen from that viewpoint. The belief base will contain various types of *conceptual items*, which can be thought of informally as denoting objects or relations or other structures within some domain or world. However, this idea of denotation is left as an intuitive way of thinking about the nature of conceptual items – we will not attempt to formalise this intuition by developing a model theory for conceptual items. (Sometimes, where there is no ambiguity, we will refer to conceptual items as 'concepts'.)

In describing storyworlds, we will have cause to allude to a few kinds of conceptual items: *individuals*, which denote objects, inanimate or animate, including people; *propositions*, which describe statements that can be true or false within the storyworld; and *rules*, which describe how propositions are related to each other. Rules can be thought of as like material implications in a traditional formal logic, in that they express inter-proposition connections, but are essentially a subtype of proposition.

Propositions may be quite fine-grained, so that a single proposition could describe an extremely small detail of the subject matter. It is convenient to be able to refer to sets or clusters of propositions which, taken together, describe some large, more intuitively natural, aspect of a scene. For example, a story might involve the idea that 'the protagonist is seeking a sexual partner', and this could comprise several propositions. We will use the term *situation* for a set of propositions like this. Although we would expect the elements of a situation to be related in some way, we have no formal specification of this, and so a situation is simply a set. We will also continue to use the term 'situation' informally, for states of affairs which would, if modelled in our framework, be represented as a 'situation' in the more precise sense.

The rules show how different portions of information are, or could be, related, and hence embody a form of reasoning system. This means that each viewpoint will, in effect, have its own self-contained reasoning system, which we will refer to as the *internal logic* of a viewpoint. Where the viewpoint is a storyworld, we may refer to its reasoning system as the 'internal logic of the story' or the 'internal logic of the joke'. We will examine this idea in more detail shortly (Section 4.5).

It follows naturally from the remarks in Section 4.3 that the storyworld's reasoning will initially mimic the audience's own view of how the real world works. The logic of the storyworld will have to be amended if the narrative introduces unreal possibilities such as telepathy or talking animals, as in science fiction, in fairy stories and in some jokes. Also, the viewpoint associated with an individual story character may contain highly idiosyncratic reasoning (a topic we will expand upon in Chapter 6).

It might be thought that the knowledge representation scheme will require, as well as a belief base within each viewpoint, a repository of miscellaneous administrative connections of various kinds, which we tend to take for granted when looking at diagrams like Figures 4.1 to 4.3. This could include an indication of which viewpoints are associated with which individual concepts (in cases where the viewpoint represents a particular character's view of the world), which concepts are counterparts of each other across viewpoints, etc. Having the noted the need for such back-office minutiae, we will continue to take these links for granted, and say little more about them. These links are not properly part of the belief base of a viewpoint, but are, relative to a viewpoint, metadata. They would be needed, for example, in a software implementation, but have no substantive function in how information is used inside a viewpoint. Some of this supplementary data would be needed for the process of inference (see next subsection) which is also at a metalevel with respect to the belief bases of viewpoints. However, the main administrative connections, such as the hierarchy of viewpoints and the links between characters and viewpoints, are intuitively natural, and hence we will not, when relying on them in joke analyses in later chapters, make any special remark about this metadata.

Audience inference

So far, we have mentioned (Section 4.2) the need for text to be converted into some representation of meaning. Although much of that process can be treated as a relatively straightforward translation between different levels of linguistic representation (Gazdar & Mellish, 1989; Jurafsky & Martin, 2000; Poesio, 2000), there may be a need for some amount of reasoning in order to resolve uncertainties in this mapping (Mellish, 1985; Ritchie, 1983). There is widespread agreement that a human reader/listener depends upon reasoning in order to reach a full understanding of a text, even if he is not consciously aware of all such processes (Foss & Hakes, 1978; Singer & Ferreira, 1983; Thorndyke, 1976). This reasoning by the audience handles many different aspects of comprehension, such as supplying default information about typical situations, predicting likely consequences of actions, detecting a character's plans or beliefs from their utterances; see also Sections 4.6 and 4.7. We will use the term *audience inference* for this process of information expansion.

A joke often relies on some crucial idea which is merely implied by a joke text, and hence most jokes rely on the audience fleshing out the bare information of the text in order to grasp the joke. This need for inference as part of the comprehension process has always been assumed in joke analysis, but most joke analysts seem to regard it as too obvious to be worth mentioning. We draw attention to this requirement merely to once again promote tacitly held assumptions into explicit desiderata for a cognitive model.

Although we use the term 'audience inference', this does not mean that this process must be solely, or even principally, based on a formal logic with a deductive mechanism. It could, for example, include some sort of 'spreading activation' mechanism (Collins & Loftus, 1975; Quillian, 1968), which might be very relevant to matters of salience (Section 4.7). We are concerned more with the overall functionality, rather than the internal mechanisms.

We will say more about the sequential nature of audience inference in Section 4.7. For the moment, we note that, as more information is obtained during text comprehension, changes may have to be made to previously adopted propositions. That is, new information is not simply added to old, building up in a constantly consistent manner to a final accumulation, in what logicians would term a 'monotonic' arrangement. In stories and jokes, the information flow is 'non-monotonic': new information can override old, rendering previous inferences invalid.

Since we are treating the comprehension of the text as depending upon the construction of a nested set of viewpoints (Section 4.3), audience inference must have the capability to manage and reason about such interrelated belief bases. There are various proposals for logics of belief (Gärdenfors, 1988; Konolige, 1986; Rescher, 2005), and we do not intend to argue the case for any particular formal mechanism.

We are leaving aside completely the question of which inferences might be intended by the writer or teller of the story/joke. This would lead into the even more complex question of how a story or joke is created, and how the teller models the reactions of the audience. All that is beyond the scope of the current volume.

Comparing the two systems

We have stated that each viewpoint has its own internal logic, and that the audience performs, during comprehension, audience inference. As these are both, loosely speaking, reasoning systems, it is helpful to emphasise how they are completely different conceptually. The main differences are as follows:

Role: Internal logic describes the patterns of information within the viewpoint, indicating, for example, why one situation is a consequence of another. It is about links between conceptual entities within the viewpoint, defining the nature of that world. Audience inference, on the other hand, attempts to build the storyworld (including any viewpoints involved), taking into account a variety of types of knowledge, including the internal logic; in particular, one of the tasks of audience inference is to figure out what constitutes the internal logic, as this may not be obvious initially (e.g. in a fantasy story, or in many jokes).

Processing: Audience inference is a process, happening in time as the text is comprehended, passing through a sequence of stages as more information is absorbed. Internal logic characterises relations between conceptual entities, and is not a sequential process.

Scope: There are, in principle, separate internal logical systems for each viewpoint, even if they will usually contain much the same content. There is a single audience inference process, and it can operate on the belief bases of all viewpoints accessible to the audience.

Levels: If we regard the internal logic as the basic level describing the objects and relations within the storyworld, then audience inference performs reasoning about that world, and may even reason about conventions of storytelling and joke structure. In that sense, audience inference is at a 'metalevel' in comparison to the 'object level' of internal logic.

Validity: The internal logic may make empirically inaccurate generalisations or treat as commonplace some situation that would be highly unlikely in the real world. There is no evidence that the audience inference is inherently incorrect, and we have to assume that the audience attempts to work out the full meaning of the text as effectively as possible. (We will return to this in Chapter 6.)

Both audience inference and internal logic need to be investigated further in the quest to understand how jokes work, but it is important to bear in mind the conceptual distinction between these two aspects. For example, the phenomenon of being misled during joke comprehension (Sections 4.7 and 7.6) is a relevant aspect of audience inference, while we will argue in Chapter 6 that the idea of 'pseudo-logic' in jokes is concerned with the definition of internal logic, but is not a mechanism of audience inference.

4.5 The nature of internal logic

Defeasible logical consequence

A traditional formal logic allows the precise statement of which propositions (consequents) follow from given propositions (antecedents). As a model of truth and falsity, it permits no intermediate status: either a formula is a consequence of some premises, or it is not. Also, inference using such a logic is 'monotonic', in the sense that the consequences of a set of propositions cannot be reduced by adding propositions to the set – additional information cannot alter the outcomes. Modern formal logics allow more flexibility, in various respects. Fuzzy logic (Zadeh, 1975a, 1975b, 1975c) associates a numerical value (which can be thought of as a degree of truth) with propositions. Probabilistic logic (Nilsson, 1986) also links statements to numbers, but in this case as measures of likelihood. We noted (Section 4.4) that the audience inference system must behave in a 'non-monotonic' way: knowledge does not necessarily accrue steadily, but can be removed. The same is true of the internal logic: any deduction is 'defeasible', in the sense that it can be overridden subsequently. Various 'default logics' (Reiter, 1978, 1980; Turner, 1984) formalise such notions. Within the strand of work on knowledge representation using 'frames' or 'scripts' (Minsky, 1975; Raskin, 1985; Schank & Abelson, 1977) a particular form of defeasible information is the 'default value' for attributes of a conceptual item. The ideas of frames and scripts have led to the development of 'description logics' (Baader, Calvanese, McGuinness, Nardi, & Patel-Schneider, 2003; Taylor, Klinov, & Mazlack, 2007), which impose certain structures on the content.

We have no aspirations to introduce yet another form of logic, nor do we have any evidence that some particular existing formalism is particularly appropriate to represent the internal logic of joke worlds. Also, it is not part of our remit here to devise a complete model of story understanding, which would almost certainly require complex representation of knowledge. Instead, we will, in keeping with one of our basic working assumptions (Section 2.3), give a rough sketch of the facilities that seem to be needed, and observe that these requirements are very modest, given the richness of representational schemes already available. There are almost certainly other logical mechanisms which are required for full text comprehension (and hence for complete joke comprehension), but we leave these as a separate research question, in much the same way that we ignore details of, for example, text parsing algorithms.

The essential nature of the internal logic can be seen as derived from two components: the underlying inference mechanism, and the rules (implication statements). As far as the underlying mechanism is concerned, we merely specify that the internal logic will require some notion of consequence as in most formal logics, since both stories and jokes rely heavily on relatively terse information being expanded (see Section 4.6 for more discussion of this). The notion of consequence must be defeasible, allowing for default reasoning and revisions of conclusions. It is possible that the logic may also require some probabilistic aspects, but we have no firm evidence of this. We believe this captures fairly accurately the intuitive judgements which joke analysts have made in describing the situations in joke worlds. Our discussion of how 'logic' fits into jokes (Chapter 6) is general enough to cover any reasoning scheme which meets this loose specification.

As for the rules/axioms of the internal logic, a small number of requirements will arise in later chapters as we examine jokes in more detail. There is one area where even non-humorous stories have a need for some coverage. Stories and jokes often depend upon the way in which the situations within the storyworld are causally linked. In particular, comprehension can be confronted with the question of why something came about in the storyworld. Hence, the internal logic should contain concepts which can be used to describe such links between situations.

There is a related issue of normality, which we will address in the next subsection.

Normality

In everyday reasoning, some notion of 'normal' plays an important part, and the idea also figures in joke analyses which allude to 'abnormality' or to 'norms'. The question therefore arises: do we need some notion of 'normality' in our joke comprehension framework?

Normality can be seen as the idea that past experience, including cultural knowledge, conditions what people will expect to happen. This was at the heart of the frames/scripts approach (see previous subsection), which stressed the powerful effects of existing knowledge upon perception and cognition.

This conception is also explored by the 'norm theory' of Kahneman and Miller (1986), in which a person's judgements are based on 'norms' derived, in response to particular circumstances, from knowledge the person has retrieved from memory. Hence, a person's judgements, even in unfamiliar settings, can be based on norms which are constructed at that moment.

These arguments address the extent to which a person's knowledge can influence their reasoning, but have few implications for the choice of logical mechanism. For example, the patterns of reasoning appealed to by advocates of frames/scripts could be captured by a knowledge representation scheme based on logic (Hayes, 1979), particularly when there are, as indicated above, such rich notions of logic available.

Another aspect of normality is embodied in the idea of knowledge being structured into 'prototypes' (Rosch, 1973; Rosch & Mervis, 1975). The idea is that people, in their use of language and reasoning, do not treat categories (such as '*bird*' or '*chair*') as a simple set with an all-or-nothing membership criterion, but rather as a collection of exemplars or subcategories which vary in how typical or representative they are of the category. A robin is a highly typical bird, a penguin is not. This notion of normality is more about degrees of category membership than about inference from experience. (Brône and Feyaerts (2004, pp. 363–364) argue for this concept being at the core of certain jokes, in which there is confusion between a typical instance of a concept and an untypical instance.) Even if this approach to categories is adopted, it still leaves open the nature of the logic which operates on these categories.

The situations within a story which are treated as normal (by the narrator or by the story-characters) are evidence about the nature of the internal logic, something which the audience has to determine (see Sections 4.6 and 6.6). We will therefore sometimes, when analysing a joke, remark upon some situation being treated as normal within the joke world. However, this does not mean that a formal notion of 'normal' is required as part of the logical apparatus, in addition to conventional logical propositions and implications. Instead, we can treat normality, like causality, as part of the content about which the internal logic has rules. We do not rule out a formal logic, possibly probabilistic, which builds 'normality' into its mechanisms, but we do not require this.

Intuitively, the informal idea of normality is related to two other ideas: 'expectation', which we will deal with in the next subsection, and 'willing suspension of disbelief', discussed in Section 4.6.

Expectation and anomaly

As will become clear later, particularly in Chapters 7 and 8, humour is often said to depend on the violation of 'expectations' or of 'predictions'. These two terms seem to be used interchangeably in discussions of joke mechanisms, and neither is very tightly defined. We would like, in later chapters, to examine this apparently central role for expectation/prediction in jokes, and therefore we will try to be slightly more precise about what we mean. We will use the term 'prediction' for, loosely speaking, forecasts of events in the future, and will deal with this in the next subsection. First, we will look at what we will class as 'expectation': patterns of normality within the storyworld.

When humour scholars refer to the 'violation of expectations' they sometimes appear to be referring to situations within the joke world which are in some way unusual, rather than forecasts of future events (our 'predictions'). The question would seem to be: how can we define this notion of 'expectation' in terms of the internal logic?

In fact, analyses of jokes rarely rely on expectation as such, but on the *violation* of expectations. That is, only when there is a conflict with an expectation does the joke analyst make any mention of expectation. In the remainder of this subsection, we will outline some notions of 'violated expectation' which we believe are useful for describing the patterns found within jokes, but we shall not attempt to define expectation itself. (It might be that a suitable definition would be that an expectation consists of information that is filled in by default, like the 'covertly entered' category of Hurley et al. (2011).)

(We will not be adopting the common usage within probability theory, where 'expectation', also known as 'expected value', is an abstract value which represents, for a numerical variable, the sum of all possible values for that variable, weighted by their probabilities.)

We start from the general point that where there is an observation of abnormality, there are, implicitly, two sets of rules being considered. There are the rules of consequence or causation which gave rise to the situation in question, and there are the rules by which this situation is deemed abnormal. The natural way to capture this within our framework is to use the differences between the internal logics of separate viewpoints. The scenario of interest here is where a lower viewpoint, such as that of the storyworld or of a story-character, has rules which give rise to some situation, but a dominating viewpoint – typically the audience's world – has rules which do not lead to that situation, and may even lead to a conflicting situation. This is makes use of the assumption, earlier in this section, that the internal logic can make statements about causation within the storyworld.

The next point is that, during text comprehension, there may be no explicit information about what rules hold within the storyworld and/or a character's viewpoint. In these circumstances, the rules of the audience's real world will be inherited into the lower viewpoint, although these can be overridden in the light of subsequent information from the text. Hence, a situation may arise in the storyworld which initially appears to conflict with the (inherited) rules of that world, but once the true rules of that world are determined, the situation is seen to follow unproblematically. Also, a text can assert information which appears at first to conflict with what the rules of the storyworld, either inherited or otherwise established, would imply. This can be because there are further propositions or rules to be revealed which will render the situation unproblematic.

We will define these different variants on violation of expectation as *anomalies*. There are three configurations to consider, for a proposition *P* (and by generalisation for a situation *S*) in a viewpoint *V*:

Apparent anomaly: There are no explicitly provided relevant rules specifically within *V* that lead to *P*, and the rules inherited from a higher viewpoint V' fail to lead to *P*.
Definite anomaly: There are relevant rules specifically within *V* which lead to an outcome different from *P*.
Relative anomaly: There are explicitly provided relevant rules within *V* which lead to *P*, but the rules in a higher viewpoint V' do not lead to the counterpart of *P* in V'.

Where rules which are local to a viewpoint lead to a proposition or situation, we will say that this provides *support* for the proposition/situation. In a case of relative anomaly, the proposition *P* will be described as *supported*, and in apparent anomaly *P* will be described as *unsupported*.

The configuration which results in a relative anomaly involves a mismatch between the internal logics of the two viewpoints. In this case, we will say that the lower viewpoint has internal logic which is *discrepant* with respect to the higher viewpoint. (We will consider the notion of discrepant logic in jokes in Chapter 6.)

These kinds of anomaly have no inherent temporal element to their definition. Each describes one particular state of the viewpoints, and although a later state may be different, temporal change is not part of the definitions. This is in contrast to what we will term 'prediction' (see next subsection).

The phenomenon of apparent anomaly, in the sense defined above, can be observed in non-joke fiction, such as novels or short stories. Opening passages are particularly convenient for illustrating this, as the audience (reader) starts with a more or less empty storyworld. For example, George Orwell's novel *1984* famously starts with a statement that, in the opening scene, timepieces are striking thirteen. This explicit assertion ensures the clock-striking is a situation in the storyworld, but it would not follow from any rules inherited from the audience's real world, and there are not yet any text-specific rules which provide support. Similarly, a more recent novel begins thus: 'They had flown from England to Minneapolis to look at a toilet'(*Juliet Naked* by Nick Hornby, 2010, Penguin Books, London). From this sentence, the audience has to accept that there is a situation in the storyworld which lacks support using rules inherited from the audience's viewpoint, and for which there is, as yet, no text-specific rules offering support. Also, there are some story-characters ('*they*') who seem to be treating this situation as relatively normal, and whose viewpoints may therefore contain some as yet unknown rules which lead to this situation. This is currently an instance of apparent anomaly, but has the possibility of becoming relative anomaly once we learn more about these characters.

These ideas of anomaly will be useful when we come to examine incongruity-resolution jokes (Chapter 7), and therefore may appear to be specialised humour-specific parts of our supposedly general account of text comprehension. However, the definitions of 'support' and 'anomaly' add no new assumptions to our text model – they simply single out certain possible configurations and allocate convenient labels to them. Thus they do not constitute covert customisation of the text model for joke purposes, as is illustrated by the occurrences in novels.

We have presented the ideas of anomaly and support as logical configurations within or between the belief bases of viewpoints. It can be helpful to think of some of these configurations in terms of how they may affect the audience's cognition. Informally speaking, lack of support for a situation within a storyworld, as in an apparent or definite anomaly, can raise a question for the audience: why has this abnormal situation arisen? Very often, a narrative goes on to answer such questions by providing, perhaps indirectly, the internal logic of the storyworld and/or its characters (as happens in novels such as those cited above (Orwell, 1950; Hornby, 2010)).

We will use the term *justification question* to refer to this perspective on an apparent or definite anomaly. That is, this is the mental reaction of the audience to these types of anomaly. A justification question will be said to be *answered* when support for the apparently odd situation is discovered within the relevant viewpoint, thereby transforming it to a relative anomaly or possibly eliminating the anomaly.

There is also the case where the narrative presents some proposition(s) explicitly, but it is not immediately obvious what inferences from this information connect to the rest of the story so far. That is, the narrative has supplied information that appears at first to be insufficiently related to existing knowledge. The question does not derive from a lack of support for these new propositions, but rather from it not being clear how these propositions support something else. As will become clear when we examine specific jokes, these circumstances usually arise in a context which indicates, by the pragmatic conventions of telling stories and jokes, that the new information is intended to contribute to support for some previously conveyed situation/proposition. In this way, the new proposition(s) can be presented as answering an earlier justification question. How it achieves this connection is sometimes not at once obvious, and hence some further audience inference is needed. We will refer to this as the audience experiencing a *relevance question*. (The concept of 'relevance' is vast and complex, and there is no suggestion here that this captures that grander notion; the term 'relevance question' is used here simply as a convenient label for this specific type of information deficiency.)

To sketch it symbolically, a text may set up an unsupported situation S, and hence a justification question Q_1: 'why is S?'. Later, a proposition P may be presented in a way which conveys the impression that P will answer Q_1; that is, that $P \Rightarrow S$. If the implicative statement $P \Rightarrow S$ is itself not yet supported, then the narrating of P has created a relevance question Q_2: 'why does $P \Rightarrow S$?'. Further inference may establish a logical path from P to S, hence supporting both S (answering Q_1) and $P \Rightarrow S$ (answering Q_2). This shows that the relevance question based on P is essentially a justification question based on $P \Rightarrow S$.

The quest for coherence (Section 4.6) could be viewed as a recurring attempt to resolve justification and relevance questions. (See also remarks in Section 4.7.)

Prediction

In the course of text comprehension, an audience may, often unconsciously, treat certain future occurrences as more likely than others, whether as a result of parsing textual material or after making further inferences from the meaning of the text. Some of these occurrences may be at a relatively low level – for example, the presence of a specific word – and hence not even inside the storyworld. We treat this phenomenon as an aspect of audience inference, rather than part of internal logic. This is a forecast of an outcome which has not yet arisen during the comprehension process; that is, something inherently based on temporal sequence. For avoidance of ambiguity, we will use the term *prediction* to refer to this, rather than the term 'expectation' discussed in the previous subsection. We will explore the idea of 'prediction' further in Section 4.7 and in Chapters 5 and 8.

Intuitively, there would seem to be a relationship between this idea of likelihood and the notion of logical consequence that we have adopted for the internal logic, since logical reasoning could indicate what will happen next. We see this as audience inference (a process which happens in time) making use of internal logic (knowledge structures within viewpoints) to make predictions. However, we do not wish to treat predictions as being only the consequences indicated by the internal logic. Audience inference has access to other sources of information (e.g. the text itself, conventions of storytelling), and so may arrive at predictions which are quite separate from conclusions within the storyworld.

We should indicate a common meaning of the word 'prediction' which we will *not* be considering. This is the sense in which a scientific theory is said to 'predict' some observable phenomenon: the theory explains why the phenomenon takes the form that it does. Even if the theory is devised after the phenomenon has been observed, it can still be said to 'predict' the observations. For example, several centuries ago, scientists sought a theory which would 'predict' the known positions and orbits of the planets. We will try to be consistent in using 'prediction' for forecasts of future outcomes during text comprehension.

It might seem that by entertaining the idea of 'likelihood', we are dabbling in probability, specifically subjective probability (Jeffrey, 2004). We certainly do not rule out a possible formalisation in which likelihood would be modelled by probability (and audience inference might be based upon probabilistic logic (Nilsson, 1986)). There are some highly developed probability theories, without complete agreement on its foundations (Shafer & Pearl, 1990, Chapter 2). However, current ideas about joke comprehension do not, at present, depend on exact details of probabilities, nor on any precise model of probability. All that we need is the less theoretical, more informal, idea of events being more or less 'likely'. Although a suitable notion of mathematical probability might prove to be a good formalisation of the informal notion of 'likelihood', we are not ready to commit ourselves on this matter, since we are, as repeatedly remarked, adopting only the level of detail and abstraction that is needed. We therefore leave open the choice of an exact formal model, such as some variant of probability. We will return to the idea of probability when we consider the more low-level aspects of text comprehension, in Section 4.7.

4.6 Filling in gaps

Coherence

The ideas in this section could be seen as related to the issue of 'coherence' in a text: that is, how well do the component ideas of the story fit together? The question of what renders a text internally coherent is complex and difficult, with many contributing factors, such as causal linkage (Black & Bern, 1981), narrative point of view (Black, Turner, & Bower, 1979), and a variety of discourse effects (Fetzer, 2012). There is no agreed theory of how best to characterise this elusive quality. We will not adopt coherence as a concept in our abstract model, but merely observe that text comprehension could be seen as a constant quest for coherence:

> ...theories of narrative text comprehension generally equate successful discourse comprehension with the construction of a coherent mental representation of the state of affairs described in the text at hand...
>
> (Nieuwland & Berkum, 2008, pp. 604–605)

> ...most of the theories developed in the area of text comprehension, for example, have put their focus on coherence relations. Consequently, these theories have posited the construction of an internally coherent representation as the ultimate goal of comprehension.
>
> (Schroeder et al., 2008, p. 238)

Alonso (2014) also emphasises the centrality of coherence.

In particular, much of text comprehension is about adding information to what has been supplied by the text, in order to make connections or to make sense of the provided information. In this section, we look at some of these effects.

Accommodation and abduction

It has often been observed that some texts, sentences or utterances make sense only if certain other propositions are true in the context of use. For example, when a speaker uses the phrase '*my sister*' in a context where this seems to be referring to a real-world entity (e.g. '*I am going to visit my sister*'), this utterance makes complete sense only if the speaker has, or soon will have, a sister. Regularities like this are usually referred to as 'presuppositions' (Levinson, 1983; van der Sandt, 1988). Although there is some disagreement about the exact theoretical account of presuppositions (Karttunen, 1973; J. Katz & Langendoen, 1976; Stalnaker, 1973; van der Sandt, 2012), there seems to be general agreement that an audience can often understand a sentence containing presuppositions without needing to know the presupposed proposition(s) beforehand. In many cases, if the audience has no information that conflicts with the presupposed material, he will simply adopt those proposition(s) as true. In the example above of '*my sister*', if the audience has, up to that moment, no knowledge about the speaker's siblings, it is quite likely that he will adopt as true the fact that the speaker has (or had, or will have, according to the surrounding context) a sister. This phenomenon, of an audience automatically, and often unconsciously, assuming the propositions necessary for a perceived text to make sense, is usually referred to as 'accommodation' (Lewis, 1979; Roberts, 2015; van der Sandt, 2012).

Since a presupposed proposition may be required in order that the perceived text be felicitous, there is a relatively close relationship between the presupposed information and the explicit statement. However, audiences also make assumptions which are much looser, more general, and less justifiable. This is where someone posits some particular propositions as being true, because this would provide a reason for some known information being the case. This pattern of accounting for observed facts was dubbed *abduction* by Peirce (Hartshorne & Weiss, 1935, pp. 358ff.). Although it could be seen philosophically as a part of the scientific method (Fann, 1970), cognitive science treats abduction as a form of everyday reasoning (Hobbs, Stickel, Appelt, & Martin, 1993). For example, Charniak and McDermott (1985, p. 453) describe it as '... the generation of explanations for what we see around us'. They give the example that from two accepted propositions, '*a drunk person cannot walk in a straight line*' and '*Jack cannot walk in a straight line*', someone may leap to the conclusion '*Jack is a drunk person*'. Famously, this is the type of reasoning that Sherlock Holmes was often depicted as using.

We will rely on both accommodation of presuppositions and abductive reasoning as mechanisms of audience inference in our later commentaries on joke comprehension. However, the audience's licence to augment explicit information is not unrestricted, as we shall see in the next subsection.

Disbelief-suspension

As we mentioned in Section 3.3, Raskin (1985) has suggested that the routine conveying of facts from speaker/writer to audience has the status of 'bona-fide communication' (BFC), but there can also be 'non-bona-fide communication' (NBFC), in which factually incorrect or misleading material is conveyed, violating certain accepted conventions about truthfulness or cooperation. Lying is a clear example of NBFC, but Raskin and Attardo (1994) state that joke-telling, being more socially acceptable than lying and more frequent than play-acting, is '... the default non-bona-fide communication mode, or the one which is closest to bona-fide communication.' (Raskin & Attardo, 1994, p. 36) They go on to propose some pragmatic principles governing joke-telling (see also Attardo (1994, 2001)).

We will leave aside the question of which NBFC mode of communication is 'closest' to BFC, but it seems clear that basic storytelling is a relatively simple instance of NBFC. What distinguishes the recounting of a truthful anecdote from the narrating of a fictional story is the status of the information content and how the audience is expected to treat that content. In particular, comprehension of fiction generally relies on the audience treating as true, within the storyworld, propositions or inferences which they might not accept within their real world. This is sometimes referred to as '(willing) suspension of disbelief', after a phrase used by Coleridge (Engell & Bate, 1983, p. 6). Most of the content in a typical story is, in a strict sense, factually inaccurate, as authors routinely introduce new characters, places, etc. These non-facts are typically accepted without problems, as long as they do not seem abnormal within the particular narrative context. Often, the introduced objects, characters or situations are fantastical or even impossible, but, in a properly constructed story, are absorbed by the audience (as remarked in the quotation from Sanford and Emmott in Section 4.3). This can be seen as the deployment of a *disbelief-suspension* convention, which allows apparently abnormal information to be incorporated into a storyworld. The abnormality here is relative to whichever rules are currently in place for the storyworld, which will often be directly inherited from the audience's real world, but could also be unreal rules established by earlier parts of the text, as happens in science-fiction, fantasy, or even tales set in other historical periods. This process is highly influenced by cultural conventions about the type of text: fairy tales, magical realism and science-fiction each have rather different constraints on what is accepted as plausible, as do jokes. This licence is most noticeable when the propositions are particularly abnormal.

It seems intuitively clear that there must be limits to the power of this convention, in the sense that overly implausible material may cause an audience to feel puzzled, dissatisfied, or even reluctant to accept propositions in the storyworld. Story writers can use this effect deliberately to raise questions in the mind of the audience (Bailey, 1999a, 1999b; Dibell, 1995).

In a relatively naturalistic text, audience inference is mostly about which propositions are true in the storyworld, whereas in a less natural storyworld, as in fantasy or science fiction, the audience has also to infer how the storyworld works – that is, what patterns of consequence operate in that world. In joke comprehension, the problem is directly comparable to this latter case, in that the audience may have to infer the rules that apply within the joke world. This means that disbelief-suspension is pertinent to all forms of conceptual items within the storyworld, both basic propositions and rules (logical connections between propositions).

Within our framework, disbelief-suspension has to be an aspect of audience inference rather than part of the internal logic of a storyworld. This is because it operates at a metalevel with respect to the content of the storyworld, passing judgement on potential additions to that content. The audience has to figure out the storyworld's internal logic as the narrative proceeds, and part of this could involve the application of disbelief-suspension conventions.

We will treat disbelief-suspension as a mechanism which assesses the suitability of potential individuals, propositions or rules for inclusion in the storyworld. This mechanism does not itself introduce new material into a storyworld – it merely assesses the *magnitude* of potential insertions into that world. In the ongoing task of figuring out the internal logic, any item which is considered for inclusion – for example, as a result of abduction – will be rated in this way. The collected assessments of 'magnitude' in the course of the text indicate how much disbelief-suspension is required, which then contributes to an overall judgement about the plausibility of the story. Disbelief-suspension could be seen as another manifestation of the idea of 'normality' which we discussed in Section 4.5.

Although there are degrees of disbelief-suspension, roughly corresponding to the magnitude of the implausibility in the element of the story, there also seems to be some sort of threshold whereby certain non-real concepts become accepted by disbelief-suspension and then are not treated as abnormal. In particular, such accepted items do not require 'support' and do not give rise to 'justification questions' (in the sense of Section 4.5).

This mechanism will take account of various aspects. These include the plausibility of the candidate addition relative to other knowledge, either about the real world or the storyworld, and also the application of specialised conventions for a particular genre, such as certain kinds of magic in fairy tales, or talking animals within jokes. Such conventions reflect, informally speaking, one aspect of the idea of a 'genre' of fiction, but this does not mean that we will, with our limited objectives, try to introduce any categorisation of narratives into genres.

We will return to this topic when we examine logic in more detail (Chapter 6) and explore incongruity in jokes (Chapter 7).

4.7 Processing

Incremental processing

Intuitively, introspection suggests that text comprehension proceeds in an incremental fashion, in the sense that small successive segments of text are interpreted rapidly as they are perceived, and the relevant cognitive processing is not postponed until the end of a larger stretch of text such as a sentence. This is not merely a naive view:

> There is ample evidence, however, that sentence comprehension is incremental: we do not wait until we have heard an entire sentence to start disambiguating and comprehending...
>
> (Levy, 2008, p. 1129)

Evidence for this has been gathered, for example, from studies involving neural ERP (Xiang & Kuperberg, 2015) or eye-tracking (Altmann & Mirković, 2009; Demberg & Keller, 2008).

We will treat these incremental steps as applying both to the conversion from text to meaning (Section 4.2) and to any further processing of the meaning relative to the audience's state of knowledge (Section 4.4). As Levy notes, one important property 'that must be accounted for by any realistic theory of human sentence comprehension' is 'inference on the basis of incomplete input' (p. 1127), because 'Comprehenders are able to make inferences about later parts of the sentence based on what they have heard earlier in the sentence.' (p. 1129)

Not only does the inferential expansion of the basic information in the text occur incrementally as the text is processed, there may well be further processing of this sort after the last item in the text. (This additional inferring may well be a significant part of joke comprehension – see Section 7.3.)

Even if processing is incremental, in the sense that some meaningful representation and inferences can be extracted at each small step, this does not mean that it provides a steady accrual of meaning, with no changes, since, as we have already observed, new information can override previous assumptions.

Cognitive effort

Generally, the processing of text, including inferences, will be extremely fast, and the audience will not be consciously aware of it. Schroeder et al. (2008, p. 237) describe the integration of new information, by the reader of a text, as 'quick' and 'effortless'. It can be hard for someone who has read or listened to a text to remember afterwards which propositions were stated directly and which were inferred automatically (Foss & Hakes, 1978, Ch. 5). However, there may be occasions when the absorption of new information requires more cognitive processing than usual, even to the extent that the audience is aware of a conscious effort, perhaps as a form of problem-solving. That is, the *cognitive effort* needed at each step may vary greatly.

Kahneman (2012), on the basis of many psychological studies, proposes that human cognition relies on two modes of processing, which he labels 'System 1' and 'System 2'. System 1 is the default mechanism which a person relies on most of the time, usually unconsciously. It makes fast inferences, often based on inadequate data, coming to conclusions which are likely to be useful but might actually be inaccurate. System 2 is a slower processing facility which operates more carefully and often consciously. It tends to take account of more information, use more resources than System 1, and to treat cognition as a form of problem-solving. Kahneman's model has System 1 in charge until a difficulty arises, for example in making sense of some stimuli. Then, System 2 is invoked to try to solve this problem.

Ventis (2015) outlines how certain accounts of joke comprehension can be seen as the audience switching from System 1 to System 2 mode on encountering the punch line (see Section 7.3). It may be the case that such switches occur more generally, not just at the punch line. That is, any occasion where the audience feels a conscious need for thought may be a change from System 1 to System 2, perhaps for a brief period.

It seems likely that the quantity of effort at any particular step in processing can be viewed as varying continuously, rather than being subdivided into distinct categories 'low' and 'high'. However, when we analyse jokes, it will be convenient to refer to those occasions when the effort is sufficient to create a sensation, in the audience, of a delay and/or a need for problem-solving.

The occasions where increased effort is required can be seen as instances of puzzlement, of which there are three cases of interest, differing not in the amount of effort but in the stage in the comprehension process at which the puzzle is solved. These are different ways in which the audience reacts to the text, not categories of texts or of dialogues. We will label them as follows:

Assimilation difficulty: The audience is able to make sense of the immediate input after some reflection, with no further information from any subsequent text, or from other sources.

Temporary gap: The audience is not able to make sense of the data on the basis of existing information, but manages this soon afterwards, once further information is obtained (typically, later in the text).

Unexplained gap: The audience is unable to make sense of the data on the basis of existing information, and still cannot do this even after further information is obtained from the entire remainder of the text.

When describing joke comprehension, we will adopt the hypothesis that what we have called 'justification' and 'relevance' questions (Section 4.5) can lead to these kinds of information gap, resulting in additional cognitive effort.

Revising interpretations

We observed in Section 4.4 that audience inference would have to be 'non-monotonic' to allow for revisions to information during comprehension. This phenomenon can happen in small and relatively uninteresting ways during text comprehension, largely unnoticed by the audience, since it is processed automatically at some unconscious level. However, sometimes new information can cause such a radical revision of interpretation that the audience becomes aware that some misunderstanding has occurred. Any processing model of text comprehension must allow for the revision of interpretations, major and conscious as well as minor and automatic.

Many psycholinguistic studies have been carried out to investigate how people process ambiguous texts. A recurring observation can be summarised thus:

> Typically, listeners are not aware of the potential ambiguity that lurks within many of the utterances they hear. They generally come up with only one conscious interpretation of the input, and in the vast majority of cases it is the appropriate one.
>
> (Foss & Hakes, 1978, p.121)

(See also Jackendoff (1987, pp. 115–119), Kuperberg and Jaeger (2016, p. 46).) On the other hand, there are experiments which suggest that, at some low and unconscious level, a listener takes account of all the possible meanings of a phrase or sentence (Carey, Mehler, & Bever, 1970). Garrett (1970) argues that this apparent contradiction can be resolved by the hypothesis that where a text has multiple possible interpretations, all interpretations are processed to some extent temporarily during the comprehension process, but only one preferred interpretation emerges at a conscious level as the final reading of the text. Moreover, where the person is initially given a bias towards one possible interpretation, but then presented with information or a question which requires the less preferred interpretation, more cognitive processing time is needed (Carey et al., 1970). That is, where later information conflicts with the earlier bias, the text is understood only after what we are calling an assimilation difficulty (see previous subsection). This is manifested in the much-studied phenomenon of 'garden-path' sentences (Bever, 1970), in which the typical reader/hearer adopts a particular grammatical interpretation early in the comprehension process, only to find that this is not syntactically compatible with a later part of the text. Such scenarios usually result in a difficulty in understanding.

This raises a key question: if the audience is, as part of normal text comprehension, constantly revising the knowledge state, what kinds of change count as 'major' – i.e. conscious repairs of misunderstandings? With our limited remit here, we do not pretend to answer this difficult question. We simply record that there seems to be some sort of distinction, and that we will refer to it when exploring joke comprehension.

Salience

During text comprehension, different abstract entities, such as meanings of words, may have differing degrees of *salience* in the mind of the audience. This idea has been assumed, implicitly or explicitly, for decades. It is central to various computational accounts of how anaphoric expressions are interpreted (Grosz, Joshi, & Weinstein, 1995; Hirst, 1981; Sidner, 1981), and, at some level of abstraction, could be seen as part of the phenomena of 'priming' (see references in Section 4.2) and 'alignment' (Branigan, Pickering, McLean, & Cleland, 2007; Garrod & Pickering, 2004). The prominence of entities, ranging from abstract meanings to actual words, can affect how likely a speaker is to use them in generating an utterance, and how likely a reader/hearer is to choose them when interpreting a text.

An item can achieve a relatively high level of prominence even if it is neither present nor true within any viewpoint of the story. If a character says '*I've never seen an elephant with six legs and two trunks*', then the imaginary concept of this creature is immediately salient. Similarly, when a proposition is negated or denied (e.g. '*I am not a crook*'), that proposition takes on a degree of salience. Comparable observations apply to concepts which arise not directly from utterances but from inference by the audience, since reasoning may lead to certain concepts being obliquely involved and hence increasing their relative prominence.

As with all the factors we are considering, we focus solely on salience from the audience's perspective. That is, we are interested in the extent to which some object, concept or proposition impinges upon the audience's consciousness, and how this can be affected by various factors, such as proximity, vocal emphasis, etc.

This notion of salience can be thought of as a partial ordering on abstract objects and propositions within the audience's viewpoint, and hence could perhaps be approximated by some sort of numerical rating.

Salience may also be related to the matter of unmentioned propositions within a storyworld. There may, in the course of a story, be facts which could in principle be inferred with high certainty and high plausibility – for example, that some story-character, being human, has a liver – but which do not enter into the audience's deliberations about the storyworld. There are a vast multitude of potential propositions like this, which are below some threshold of awareness or attention, but may at any moment be dredged up into focus by a step in the discourse. We will distinguish two particular degrees of salience in the audience's viewpoint. These correspond roughly to the audience either being consciously aware of something, or being wholly unaware of it, at least at any conscious level. We will use the terms *aware of* and *unaware of* to describe these two possible relationships between an audience and some entity.

It is possible that the various phenomena described in this section actually result from disparate mechanisms. For example, there might be different principles governing the priming of a lexical item and the audience's awareness of certain background propositions. However, we are mainly concerned with setting out a overall abstract interface which our analyses of jokes can use. It does not matter, for our purposes, if these are all distinct in their underlying mechanisms. We want our text comprehension interface to manifest these effects, without regard for how they come about. This means that we are adopting the observed phenomenon, rather than any theoretical explanation, as past of our minimal specification of a text comprehension model. We will, for convenience, treat all these effects as manifestations of a scale of mental prominence for which we adopt the umbrella term 'salience'. If it were to be shown that there are a few different causes at work, that would make little or no difference to our joke analyses.

The audience's immediate interpretation of the text is affected only by the audience's idea of salience. However, when we examine certain jokes (Section 9.2), it appears that we must allow for story-characters having salience measures which differ from that of the audience. For the audience to be able to comprehend such jokes, it must be possible for the audience to make inference about the salience measures within viewpoints, just as there is inference about propositions and rules within viewpoints (see Section 4.4).

Probability in text processing

We have briefly (Section 4.5) mentioned probability in the context of general knowledge organisation. However, it has also been at the heart of a widely supported view of the text-processing aspects of language comprehension over the past two decades (Jurafsky, 1996; Kuperberg & Jaeger, 2016; Levy, 2008). This often includes an arrangement in which there can be inter-communication between relatively high, conceptual levels and lower, concrete linguistic levels – 'a multi-representational hierarchical actively generative architecture' (Kuperberg & Jaeger, 2016, p. 33). However, these probability models are usually narrowly focused on the task of incremental text parsing, and typically do not apply probabilistic methods to general reasoning about the world. That is, the probabilities involve relations between linguistic entities such as words and syntactic structures, rather than between higher conceptual units.

In this approach, to simplify somewhat, two sets of entities are given probabilistic ratings at each stage of comprehension:

Partial interpretations: The probabilistic model represents multiple possible interpretations of a text by positing a probability distribution across all interpretations of the text so far.

Possible continuations: A widespread (and intuitively natural) idea is that the text so far processed makes certain continuations more or less likely.

> The probabilistic model represents this as a probability distribution across possible future continuations of the text.

A probability distribution over possible textual continuations could be seen as a form of probabilistic prediction, in the sense that we will discuss in Chapter 5. Intuitively, the probabilities allocated to potential continuations could be assigned at a very low lexical level, as when the start of a famous quotation may result in the rest of that known phrase taking on a high probability. Or probabilities might be attached to high level concepts, for example, what will occur next in a story. Probabilities may vary across these levels. For example, a specific phrase could simultaneously be the conclusion of a particular known quotation, a play on words, and a sexual innuendo, and these could have different probabilities. However, current probabilistic models of language comprehension apply primarily to lower, more linguistic, levels.

Although there has been much theoretical work to elaborate the workings of probability distributions over linguistic structures (e.g. Linzen & Jaeger, 2014), we do not require that level of detail here. In particular, there seems to be no need to adopt the idea of a probability distribution over partial interpretations. That would depend to some extent on what consequences such a distribution would have for the subsequent understanding of the text, and in particular for any joke-related effects.

For example, it would be interesting if the probabilities in this distribution were to represent the salience of the possible interpretations, in a manner that accurately reflects the way in which salience affects the audience's treatment of subsequent text. That could then, as proposed by Mayerhofer and Schacht (2013), provide a more precise model of the phenomenon of the audience usually being aware of only one interpretation of the text so far, and possibly of some form of prediction (see Chapter 5). We will leave it open whether the relative salience of different interpretations could be represented probabilistically, as this allows us to avoid details which are not directly germane to joke comprehension.

We will say more about linguistic aspects of joke comprehension in Chapter 9.

4.8 Narrative aspects

Absence of narrative structure

Because it is important to recognise what is and is not distinctive about joke comprehension, we have emphasised that joke comprehension shares many of the general properties of story comprehension. It is also obvious that many jokes are miniature narratives. Where a joke clearly constitutes a story, then a better model of narration will help in giving a fuller account of the comprehension of that text. However, we have refrained from incorporating aspects of genuine narrative, such as plot structure, into our outline of essential requirements for joke comprehension. There are three reasons for this:

- Not all jokes are recognisable as conventional narratives: there are various forms of pun, riddles, 'knock-knock' jokes, aphorisms, etc.
- It has been observed (Attardo, 1994; Ritchie, 2004) that it is sometimes possible for the same joke (in essence) to be delivered in ways which differ in their linguistic structure, either at the sentence or the discourse level. This is one relatively superficial way in which a joke can take on a non-narrative appearance. (Attardo and Raskin (1991) refer to this as a variation in 'narrative strategy'.)
- Higher-level narrative constructs, such as subplots or three-act structure (McKee, 1999) have not been used in previous analyses of jokes to describe why a particular text is humorous.

As we have set out in the earlier sections of this chapter, general text comprehension involves the audience encountering information in stages, and attempting, using inference as necessary, to integrate this into a coherent interpretation. Story understanding and joke comprehension both inherit these attributes, and also rely on the depiction of a fictional world in which there can be imaginary characters and in which different norms can apply. However, we are taking no position about higher narrative structure.

Conventions of narrative

As well as disbelief-suspension (Section 4.6), narrative relies on other conventions established within a particular society and culture.

One obvious class of convention is the *stock character*: a type of story-character who has several attributes which often cluster together within stories, or some particular subclass of stories. Fairy tales abound with these: the handsome prince, the beautiful maiden, the wicked witch, the evil stepmother, the wise magician, etc. A crime novel may feature a world-weary, wise-cracking, superficially tough but inwardly gallant private detective. Another conventional construct within stories is the *standard situation*. Westerns have their cavalry charges, public hangings, one-to-one shoot-outs, etc., and a certain type of crime novel may feature a closed set of suspects, the surviving members of which are gathered together at the denouement by the brilliant detective, another stock character.

All of these are handy devices for the storyteller, and they also simplify the story comprehension, as the audience can quickly absorb the story if many of the component parts are highly familiar and standardised. As Hurley et al. (2011, p. 163) put it: 'A stereotype functions as a data-compression device that instantly references a huge library of exaggerated or oversimplified information'. Of course, such instruments of narration quickly lead to clichés, but we are not considering literary merit here, merely the constructs which the audience may encounter. Such ready-made components are particularly useful for jokes, where a situation has to be established within a very short text. Like the conventions for disbelief-suspension (Section 4.6), they can be deployed by an audience when a text contains indications that they are applicable.

Popescu (2011, p. 177) suggests that some of these ready-made packages of content may function merely to enhance a joke (see Section 3.5), or even simply to signal that a joke is intended (see Section 3.4).

Raskin (1985) suggests that standard devices like these can be seen as specific forms of 'scripts', as part of his script-based theory of jokes (see Section 7.7). Oring (1992a, pp. 8–9) and Davies (2004) agree that scripts would be suitable for expressing these unreal patterns found within jokes, but observe that these clichés are mere narrative or humorous conventions and do not reflect how people reason about reality, as would be the case for actual stereotypes. (As noted in Section 4.5, even if we accept that it is useful to make use of such stereotypical knowledge, this does not necessarily mean that it must be represented as frames or scripts.)

4.9 The results of comprehension

In the light of our objectives, as set out in Chapters 1, 2 and 3, and the various mechanisms and facilities reviewed in the current chapter, two questions arise. Firstly, what is the overall result of text comprehension? Secondly, which abstract entity should be considered as the object of predications such as '... is a successful joke comprehension' or '... results in amusement'?

To answer these two questions, we first have to describe in slightly more detail the process of text comprehension. We regard this process as progressing through a sequence of *comprehension states*, where a comprehension state contains a single hierarchical arrangement of viewpoints, along with any conceptual items in the belief bases of those viewpoints. At the start of the process, there is an initial comprehension state containing only those viewpoints which the audience has available generally, without any viewpoints specific to the text which is about to be encountered. As the comprehension proceeds, viewpoints are created and their belief bases develop, so that at each stage of comprehension there is a slightly different comprehension state; that is, the content of the interlinked viewpoints changes.

Of particular interest is the last in this sequence of comprehension states. That is, the comprehension state which results from post-text inference: a complete hierarchical structure of viewpoints, each with its own belief base. This is what the audience believes about the storyworld and any subordinate viewpoints, at the conclusion of the text. We will call this the *final comprehension state*, or sometimes *final state* for short.

However, it will become clear in later chapters that the success of joke comprehension depends on more than simply the final comprehension state.

To determine whether a text is a joke, and possibly amusing, it may be necessary to consider certain aspects of how the final state came into being. Hence, to provide enough information to determine verdicts such as jokehood and funniness we require a more comprehensive structure, representing the course of the comprehension process. We will use the term *comprehension history* to refer to an abstract entity that contains

(i) the ordered sequence of all comprehension states through which the comprehension process has passed;
(ii) the amount of cognitive effort expended in passing between consecutive comprehension states;
(iii) the time expended in passing between consecutive comprehension states.

This could be seen as a formal representation of what the audience experiences during joke comprehension, and it should contain sufficient information to determine, relative to the audience for whom this comprehension history has come into being, jokehood (is this text a joke?), funniness (how funny is this text?), and various socio-cultural reactions (e.g. is this joke offensive?). A full theory of jokes would state how these judgements are determined by the content of the comprehension history.

Since a comprehension state contains all the conceptual items in each of its viewpoints, and all of these are derived by audience inference based on audience-specific beliefs, a great deal of audience-dependent information is already held in the comprehension history. Also, the comprehension history contains, as an element of the viewpoint hierarchy, the audience's view of the real world. Hence, it could be that a theory of jokes would be able to state the conditions for jokehood or funniness solely in terms of the comprehension history, without including a model of the audience as a further source of information.

As noted in Section 3.6, joke analysis seems to involve hypothesising a Natural encounter with the joke. Hence, it could be that both jokehood and funniness are determinable from the hypothetical comprehension history for such an imagined encounter. The exact aspects of the history which are relevant to joke recognition or joke appreciation would depend on the details of the theory of jokes.

4.10 Summary

In later chapters, we will, following the research strategy set out in Section 2.3, assume availability of the text comprehension facilities described in this chapter. For convenience, we will, below, give a very brief reminder of the more prominent aspects of those facilities; fuller details can be found in the relevant sections earlier in this chapter.

We are considering text comprehension by a single idealised individual, the audience, and all relevant influences, such as context, are treated as being part of that audience's internal state. Text comprehension maps input text, spoken or written, into a literal meaning. Audience inference then draws out further information. This proceeds incrementally, in the sense that inference occurs as soon as an item of information can be extracted from the text so far. The inference process causes the construction of a hierarchical set of viewpoints, in which the root viewpoint is the audience's view of the real world, and that viewpoint has a directly subordinate viewpoint which is an abstract storyworld. In following chapters, we will refer to the storyworld that is built up during joke comprehension as the *joke world*, to allow for the possibility that it has particular characteristics not shared by all types of storyworld.

Each viewpoint contains a belief base, in which knowledge is structured into certain kinds of conceptual item which may have varying degrees of salience. Some of these items represent logical implications, within a logic with some default mechanism. This constitutes the internal logic of the specific viewpoint, which is to be distinguished from the audience inference that goes on as the audience makes sense of the text, which includes determining the internal logic of the storyworld. That determination of the logic is subject to the conventions of disbelief-suspension, which rate possible material for its plausibility.

During the comprehension process, audience inference may make predictions about possible outcomes later in the process. At some stages, the audience may become aware of a brief need for additional cognitive effort.

The contents of the belief base of a subordinate viewpoint are typically inherited from a superordinate viewpoint, although inherited material has a default status, and may be overridden by more definite evidence. There are other ways in which audience inference can fill in propositional content that has not been expressed explicitly, including accommodation of presuppositions and abductive reasoning. Despite these, there can be gaps and questions, where audience inference has hypothesised the existence of some situation in a viewpoint, but there is no support for it.

This chapter has been concerned only with the underlying text comprehension process, and does not cover all the factors which contribute to joke comprehension. So far, we have merely laid down the basic foundation which we regard as being shared with the comprehension of general text, particularly fiction. For jokes, these facilities mainly affect what we have called (Section 4.1) the 'conceptual' mechanisms. For the next few chapters (Chapters 5 to 9), we will continue to consider conceptual matters, but from the perspective of joke mechanisms rather than general text comprehension. The 'attitudinal' components of joke comprehension will be examined in Chapters 10 and 11. There will of course be further effects of the whole process, such as emotions and physical reactions like laughter, but we regard those as falling outside the remit of this book.

Chapter 5

Processing and prediction

5.1 Variants of prediction

As we noted earlier, the expressions 'expectation' and 'prediction' seem to be treated as equivalent by humour analysts. In Section 4.5 we adopted distinct interpretations for these two terms: 'expectation' concerns relations between situations within the internal logic, 'prediction' is about events occurring during audience inference. We will now consider different notions of how prediction comes about.

One notion of prediction involves the assignment of differing probabilities to possible future events, as used in some current approaches to text parsing (Section 4.7). We will refer to this as the *probabilistic* notion of prediction.

Another notion of prediction is advocated by Wyer and Collins (1992), who note that the comprehension of each segment of a stimulus brings particular knowledge structures to the fore; in our terms, these items become more salient. Furthermore, new information is interpreted primarily with respect to what is most accessible at that moment. Hence, the early part of a text causes the audience to have certain concepts more readily available, and the ease of comprehension of subsequent segments of text will depend on the degree of accessibility of appropriate items of knowledge. Increased cognitive effort (see Section 4.7) can occur where the necessary knowledge is not easily accessible, even if the audience does possess that knowledge. Predictions are then implicitly represented as the set of continuations which are processed relatively easily using the currently accessible knowledge structures. This notion of prediction is graded, in the sense that ease of processing is not an all-or-nothing category. We will refer to this as the *accessibility* view of prediction.

A third way of formulating prediction reflects fairly closely the everyday usage of the word. In this, a prediction specifies a set of future outcomes and excludes certain other outcomes. For example, in normal parlance, predicting sunshine and clear skies excludes the possibility of heavy rain. Although a prediction of this sort seems at first glance to specify a single outcome, in fact it describes a set of possible outcomes, since any concrete statement of a prediction is bound to be at some level of abstraction, omitting finer details.

Different values for these finer details can lead to different variants of the predicted outcome. For example, predicting warm weather omits an exact temperature, and so may be satisfied by a range of values; predicting that a particular athlete will win a certain race omits details of the winning margin of time or distance, again allowing the prediction to become true in a number of different ways. In the case of text comprehension, there might be a semantic prediction that a phrase describing a form of transport is imminent, so that '*train*' or '*bus*' would fulfil the prediction, but '*cauliflower*' would violate it. It is important that some possible outcomes are excluded by the predicted set, otherwise the prediction is vacuous. We will refer to a prediction of a particular set of possibilities as a *specified outcome* prediction. It could be seen as a special case of probabilistic prediction, in which the probability distribution has a particular form.

As we will see in Chapter 8, there are different models of 'surprise' depending on which version of prediction is adopted.

5.2 Violations of predictions

When trying to analyse predictions in detail, the following states of knowledge might be involved, when some situation or information E is perceived or discovered:

Prior: immediately before E is encountered;
Posterior: immediately after E is encountered;
Integrated: after an explanation has been composed for E;
Alternative: a hypothetical state (following Prior) in which E did not take place.

As we will see in Chapters 7 and 8, some authors link humour to 'violation of predictions'. For the three variants of prediction in Section 5.1, there are three corresponding notions of 'violation'.

For the probabilistic notion of prediction, a violation can be defined in terms of a comparison of two probability distributions, from the knowledge states Prior and Posterior. There is no single accepted definition, but presumably a violation occurs when the Posterior distribution is noticeably different from the Prior distribution. As we will see in Chapter 8, there is at least one rigorous mathematical definition of 'difference between distributions' which has been offered to capture the idea of 'degree of violation' of a probabilistic prediction.

As we remarked in the previous section, specified outcome prediction could be seen as a special case of probabilistic prediction. Hence, any definition used for a probabilistic prediction violation could be adapted for use with this other variant. There could also be a more specific, and intuitively natural, definition of violation, in which the actual event is found, in the Posterior state, not to fall within the class of events in the prediction (which would have given rise to an Alternative state).

As noted earlier, the accessibility definition of prediction assigns degrees of prediction based on ease of processing. This means it could lead to a definition of degrees of violation. Alternatively, a violation could be any event which results in higher processing, in some sense which would have to be defined. This would occur in the transition from Posterior to Integrated.

We will return to these ideas when we consider formal accounts of surprise, in Chapter 8.

5.3 Prediction: fast or slow

When exploring the role of prediction in joke comprehension, particularly as part of a surprise, we are interested in predictions which happen more or less automatically, rapidly, and quite possibly unconsciously, as the text unfolds for the audience. For example, in (2), it could be argued that the audience tacitly predicts a word such as '*engine*' or '*part*' for the end of the last sentence.

(2) A plane was delayed nearly an hour on take-off. When it eventually took to the air, the passengers asked the stewardess the reason for the late departure.
'Well,' she explained, 'the pilot was worried about a noise he heard coming from one of the engines and it took us a while to get a new pilot.'
(Tibballs, 2000, p. 40)

This is in contrast to considered predictions which someone might adopt after some pondering. (This distinction seems, intuitively, to reflect the 'System 1'/'System 2' distinction of Kahneman (2012) – see Section 4.7).

This point is of particular relevance to studies (Martin & Fearman, 2016; Pollio & Mers, 1974) which seek to find a relationship between the funniness of a joke and the ease with which people can, given a specific set-up, predict the punch line. When someone is explicitly asked, as in these studies, to supply an ending for a text, this conscious problem-solving task is distinct from the rapid predictability which is routinely established by conditional probabilities between linguistic items and by unconsciously accepted patterns of what is usual. (There is the additional but separate complication that responses in such studies may be influenced by a participant attempting to create a humorous ending, rather than merely trying to comprehend a segment of text.)

The above remarks refer to the extent to which the effort of formulating the prediction is conscious or not. There is also the question of whether the predicting agent (here, the audience) is consciously aware of their own prediction, once made. Everyday usage of the word, for sporting events, elections, weather, etc., tends to refer to predictions which are known to their creator, rather than remaining wholly unconscious. However, when we are discussing the details of cognitive processes, we have to also take account of predictions which may be much more obscure and subtle, being below the threshold of conscious awareness.

Of the three types of prediction discussed in Section 5.1, a specified outcome prediction could plausibly be of either sort: tacit and unconscious, or explicit and conscious. The other two types of prediction, probabilistic and accessibility, are perhaps most naturally seen as describing unconscious, implicit predictions. This avoids the awkwardness of claiming that a person consciously assigns probabilities to every conceivable future outcome, no matter how unlikely and how numerous these might be. Similarly, the accessibility model involves the treatment of a very wide set of information items and instantaneous reactions at a very low level.

It seems quite plausible that the violation of a prediction might reach an audience's consciousness, even where the original prediction has not been conscious. This seems to be the case for psycholinguistic parsing models (see Section 4.7) and also for the account of text understanding adopted by Suls (1972) in analysing jokes (see Section 7.3). When an analysis of a joke suggests that a particular prediction has occurred, often the only evidence of prediction consists of a feeling that a violation of prediction has been detected. That is, rather than there being an intuition about the prediction itself, a subjective reaction is registered to the non-predicted outcome. This sense of a violation may, in turn, stem from a sensation of increased processing effort (see Sections 4.7 and 5.4). Also, the occurrence of 'surprise' is sometimes equated to a 'violation of prediction' (see Chapter 8). Hence, there is a sense in which this one intuitive feeling, of additional processing effort, leads to the sensation of a prediction violation and surprise, which in turn may bring to light a prediction. Hence, these are not independently attested phenomena – effort, violation, prediction, surprise – but rather the observation of effort and some of its consequences.

5.4 Post-text processing

Two observations have been made about the cognitive processing in joke comprehension after the audience perceives the final segment of text, and possibly parses it into some linguistic representation of meaning: the effort involved is slightly elevated and this may require additional time. For example, it is possible that the audience might take a few hundred milliseconds to realise the implications of the final words of the joke (3).

(3) Last night I went to see the worst faith healer I've ever seen. He was so bad a guy in a wheelchair got up and walked out.

(Haskins & Arnott, 2017, p. 180)

Past analyses of humour never deny – but often do not highlight – the need for the audience to make some extra cognitive effort in order to comprehend a joke. Within joke comprehension, the pattern appears to be that some additional effort may be required after the initial interpretation of the last segment of text.

> It has been noted that the resolution of incongruity in humor involves mental expenditure . . ., so it is clear that the hearer of a joke must infer some implicit information, or perform some cognitive task.
>
> (Attardo, 1994, p. 289)

> If the audience is to experience a mental shift, they must be caught offguard with something that they cannot smoothly assimilate.
>
> (Morreall, 1983, p. 84)

As we will discuss in Section 7.3, post-text cognitive effort, as implied by the above two quotations, is at the forefront of, and perhaps the central point of, the joke-comprehension model of Suls (1972). Suls's ideas are widely cited as the basis of the incongruity-resolution model (Chapter 7), which means that many authors implicitly adopt this central component of joke comprehension. O'Shannon (2012) offers a classification of humorous items along two dimensions: incongruity and cognitive process. In this scheme, a joke can lie anywhere in the space defined by these two axes, for example having very low incongruity but a high demand for cognitive process. Oring (1992d, pp. 89–90) emphasises that there must be just the right amount of effort by the audience, as too much or too little can spoil the humorous effect. Wyer and Collins (1992, p. 673) make a similar claim regarding comprehension difficulty, in which they see humour as being an 'inverted-U' function of both time and effort. They cite a number of studies which appear to support this hypothesis. Interestingly, Apter and Desselles (2012) see cognitive effort, particularly the formulation by Wyer and Collins, as an 'enhancer' (Section 3.5) rather than a core component. This could be because Apter and Desselles consider humour in general, not merely jokes, and it may be that the role of cognitive effort is more crucial in the joke, a constructed form, than in some other types of humour.

In many jokes, the climax of joke comprehension consists of the audience uncovering, via post-text inference, some key material which has, until the final moment, not even been considered as a possibility. This is the case, for example, in (4).

(4) A husband and wife were sitting watching a TV program about psychology explaining the phenomenon of mixed emotions. The husband turned to his wife and said, 'Honey that's a bunch of crap. I bet you can't tell me anything that will make me both happy and sad at the same time.' She replied, 'Out of all your friends, you have the biggest penis.'

(Hurley et al., 2011, p. 139)

More specifically, the inference transforms the propositions from being something that the audience is 'unaware of' to something that the audience is 'aware of', in the terminology of Section 4.7. We will refer to any information which the audience infers only in the final state as a *final revelation*.

Another aspect of joke comprehension that many writers take to be obvious is the need for the final revelations to arrive suddenly: '... In any event, the recognition brought about by the punchline must be *sudden*. The punchline must bring about an abrupt cognitive reorganization in the listener.' (Oring, 1992b, p. 83). Similar remarks are made by Gruner (1997, Chapter 1), Hobbes (1840 [1650]), Hurley et al. (2011, p. 288), Morreall (1983, pp. 48–51), Schopenhauer (1964 [1883]), Suls (1983, p. 54). Some authors see this as an *incongruity* coming to light suddenly, whereas others state the need for a rapid *resolution*; these two concepts are explored in Chapter 7.

In the theory of Veatch (1998), the need for two interpretations to be juxtaposed 'simultaneously' implies a fast deviation from predictions. This is reminiscent of a suggested neural model of humour (B. Katz, 1993, 1996) in which rapid switching between meanings is central, and also of psychological findings about the periods during comprehension for which particular meanings are active during joke comprehension (Vaid, Hull, Heredia, Gerkens, & Martinez, 2003).

All this means that as well as the post-text cognitive effort affecting the success of a joke, the duration of this effort is also critical. Since the crucial content comes to the audience's awareness only as a result of the audience's own post-text inference, the timing depends entirely on the pace of that cognitive work – the insight arrives literally at the speed of thought. Hence, the question of timing is not wholly separate from the matter of cognitive effort.

At present, we are not sure how to make the informal notion of 'sudden' precise and operational, and mere inspection of joke texts does not provide clues. Morreall (1983, p. 49) suggests that the suddenness that is essential to laughter depends not only on the speed, but also on the magnitude of the change which is perceived. That is, if either the change is too small, or the speed too slow, then this will be too easy for the audience to assimilate, and not sudden enough for laughter. This remains to be properly tested. Humor-creating suddenness may be a subtle characteristic of cognitive processing, to be determined only by careful experimental work.

5.5 Summary

In this brief chapter, we have made the following points:

- We need to distinguish three different ideas of 'prediction': probabilistic, accessibility and specified outcome.

- Violations of prediction, typically detected on the grounds of increased cognitive effort, are defined slightly differently for the three variants of prediction.
- Predictions are not necessarily at a conscious level, but the audience is usually aware of violations of predictions.
- The speed of post-text inference and the effort involved may be critical factors in creating a humorous effect, but the exact influence of these factors has yet to be determined.

Chapter 6

Logic in jokes

6.1 The idea of pseudo-logic

The idea recurs, within the research literature on humour, that jokes crucially involve a distorted logic of some sort. One of the joke techniques of Freud (1966 [1912]) is 'faulty reasoning'. According to Ziv (1984, p. 98), jokes have a 'local logic', which occupies '...a middle position between logical and pathological thinking'. Attardo (1994, p. 148) lists a number of past authors who '...have attempted to define the types of playful logic that seems to operate in humor'. Attardo and Raskin (1991) allude to 'paralogisms', and the 'logical mechanisms' of the General Theory of Verbal Humour (GTVH) are said to be 'paralogical' (Hempelmann & Attardo, 2011, p. 147), and to embody 'a distorted, playful logic, that does not hold outside the world of the joke' (Attardo, 1994, p. 226). Oring says that 'The techniques of jokes are often paralogical, pseudological, or spurious', involving '...the drawing of conclusions from antecedent statements and facts even if those conclusions are not necessarily sound' (Oring, 2011, p. 151).

Some of the above authors do not present clear example jokes to illustrate their concept of flawed logic, but Freud says that (5) uses 'faulty reasoning', and Attardo and Raskin offer (6) as an instance of a 'figure-ground reversal' logical mechanism. Example (7) could perhaps be seen as relying on dubious logic.

(5) A gentleman entered a pastry-cook's shop and ordered a cake; but he soon brought it back and asked for a glass of liqueur instead. He drank it and began to leave without having paid. The proprietor detained him. 'What do you want?' asked the customer. – 'You've not paid for the liqueur.' – 'But I gave you the cake in exchange for it.' – 'But you didn't pay for that either.' – 'But I hadn't eaten it.'

(Freud, 1966 [1912], p. 60)

(6) How many Poles does it take to screw in a light bulb? Five. One to hold the light bulb and four to turn the table he's standing on.

(Attardo & Raskin, 1991, p. 295)

(7) A couple woke up in the morning. 'Did you hear the storm last night?' asked the husband.
'No,' said his wife. 'Was there thunder?'
'Yes, it was terrible. It sounded like the end of the world.'
'Why didn't you wake me? You know I can never sleep when it thunders.'
(Tibballs, 2000, p. 300)

None of the authors cited above define what they mean by 'logic', but their use of this term (and related terms such as 'syllogism' and 'drawing of conclusions') suggests that they do not mean merely that there is something vaguely odd going on inside jokes. It is not clear whether they have in mind a formally defined system of inference – as 'logic' would denote within mathematics, philosophy and formal semantics – but they must be alluding to some form of systematised reasoning, and this is the broad claim that we will examine here. We will, for clarity, examine the issue assuming a traditional notion of formal logic, but we see the arguments as applying equally to any systematic and formally defined notion of rule-based reasoning.

We will consider the following questions:

- Where, within the process of joke comprehension, does the faulty logic occur?
- Does the faultiness mean that there is a non-standard inference apparatus at work?
- How faulty can the humour-creating logic be?

These matters are closely related to the influential 'incongruity-resolution' account of humour, which we will explore in more detail in Chapter 7.

6.2 Which reasoning is faulty?

In Section 4.4, we set out a distinction between 'internal logic' (which describes propositions within the joke world) and 'audience inference' (the process that the audience goes through in making sense of the joke). (See Table 6.1 for a brief comparison of these two notions.)

This raises a question: to which of these two reasoning systems are writers on humour referring when they mention 'faulty logic'? We have already observed that the internal logic can deviate from accuracy in the interests of creating a fictional world, and that there is no reason to assume that the audience would deliberately reason incorrectly. This suggests that the internal logic is the prime candidate for being 'faulty' in this humour-related way.

Although Hurley et al. (2011) make no mention of faulty logic, they remark that 'The humor in fictions is the humor of a logic internal to the story...' (p. 193), which seems unambiguous. However, many of the authors quoted in the previous section do not make it clear which of 'internal logic'

Table 6.1 Internal logic and audience inference

	Internal Logic	*Audience Inference*
Role	Defines possible situations	Builds interpretations
Process in time	No	Yes
Scope	Separate for each viewpoint	Across all viewpoints
Level	Inside joke world	Metalevel
Validity	May not match real world	As correct as possible

and 'audience inference', are to be regarded as 'pseudological' or 'paralogical'. Some of Ziv's remarks about 'local logic' apparently describe what we term 'internal logic', but he sometimes seems to imply that the audience uses the flawed logic:

> '... to resolve incongruities, one can either use logic or employ a different mode of thinking. The particular way of approaching incongruity in humor is what I call *local logic* ...' (p. 81).
>
> 'We are accustomed to logical thinking, and all of a sudden it does not work. Failing to solve a joke's incongruity by logic, we try the thought mode of local logic.' (p. 96)
>
> (Ziv, 1984)

The GTVH approach seems to make a similar conflation. The quotations in Section 6.1 above seem to have the logical mechanism (LM) describing aspects of the joke's meaning, thus involving logical connections within the joke (internal logic). Similarly, many illustrative examples of LM (Attardo, 1997; Attardo, Hempelmann, & Di Maio, 2002; Hempelmann & Attardo, 2011) seem to be statements of semantic or other relationships within jokes, rather than processes. Raskin, Hempelmann, and Taylor (2009, p. 292) say that the LM is '(situationally-)false reasoning', a description which could apply to either audience inference or internal logic. On the other hand, some statements seem to place the LM within audience inference: it is a 'dynamic cognitive process' (Hempelmann, 2004, p. 383), and 'the LM is the resolution itself, not just an enabling mechanism thereof... the resolution is a dynamic phenomenon, the enabling mechanism is a static component of the text' (Attardo, 1997, p. 409).

The distinction between internal logic and audience inference is important. If we are trying to elaborate the ways in which joke worlds can operate, we should concentrate on the internal logic of the joke, without the distraction of possible cognitive processing by an audience trying to understand the joke. Conversely, in mapping out the comprehension process, we should not confuse it with possibly faulty logic which joke-characters may adopt (although the audience inference is about the internal logic).

As we have outlined (Section 4.3), the information within a story or joke, including logic implications, can be regarded as belonging to one or more separate 'viewpoints', each with contents (the 'belief base') defining what implications hold in that viewpoint. As remarked in Section 4.4, stories may deviate from reality, and we suggested that this was a characteristic of the internal logic, not of the audience inference; the latter, in contrast, is as accurate as the audience can achieve. There is no reason to change this position for the special case of jokes. Any deviations from strict real-world validity in the implications within jokes can be confined to the internal logic, often within one specific viewpoint. For example, (8) has a farmer-character, in whose viewpoint there is some non-standard reasoning.

(8) Farmer Giles goes out and ploughs one of his fields with a steamroller. 'What are you doing?' asks his wife. 'Isn't it obvious?' he says. 'I'm growing mashed potatoes.'

(Haskins & Arnott, 2017, p. 182)

Many jokes can be found in which there is unsound reasoning within the joke world, typically attributed to a specific story-character. In contrast, there is no evidence that the cognitive work which the audience carries out in order to understand the joke contains flaws that have particular effects on humour.

This does not imply that audience inference will never make mistakes while interpreting a joke, since many jokes, such as (9), involve the audience being temporarily misled (see Section 7.6 for more on this).

(9) I woke up at six o'clock this morning and lay there with a terrible hangover. Already my next-door neighbour was out mowing his front garden. At first I thought I'd smack him in the mouth. But then I thought, 'No! Blow it! He'll just have to mow round me.'

(Haskins & Arnott, 2017, p. 156)

However, such transient misinterpretation is a distinct phenomenon from the way that the internal structure of the joke can involve flawed logic.

Typically, the joke depicts or implies the anomalous situation, but does not spell out explicitly an ordered sequence of logical steps leading to that situation. The audience, in order to account for the unlikely situation, then may guess that some fictional character subscribes to reasoning which seems erroneous in the audience's own viewpoint. Audience inference always has the assumption – based on the fact that a joke is being interpreted (Section 3.3) – that whenever the material being considered is a joke, there may well be strange reasoning. Sometimes, this is emphasised by the presence in the joke of some conventionally 'stupid' character or social setting, as in example (13) in Section 6.4.

6.3 Faultiness and viewpoints

Within jokes, faulty logic involves what we have labelled (Section 4.5) as 'discrepant logic': a difference between the internal logics of two viewpoints. In particular, some situation occurs within the joke world, but lacks support in some dominating viewpoint; i.e. there is a 'relative anomaly'. For example, the actions of the patient-character in (10) seem to require an internal logic for that character's viewpoint which is different from real-world normality.

(10) Patient: 'My wife thinks I'm crazy because I like sausages.'
Psychiatrist: 'Nonsense, I like sausages too.'
Patient: 'Great – you should come and see my collection. I've got hundreds of them.'

(Tibballs, 2000, p. 256)

Often, the dominating viewpoint is one which could reasonably be taken as a standard, such as the audience's view of the real world. This could contribute to the feeling that there is flawed logic – the very notion of 'faulty' suggests that not all viewpoints have equal authority. The idea is not so much that one of the interpretations is 'correct' (in the sense of accurately matching the real world), but that one of the viewpoints is taken as the norm with respect to which propositions and rules in the other viewpoint may be seen as deviant.

Sometimes, a joke narrative will establish fictional norms which may not match the real world, but against which there can be violations. For example, (11) sets up a world in which, somehow, a tap-dancing duck is normal, only to violate this norm before the end of the set-up, thereby creating a justification question which is answered by the punch line (see Section 7.4).

(11) A circus owner walked into a bar and found everyone gathered around a table. On the table was a duck tap dancing on an upturned flower pot. The circus owner was so impressed he immediately bought the duck and the flower pot for 1,500 dollars. Hundreds flocked to see the duck's first performance in the Big Top but, to everyone's disappointment, the duck didn't dance a step. The angry circus owner went back to the bar to seek out the man who had sold it to him.
'That duck is a fraud,' raged the circus owner. 'He hasn't danced a step for me.'
'That's odd. Did you remember to light the candle under the pot?'

(Tibballs, 2000, pp. 56–57)

In jokes, the viewpoint in which faulty reasoning occurs is almost always the viewpoint of a story-character, as in (8) (ploughing mashed potatoes) and (10) (the collector of sausages). (As will be discussed in Section 11.5, there are occasional examples where it is the top level of the joke world, or even the audience's view of the real world.) The views of that story-character are then deemed erroneous, and often stupid, relative to either the norms of the joke world or the way that the real world operates, which the joke world will inherit by default. Where there are two story-characters with differing views, as in (10), the information associated with one story-character will usually be shared with a higher viewpoint, such as the joke world or the real world. This could come about because the information originated in the higher viewpoint and was inherited by default into the story-character's viewpoint. The discrepancy between the two character viewpoints is then also present between one character viewpoint and this higher viewpoint. For example, in a successful comprehension of example (10), the audience's viewpoint is likely to agree with that of the psychiatrist-character.

As we shall see in Section 6.6, for a joke to give the intuitive feeling of humorously faulty logic there may have to be further factors, not merely discrepant logic.

6.4 Some illustrative examples

We can use some examples to illustrate the distinction, within joke comprehension, between audience inference and faulty internal logic.

(12) A woman sat down in a psychiatrist's office. 'I think I may be a nymphomaniac,' she said.
'I see. Well, I can help you, but I ought to tell you in advance that my fee is 75 dollars an hour.'
'Hmmm,' she said. 'How much for all night?'
(Tibballs, 2000, p. 254)

In (12), both the internal logic and the audience inference rely on a (perhaps socially unacceptable) stock character (Section 4.8), the nymphomaniac, deemed to have an absurdly inflated sexual appetite. The internal logic in the woman-character's viewpoint is something like this:

The psychiatrist-character has offered services for a fee; this is an offer of sexual activity; an hour is not sufficient; hence a longer session should be requested.

Once again, this is not reasoning that the audience needs to concur with, but involves a perspective attributed to a story-character. This attribution occurs as a result of audience inference about the circumstances and dialogue in the story, working back from the punch line:

The patient-character has asked the price for an all-night session. Hence, she is interested in an all-night session with the psychiatrist-character. She is a potential nymphomaniac. Hence, she may be proposing an extensive sexual encounter. This could be because she has interpreted the psychiatrist-character's offer of help as an offer of sex, in return for a fee.

This sketch emphasises that the audience inference process has to discover the internal logic.

Assuming that the audience does not regard the sexual interpretation as justified by the circumstances, we have a discrepancy between the audience's and the patient-character's viewpoint. At an early stage where the audience has not yet worked out the internal logic as sketched here, there would be, in our terminology, an apparent anomaly. Once the audience has detected the internal logic of the patient-character, thus discovering the support, there is a relative anomaly.

The next example, (13), uses the traditional stock characters of stupid Irish.

(13) Did you hear what happened to the Irish Sea Scouts? Their tent sank.
(Tibballs, 2000, p. 172)

In (13), the internal logic may be something like this:

Within the viewpoint of the supposed 'Irish Sea Scouts': Scouts put up tents; therefore Sea Scouts will put up tents; Sea Scouts engage in activities on the sea; therefore Sea Scouts will put up tents on the sea.

There is the additional step, in a wider viewpoint:

Within the viewpoint of the joke world: a tent put up at sea will sink; therefore the tent in these circumstances would sink.

This illustrates how discrepant internal logic may be attributed to some character(s) in the story, and so takes place within the corresponding viewpoint, but the consequent actions by the character(s) take place within the wider viewpoint of the joke world, and so further consequences, such as a sinking tent, may follow within the joke world, using sound reasoning. In this example, there is discrepant logic and a relative anomaly.

In contrast, the audience inference involves unpicking the information, perhaps like this:

The tent sank, so it must have been on a body of water. It belonged to the Irish-Sea-Scout-characters, and hence the reason for being on water may well be due to reasoning in that viewpoint. Within the Irish-Sea-Scout-character viewpoint, non-sensible reasoning could lead to this in the following way: Scouts are expected to put up tents, and sea-related groups are expected to carry out activities at sea.

Once again, the audience inference process discovers the internal logic.

These examples typify the way in which discrepant internal logic operates within a joke. A character's viewpoint may contain faulty beliefs, including implications, and the character may make some steps of reasoning, using those beliefs. Some of these steps may be faulty in some way. At some stage, this causes the character to act in a particular way, and the action is in some way inappropriate, in that either it violates some conventions of behaviour or of commonsense, or it leads to some unfortunate consequences, or both. Not all of the steps of the logic are made explicit, and they may not be presented in logical order. The audience inference is an attempt to make sense of the information supplied, often working backwards from the punch line, figuring out what may be going on in the fictional world of the joke, in order to construct a coherent interpretation. This may require the consideration of possibly discrepant logic within some internal viewpoint. As Ziv observes: 'The cognitive process aims at understanding and "solving" an incongruity, thus restoring balance...' (Ziv, 1984, p. 96).

As we shall argue in Section 6.6, there is more to the question of humorous faulty logic than mere logical discrepancy between viewpoints. Our view of the operation of faulty logic within a joke contributes to our reformulation of the incongruity-resolution analysis of humour, in Chapter 7.

6.5 The soundness of the inferential mechanism

Although, as indicated in Section 6.1 above, there is widespread agreement that jokes involve pseudo-logic, the exact details of this empirical claim have not been fully explored. We turn now to one particular aspect which seems to have been accepted with insufficient evidence.

Some authors strongly suggest that the faulty logic which is central to a joke is based on a *different kind of logic*; that is, an apparatus which is qualitatively different from conventional logical reasoning. The widespread use of terms such as 'pseudo-logic' or 'paralogic' (see the quotations in Section 6.1) hints at a different specialised reasoning device. Ziv says that to enjoy humour 'one has to ... take momentary leave of Aristotelian logic' (Ziv, 1984, p. 77), Apter says that '...the structure of the comic synergy is such that it appears to escape from the restrictive demands of logic' (Apter, 1989, p. 139), and Attardo and Raskin remark that 'the use of paralogisms instead of correct syllogisms in humor is quite permissible' (Attardo & Raskin, 1991, p. 304). All this prompts the question: if joke logic is non-standard, which formal aspects of standard logic are altered? In particular, are different inferential mechanisms required?

The examples usually adduced to support the need for 'pseudo-logic' simply demonstrate that reasoning within the joke world has arrived at a conclusion which is somehow strange, as shown in our examples earlier in this chapter. The strangeness may involve being empirically incorrect, being far less likely than other possible conclusions or violating socio-cultural conventions. None of these indicate that the underlying reasoning apparatus is itself faulty – it may just be that the agent performing the reasoning is working from unusual or false data. A completely sound and conventional reasoning process can arrive at dubious conclusions if it starts from incorrect information. That is, empirically incorrect beliefs or other forms of misconception can appear as statements in the logic, leading to strange outcomes, even when the underlying logical machinery is completely correct from a logic standpoint.

This means that oddities in the internal logic of a joke need not be based on a faulty underlying mechanism – one or two simple propositions which deviate from reality may be sufficient to derail the reasoning within the joke. We shall see examples of this when we consider 'absurd' jokes, in Section 6.6.

It might seem that there are plenty of examples of jokes which depend not on sound reasoning from incorrect premises, but on a particular flawed step in the reasoning, and that such humour suggests the need for a non-standard mode of inference. However, potential relationships between propositions can be expressed within a logic as implicative statements (what we have called 'rules'), and these can cause the underlying inference apparatus to derive specific consequences. Hence, a faulty relationship between propositions can be stated in the logic, thus luring a perfectly well-designed reasoning mechanism into arriving at incorrect conclusions. An empirically incorrect belief, within a particular character's viewpoint, about how one proposition follows from another can be represented as statements in the logic. These can then lead completely valid inference methods to deduce incorrect or even bizarre consequences, as in examples (8), (12) and (13) above.

Example (14) illustrates both that the fault in the internal logic may simply be a mismatch with reality (i.e. incorrect assumptions), and also that the discrepancy may be comparatively small.

(14) Some rabbits are explaining to a hedgehog the safest way to cross a busy road at night. One says 'If you see some headlights coming, just line up between the two headlights, roll yourself up, and you'll be fine.' The hedgehog nervously sets out across the dark highway. Then, some headlights appear, approaching fast. He lines up between the beams, rolls up, and waits. Splat! He gets completely squashed. One rabbit turns to the other and says 'It's rotten luck to get a Reliant Robin on your first time.'
(edited from various versions online; see also Tibballs (2000, p. 29))

To interpret this slightly dated British joke, it is necessary to know that a 'Reliant Robin' was a well-known UK model of three-wheeled car, with its single front wheel centrally mounted. (In addition, this model of car was sometimes viewed as faintly ridiculous, perhaps adding an 'enhancer', Section 3.5, to this joke.) In this tale, the animals operate with a near-correct statement about motor vehicles: '*in the centre of a motor vehicle, there are no wheels to squash a small animal*', instead of a more accurate – but very similar – statement, '*in the centre of a conventionally four-wheeled motor vehicle* . . .'. As in the earlier examples of this section, there is no indication that the scenario depicted in the joke requires the reasoning apparatus to be faulty.

The default assumption would be that there are no inference devices which are peculiar to jokes. Although humorous phenomena are interestingly different from non-humorous ones, we should be reluctant to multiply the number of constructs that are used only in humour, unless there is good evidence that they are needed. Any proponent of the more radical position – that joke logic requires inferential devices formally different from ordinary logic – bears the onus of proof. So far, no real evidence for the existence of non-standard inferential mechanisms has been put forward.

6.6 Limits to the faultiness of the logic

One important question remains about the use of faulty reasoning within jokes: what sort of inaccuracies can be used in this way to create humour? We have to consider whether there is some principled limit or whether any inaccuracy whatsoever can be pressed into service.

Ritchie (2014) argues that the faulty logic in a joke cannot be arbitrary or random, but must bear a close similarity to some possible valid statement(s) of logic. Also, for the joke to be comprehended, it must be possible for audience inference to work out the nature of the internal logic – if the internal logic were too bizarre, this detective work might prove to be impossible. That article concludes that only empirical study of the logic of many jokes will give some idea of how to specify this notion of 'mildly and systematically incorrect'.

We will now look more closely at the way in which audience inference can figure out the internal logic of a joke. This can be seen as having two aspects: devising candidate logical statements to be added to the joke world, and assessing these statements with respect to disbelief-suspension (Section 4.6).

For example, we outlined earlier how joke (14) above relied on a very slightly inaccurate rule about the layout of vehicle wheels. Discovering this does not present much difficulty for audience inference, given the amount of information in the text. Also, the incorrect rule is sufficiently plausible that it may well be accepted by the audience during the set-up without any conscious effort; that is, without a high degree of required disbelief-suspension.

Let us now consider a joke which might be more difficult for the audience.

(15) A man at the dinner table who was being handed fish dipped his two hands twice in the mayonnaise and then ran them through his hair. When his neighbour looked at him in astonishment, he seemed to notice his mistake and apologized: 'I'm so sorry, I thought it was spinach.'
(Freud, 1966 [1912], pp. 138–139)

In (15), the internal logic, within the viewpoint of the man-character, seems to deviate from everyday rationality. However, this does not mean that audience inference cannot possibly devise a candidate for the internal logic. It is not too difficult to surmise that the text could be rendered intelligible by adding to the joke world conceptual items roughly summarised as '*spinach and mayonnaise appear very similar*' and '*spinach should be applied to one's hair*', which together establish an alternative logic which renders the story coherent and unpuzzling. However, these additions might be rated highly implausible by the disbelief-suspension mechanism.

Oring (2003c) says that (15) is 'entirely absurd'. Our analysis suggests that this feeling could emanate from the judgement that a high degree of disbelief-suspension is needed, rather than because it is impossible to construct the necessary logic. Oring also says that (16) is an example of 'nonsensical' or 'absurd' humour.

(16) He's so perverse, he likes meat better than any vegetable, except ice cream.
(Oring, 2003c, p. 13)

This sentence does seem, at first glance, to be very odd. However, even here it is possible to complete the first phase of devising the internal logic: we need simply the statement that '*ice cream is a vegetable*'. (The initial goal is simply coherence, not humour, and this potential addition may not create humour.) For the second phase, this candidate fragment of logic is likely to have a very poor (i.e. high) score on disbelief-suspension. It may be that what is sometimes referred to as 'nonsense' humour or 'unresolved incongruity' (Oring, 2003c; Rothbart & Pien, 1977; Samson, Hempelmann, Huber, & Zysset, 2009) is a consequence of exactly this scenario: a failure by the audience to find adjustments or additions to the internal logic of the joke world which make the text semantically coherent and which also do not demand an excessive degree of disbelief-suspension. This way of looking at the problem means that we do not have to partition jokes (or stories) into separate classes of 'intelligible' and 'nonsense', but can treat texts has involving some degree of nonsense, based on the degree of disbelief-suspension required (see Samson and Hempelmann (2011) for evidence of the link between nonsense and disbelief-suspension in jokes). For example, the earlier example (13) (the Irish Sea Scouts) depends on a certain amount of disbelief-suspension, and so has a measure of absurdity, though not as much as (15) or (16). This analysis in terms of disbelief-suspension is relevant to the incongruity-resolution account of humour, which we will examine in detail in Chapter 7. In particular, we shall see internal logics which require considerable disbelief-suspension when we look at elephant jokes, in Section 7.8.

Examples (15) and (16) illustrate the point made in Section 6.5: the supposed incorrectness of the internal logic may hinge on just one or two statements. Also, the internal logic may involve some general implication statements which seem valid, but are flawed or odd when applied to the conceptual items in a particular joke. In such cases, the judgement of how much disbelief-suspension is required should be based on the application of the general rule to the elements in the joke, not the rule itself in isolation. In many cases, a bizarre application of an apparently general rule is in fact a demonstration that the rule is not wholly general, but has some pre-condition that was not at once obvious. For example, in the squashed hedgehog example, (14), there was an overlooked pre-condition 'in a conventionally four-wheeled vehicle'. (There will be more examples of this in Chapter 13.)

In this way, we treat the problem of determining the internal logic as having two aspects, decomposing the question 'what kind of faulty logic is workable in a joke?' into two slightly less mysterious questions: 'what kind of logic can be devised by audience inference in order to render a text coherent?' and 'how does a potential addition to a storyworld acquire an assessment of disbelief-suspension?'.

The first of these questions can be seen as asking about the power of the inferential mechanisms discussed in Section 4.6. There will be jokes where a situation is completely baffling – an 'unexplained gap', in the sense of Section 4.7. However, the usual challenge for the audience is to divine the internal logic on the basis of a known outcome together with the conditions leading to that outcome. That is, often the start and end points of the reasoning are provided, with only some link(s) to be filled in. In such scenarios, it can be relatively straightforward to render the text coherent by the careful addition of a customised proposition or rule, since the only requirement is to connect up the content of the original text, and there is, in this phase, no ban on outlandish statements. This process will fail if the audience cannot come up with any candidate assumptions to achieve coherence. The conjecture is that such a failure would result in the joke being deemed to be incomprehensible.

Assuming that there is at least one candidate amendment to the internal logic, the second aspect of the process, assessing for disbelief-suspension, becomes applicable. Various degrees of necessary disbelief-suspension will lead to different reactions. If audience inference has achieved the coherence by devising overly bizarre concepts, then the audience may regard the candidate logic as unacceptable, so that the joke is deemed to be nonsense. More interestingly, the need for a slightly less striking degree of disbelief-suspension may lead to a judgement that the internal logic is 'faulty' or 'pseudo', as in many jokes. If there is an acceptably low level of required disbelief-suspension, taking account of whatever storytelling conventions apply, then there may be no sense of pseudo-logic. We will use the term *fanciful* to describe any elements of internal logic which require a non-trivial amount of disbelief-suspension. This is a matter of degree, depending on how severe the disbelief-suspension is.

This is a small improvement on the position taken by Ritchie (2014), which left the idea of humorous pseudo-logic as 'theory-internal'; that is, the definition of faulty logic was seen as peculiar to jokes and not based on external non-humorous principles. Here, we have expressed the problem in terms of two mechanisms – finding candidate statements and assessing them for disbelief-suspension – which are also needed for ordinary story comprehension, and which therefore are non-humorous (see Section 2.3). A fanciful logic is acceptable in a joke if it can be constructed by the normal methods of audience inference and does not demand too much disbelief-suspension. Both these constraints still need further elaboration, but as story-understanding constructs, not as humour-specific devices.

These steps do not wholly resolve all questions about the nature of pseudo-logic in jokes. Disbelief-suspension is still a complex issue, particularly as it is clear from both stories and jokes that, as commented in Section 4.6, some very unreal situations may be quite acceptable in fiction, with the details varying across genres. In this context, jokes can be seen as a genre of text, which leads to the possibility that jokes have a particular set of disbelief-suspension conventions, yet to be determined. That eventuality might seem to undermine the quest to express humour mechanisms in non-humorous terms, but this would depend on exactly what was discovered. If there were to be a specialised set of customs associated with the cultural phenomenon of jokes, and these were of the same general form as disbelief-suspension conventions for other genres, differing only in minor parameters, that would not be problematic. For example, the disbelief-suspension for oddities in a joke set-up (Section 7.8) appears to be similar to that applied in general storytelling and not to be humour-generating in itself. If this licence were found to also be appropriate for all cases of what we have called 'final revelations' (that is, at the stage where the amusement is experienced), that would be an elegant outcome.

6.7 Summary

We have argued:

- The faultiness or pseudo-logic that many authors have commented upon appears, from inspection of examples, to be located in the internal logic (propositions and relationships within the joke world) rather than the audience inference (the cognitive process of making sense of the joke).
- There is as yet no evidence that logical dysfunctions within jokes are best described by positing a faulty inference apparatus, as opposed to flawed statements or rules within the logic.
- The faulty reasoning is often localised to a particular viewpoint within the joke world, such as the viewpoint of a stupid character, while the rest of the joke world operates with a non-faulty logic.
- Any incorrectness of the logic within the joke is relative to the internal logic of some dominating viewpoint which is taken as having more authority.
- For successful joke comprehension, it must be possible for audience inference to determine the nature of the internal logic, and this indirectly constrains how bizarre that logic can be, in two ways: the audience must be able to construct statements which would achieve coherence and those statements must require an acceptable level of disbelief-suspension.

- The degree of absurdity of a joke depends on the amount of disbelief-suspension required to accept its internal logic.
- The pre-theoretic notion of faulty logic in jokes seems to correspond to what we are calling 'fanciful logic': discrepant internal logic which requires a non-trivial degree of disbelief-suspension.

In Chapter 7, we will build on these points in our discussion of incongruity-resolution.

Chapter 7

Incongruity and resolution

7.1 Incongruity in humour

Incongruity, as a key to humour, has been discussed for centuries, although not always under that name; for reviews, see Martin (2007, pp. 62–75), Morreall (1983, pp. 15–19), Raskin (1985, pp. 31–36). The central idea was described thus:

> ...the bringing together of images which have contrary additional ideas, as well as some resemblance in the principal idea...
> ...bringing resemblances from subjects of a quite different kind from the subject to which they are compared.
>
> (Hutcheson, 1987 [1750])

A more recent comment comes from a medical study on the effects of jokes: '...nearly all formulations about jokes stress the importance in humor of incongruity' (Brownell, Michel, Powelson, & Gardner, 1983, p. 21). Incongruity theory has been described as 'the dominant theory of humour' and 'the most widely accepted account' of humour within philosophy and psychology (Morreall, 2009, p. 10 & p. 12). Despite this long tradition, the concept of 'incongruity' is not tightly defined. Apter observes that '...there are so many different forms of incongruity theory that the category is not as helpful as that of relief theories, ...or of superiority theories.' (Apter, 1982, p. 192). (See also Hurley et al. (2011, p. 46).)

The term 'incongruity' is typically seen as close in meaning to other words such as 'absurdity', 'abnormality', etc. Sometimes slightly more specific explanations are offered: that it stems from the bringing together of two 'incompatible' ideas, or that it inherently involves the violation of expectations (see Ritchie (2004, Section 4.1) for more discussion). In Section 4.5, we made the distinction between temporal forecasts which are part of the audience inference process, which we labelled 'predictions', and statements of causality and consequence within storyworlds and subordinate viewpoints, which can lead to 'violation of expectation'. In the later sections of the current chapter, we will see that some examples of 'incongruity', in the terminology of past authors, are best seen as violation of predictions, and others can be seen as violation of expectation, in our narrow senses of these terms.

7.2 Adding resolution to incongruity

The elastic nature of the term 'incongruity' may have helped to hide the involvement of other factors. Although it is quite hard to find a viable textual joke which relies solely on incongruity, Morreall (2009, p. 13) observes that it was only in the late twentieth century that scholars realised that incongruity alone was not sufficient to create humour. While some have proposed quite different factors (see Chapters 10 and 11), a widely advocated idea is that incongruity must, for the creation of humour, also be 'resolved'; that is, the incongruous situation must be made to seem less odd (Attardo, 1994; Forabosco, 1992).

(17) A guy in the garment industry has a son who asks him, 'Daddy, what kind of flower is that?'
He says, 'What am I, a milliner?'
(Oring, 2003c, p. 14)

In (17), the father-character's implication that a milliner would be a suitable expert on flowers may initially seem incongruous, but the father-character can be seen as taking a garment industry perspective, in which milliners are more concerned with flowers than other specialists in that sector. This then 'resolves' the incongruity.

Although the additional stipulation of 'resolution' has become particularly dominant in the past half-century, Hutcheson's outline from the eighteenth century (see Section 7.1) includes the phrase 'as well as some resemblance in the principal idea', which could be seen as foreshadowing this development, and another eighteenth-century writer also hinted at this condition:

> Laughter arises from the view of two or more inconsistent, unsuitable, or incongruous parts or circumstances, considered as united in one complex object or assemblage, or as acquiring a sort of mutual relation from the peculiar manner in which the mind takes notice of them.
>
> (Beattie, 1776)

In the 19th century, Schopenhauer (1964 [1883], pp. 76–77) proposed that laughter results from concepts being treated in a way which is incongruous from one view, but seen as correct from another.

More recently, the incongruity-resolution (IR) model has been referred to as being '... by and large ... the accepted cognitive model of humor...' (Hempelmann & Attardo, 2011, p. 130), and as being the only 'serious contender' (Hurley et al., 2011, p. 60) amongst past models. Despite all this attention, the IR account of humour still does not have a single agreed version, and lacks detailed definitions of its central concepts (Latta, 1999; Morreall, 2009; Ritchie, 2004, 2009; Warren & McGraw, 2016).

It would quite possible to adopt the position that IR is a very general abstract description of humour which can be manifested in a wide variety of configurations within jokes. This seems, for example, to be the position of Dynel (2012), who describes various possible IR arrangements within jokes. However, articles which advocate IR as the key to humour usually present exactly one configuration as defining IR theory. Since some of these configurations are logically distinct, these authors are in effect offering competing IR 'theories' (Ritchie, 2009). We will not opt for any specific version of IR from this range, but will, in the current chapter, review the existing positions and suggest how each of these proposals could be described in our terms. That is, we will outline, using our assumed model of text comprehension (Chapter 4), how the principal versions of IR, and some related constructs, can be described in slightly more detail, thus replacing these under-defined notions with more precise and fine-grained constructs.

We will start with the most typical variants of IR theory, before moving on to some of the slightly more peripheral manifestations of incongruity in jokes. By doing this, we intend not only to show more clearly the commonalities and differences between these variants of IR, but also to make a step towards the expression of humour-theoretic constructs in terms of more general, non-humour-specific concepts (Section 2.3), and filling in more detail of the ways in which joke mechanisms operate.

7.3 Post-text puzzlement

Perhaps the most influential IR description of jokes was offered by Suls (1972, 1983), who sees the incongruity as arising at the end of the joke, triggering some additional cognitive effort which leads, if successful, to resolution: 'Humor occurs when an incongruity can be made to follow and sense can be made from the parts of the joke' (Suls, 1972, p. 83). In Suls's description, incongruity is equated with failure of the punch line to match a prediction, and Suls remarks very briefly that this mismatch leads to surprise (we will discuss surprise in Chapter 8). Then '... the perceiver engages in a form of problem solving to find a cognitive rule which makes the punch line follow from the main part of the joke and reconciles the incongruous parts' (Suls, 1972, p. 82).

Ventis (2015) suggests that this move into problem solving is a switch by the audience from System 1 thinking to System 2, in the sense of Kahneman (2012); see Section 4.7. The mention of finding a cognitive rule suggests that this phase of processing might involve audience inference to figure out some internal logic (as in Section 6.6).

This account of resolution seems to assume that the punch line is initially perceived as not following from the set-up, and that the resolution remedies this. Although Suls's algorithmic statement (a flowchart) specifies simply a mismatch with a prediction, these remarks about the relationship between set-up and punch line suggest that there is something more to incongruity, but this is not fully explained.

Suls's model appears to adopt what we have called a 'specified outcome' prediction (Section 5.1), in which the process of comprehension gives rise to forecasts of particular words and phrases. However, he offers no evidence that jokes, even the two examples he quotes, involve such specific predictions, and this claim is not persuasive. Subsequent versions of this variety of IR take the more general view that it is the meaning of the punch line, not its textual form, which is predicted, or even omit the requirement that there be any prediction (e.g. Dynel, 2012, p. 8). We will consider only this latter position, without the requirement that any incongruity triggered by the punch line is dependent on a specific prior prediction. (There is a separate question of whether a mismatch with an prediction would act as an 'enhancer', in the sense of Section 3.5.)

Suls's articles are sometimes cited as if they gave the defining statement of IR theory (e.g. Miczo, 2014; Ruch, 1992). Brownell et al. (1983) adopt this version of IR in describing experiments which found evidence of a distinction, within the brain's faculties, between 'surprise' in a joke punch line, and 'coherence' in the overall correct interpretation of a joke. Dynel (2012), as remarked earlier, treats IR as having several patterns, dubbing this one the 'red-light' mechanism within IR. Wyer and Collins (1992) adopt Suls's model, but augment it in various ways, including a hypothesis that the funniness of a joke is affected by the amount of cognitive effort used in resolving the punch line puzzlement.

Despite all this acceptance, the Suls model is not very detailed. In our terminology, it says only that the punch line causes an assimilation difficulty, occasioning some perceptible audience inference. Nothing is specified about what it means for a punch line to follow (or not) from the set-up, about the nature of the post-text inference, or about the knowledge state at the final stage. The idea that the final interpretation, after the resolution, may still contain incongruity (see Section 7.7), is not explored, nor is there any mention of flawed logic (as in Chapter 6). If we retain the idea that a specific textual prediction is required, then the model has slightly more substance, but is both less convincing and less similar to later proposals. Despite all this, Suls's sketch can be seen as a general template to which some later versions of IR add more detail. Also, we will adopt the idea of post-text assimilation difficulty as one of the constructs in our description of joke comprehension (see Chapter 12).

One of Suls's illustrative examples is (18).

(18) Fat Ethel sat down at the lunch counter and ordered a whole fruit cake. 'Shall I cut it into four or eight pieces?' asked the waitress. 'Four,' said Ethel, 'I'm on a diet.'

(Suls, 1972, p. 83)

Let us examine in more detail the logical gaps created by the punch line, which we take to be the final sentence '*I'm on a diet*'. Within the joke world, the waitress-character, in the set-up, has posed a question. An explicit question in the story sometimes indicates a justification question, which in turn might well trigger audience inference in search of an answer within the relevant viewpoint. However, here the question is simply a request for information, rather than raising matters of why something is the case. In any case, by the time the audience reaches the punch line, there is no need to look for connections back to the waitress-character's question, as the Ethel-character has already answered it with the reply '*Four*'. What is puzzling, and hence in need of audience inference, is the connection that the Ethel-character implies between being on a diet, and answering '*Four*'. This is exactly the situation we outlined in Section 4.5, where some new proposition, '*I'm on a diet*', is presented as implying some other proposition, in this case the preference for four pieces rather than eight. That is, there is a relevance question derived from '*I'm on a diet*', which reduces to a justification question based on '*I'm on a diet* ⇒*four pieces*' – why is this implication believed by the Ethel-character? To answer this, the audience inference has to find a logical sequence from '*I'm on a diet*' to '*four pieces*' within the viewpoint corresponding to the Ethel-character. It can be achieved by attributing some dubious reasoning to the Ethel-character, perhaps roughly as follows (see also Suls (1972, p. 83)):

> *When on a diet, one should eat less. This means eating fewer items. Hence four cakes are preferable to eight cakes. Hence four pieces of cake are preferable to eight pieces. This holds even when the pieces are made up of exactly the same cake.*

In this way, the relevance/justification question is answered, subject to the assumption of certain elements of the internal logic of this character's viewpoint, thus removing this gap in the coherence of the text. The Ethel-character's viewpoint then contains what would be seen as discrepant logic when compared with the audience's real world or the broader joke world, which inherits directly from the audience's view of the real world. Thus there is a relative anomaly, in our terminology. Following our observations in Section 6.6, we can also say that the proposed internal logic is fanciful since it requires a noticeable amount of disbelief-suspension to be acceptable.

(After the text has been fully comprehended, it is not clear whether the final humour-creating oddity lies in the proposition that four slices will have less dietary impact than eight, or in the reasoning that the character has applied in coming to this decision; see Section 7.10.)

7.4 A question in the set-up

A slightly different arrangement is offered by some authors as defining IR. In this version, the set-up raises some question or puzzle – the incongruity – and the punch line provides the answer – the resolution. This variant of

IR, which Dynel (2012) calls the 'crossroads' mechanism, has appeared since the early days of IR theorising, and is still seen by some as the definitive form of IR. (In 2014, a reviewer of a submission for the *Humor* journal stated: 'Incongruity-resolution theory seems to imagine that a joke sets out an incongruity in the set-up and then resolves it in the punchline.')

(19) What is grey, has four legs, and a trunk? A mouse on vacation.

Rothbart (1977, p. 91) says of (19) that '... there is incongruity or surprise in the joke body before we reach the punch line.' That is, the riddle question introduces incongruity, which the punch line resolves. (Rothbart does not explain how the question manifests surprise.) In describing psychological experiments exploring the IR model of joke comprehension, Vaid et al. (2003) analyse the joke (20). They indicate that the incongruity (which they do not spell out) occurs just before the final sentence, and that the resolution (also not described in detail) arrives with the punch line.

(20) Woman walks into bar with duck on leash. Bartender says, 'Where'd you get the pig?' Woman says, 'This is not a pig, it's a duck.' Bartender says, 'I was talking to the duck.'

(Vaid et al., 2003, p. 1436)

Example (11) (the tap-dancing duck) could also be seen in this way, and there will be more examples of this type of analysis in Section 7.8.

In terms of our text comprehension model, this pattern of incongruity and resolution can be viewed as an apparent anomaly occurring in the set-up, giving rise to a justification question. In processing terms, this leads to a temporary gap (Section 4.7). The punch line supplies information which answers the justification question by giving support within some viewpoint. In the resulting final state, it may be that this leaves some propositions which are still unsupported within the audience's own viewpoint, resulting in a relative anomaly.

The proponents of this variant of IR do not usually mention any puzzlement or problem-solving *after* the punch line. This could be because they assume that the audience can directly detect the way in which the punch line content answers the set-up question, without unusual cognitive effort, or they believe that any such effort is not germane to the humorous effect (in contrast to Suls, for whom this cognitive effort is central). Nevertheless, it seems intuitively clear that some of these punch lines do require a modicum of additional cognitive effort; that is, there is an assimilation difficulty. Sometimes this arises from the punch line causing, in our terminology, a relevance question.

In this section and in Section 7.3 above, we have shown how certain patterns of information flow noted by previous authors can be stated in terms of our text comprehension model. We are not arguing that these patterns are necessary and sufficient conditions for texts to function as jokes, even if some of these earlier authors may have implied this.

7.5 The direction of reasoning

Suls (1972) strongly suggests that the connection, found by post-text inference, is *from* the set-up *to* the punch line: the audience engages in '... problem solving to find how the punch line follows from the main body of the joke' (Suls, 1972, p. 87); see also the second quotation in Section 7.3. In considering this claim, the distinction between internal logic and audience inference (Section 4.4) is important. It could be that Suls is suggesting that there is a logical chain, within the internal logic of the joke world, from the set-up to the punch line; alternatively, the claim might be that audience inference will start from the set-up to reach the content of the punch line. Either of these ways of interpreting Suls's statement is too restrictive to cover a wide range of jokes, or even, arguably, Suls's own example, (18), Ethel and the cake. In many jokes, audience inference will work back from the new information in the punch line (as illustrated in Section 6.4), but that still allows the connection(s) discovered, within the internal logic, to be anywhere within the network of propositions that represent the joke world. For example, in the analysis above of (18), it seems that the logical connections to the punch line run not from the set-up as such, but from beliefs attributed to a story-character as a result of the content of the punch line. In a sense, the audience inference has been abductive, finding support for a given proposition by assuming other propositions that could have led to it, within the embedded viewpoint (see Section 4.6).

To emphasise this point, we can describe (21) in either way, without altering the substance of the analysis.

(21) A couple from Seattle were talking about their holiday to their friend. 'Sounds as if you had a great time in California,' said the friend, 'but I didn't know you were planning to take in Florida as well.'
'We weren't,' said the wife, 'but Ted simply will not ask for directions.'
(Tibballs, 2000, p. 312)

The set-up, up to the phrase '*said the wife*', poses a question: why did the holiday-makers visit Florida when it was not part of their plans? After the punch line, audience inference uncovers the internal logic, which then answers this question. Thus there is an account in keeping with that outlined in Section 7.4: a question in the set-up is answered, after inference, by the punch line. On the other hand, even in this same commentary, the audience inference that leads to discovery of the internal logic could be triggered by an assimilation difficulty, caused by a relevance question, at the post-text stage, in which case there could be a Suls-style analysis, as in Section 7.3. (As we remarked earlier, the Suls model has relatively few defining factors.) The same internal logic, and even the same sequence of audience inference steps, can be viewed as manifesting either of these two characterisations of the IR joke. These are alternative ways of talking about the same solution, emphasising different aspects of that solution. To some extent, this is because the Suls account emphasises the steps of the process (the audience inference), while the 'set-up puzzle' approach emphasises the logical relationships between parts (the internal logic). The two accounts may attribute the humour to different aspects of the comprehension, but they are not competing descriptions of what happens in that comprehension. (We will say more about this example in Chapter 13.)

Rather than thinking of the logical relationships simply as being 'to' or 'from' the punch line, we should think of the post-text effort as constructing an overall interpretation, in which all the information from the various stages of the text is coherently incorporated. As a result of this, various gaps/questions may be remedied/answered. In the resulting edifice, the logical connections may run from set-up to punch line, or vice versa, or from both these sources to some proposition(s) not strictly located in either. The analyses given above of (18) and (21) follow this general pattern.

This would be compatible with other, broader, phrases used by Suls to describe the result of the audience's cognitive effort, such as '... the punch line ... is congruent with the preceding text' (Suls, 1972, p. 87). O'Shannon also suggests the need for the integration of information, but sees incongruity as the outcome rather than the starting point: 'The line of cognitive process represents the work done by the receiver to combine the set-up and the punch line, resulting in the creation of the incongruous image' (O'Shannon, 2012, p. 117).

7.6 Forced reinterpretation

The 'forced reinterpretation' (FR) construction (Ritchie, 2002, 2004) is a type of joke structure which has been widely remarked upon. In this arrangement, the set-up of the joke has two possible interpretations, one of which is sufficiently obvious that the other interpretation is not, in a successful instance of joke comprehension, noticed by the audience; in our terminology, the audience is unaware of this interpretation. The punch line is in some way inconsistent with this adopted interpretation, which causes the audience to reconsider, and to become aware of the less obvious interpretation, which is compatible with the content of the punch line. Earlier examples (9) (the hang-over on the lawn) and (10) (the sausage collector) have this form, as does (22).

(22) A senior citizen is driving on the highway. His wife calls him on his cell phone and in a worried voice says, 'Herman, be careful! I just heard on the radio that there was a madman driving the wrong way on Route 280'. Herman says, 'Not just one, there are hundreds!'

(Hurley et al., 2011, p. 170)

Wyer and Collins claim, in a postulate labelled 'incongruity resolution', that when the audience fails to make sense of input using readily accessible knowledge, there is a search for a different 'knowledge domain' which will allow a reinterpretation. They do not offer any illustrative jokes which take this route, but it seems to describe FR examples such as (9), (10) and (22).

This scheme has sometimes been deemed to be what defines the IR mechanism, or even all joke comprehension – see the model proposed by Hurley et al. (2011) or the quotations in Ritchie (2004, p. 60). Other authors see FR as just one variant of IR (Dynel, 2012; Morreall, 2009, p. 141).

Most previous accounts of this construct, including Ritchie (2004), imply that the reinterpretation applies to the set-up; that is, the audience changes their understanding of the whole text that precedes the punch line. However, closer inspection of the relevant illustrative examples suggests a subtler analysis of the phenomenon. In an FR joke, revisions of interpretation are usually confined to some particular viewpoint, usually that of a story-character (see Ritchie (2006)). That is, it is very common for only specific viewpoints within the overall interpretation to be subject to revision, with the broad understanding of the set-up text being relatively unaltered.

(Ritchie (2004, Section 8.1.1) conjectured that linguistic ambiguity would be used for humorous purposes only in 'nested' parts of the set-up, not in the top-level narrative. As Ritchie (2006) points out, this hypothesis is false, as the viewpoint requiring reinterpretation may, in relatively rare instances, be the joke world itself – see Section 11.5.)

In many cases, the content that has to be amended in the viewpoint in question is something that has arisen either by default inheritance from some superordinate viewpoint or by inference from such default information. That is, the overridden content consists of assumptions about the joke world, not explicitly stated facts. Hurley et al. (2011), who class this as 'covertly introduced' material, would probably argue that this is the case in all jokes. It appears that most FR jokes rely either on this alteration of default material or the discovery of an alternative linguistic analysis for a text segment. A more wide-ranging examination would be needed to determine if this is true for all FR jokes.

All this means that we can describe the FR pattern in the following way. By the post-set-up stage, the audience has built up a coherent joke world. There is then an assimilation difficulty as a result of the content of the punch line. Further inference leads to the conclusion that some situation which had been filled in (by one of the mechanisms discussed in Sections 4.5 and 4.6) must now be treated as inaccurate and should be replaced with propositions of which the audience had not been aware until this final stage.

Our brief summary says nothing about the nature of the content of the text or its interpretation, and offers no comparison between the old and new content of the viewpoint. However, this directly reflects previous presentations, by various authors, of FR: they simply describe the sequence of information processing steps. This limited level of description has two consequences.

Firstly, the FR account is largely an elaboration of the Suls model (Section 7.3) in which the nature of the post-text cognitive processing is specified in more detail; that is, there is the additional requirement that the post-text processing involves the revising of the content of some viewpoint. Ritchie (2004, Section 5.3.1) suggests that the Suls IR model differs from the FR model because Suls does not mention multiple interpretations for the set-up. This is partly true and partly misleading. It is true that nothing in Suls's model *stipulates* a need for multiple readings, but this is a symptom of the fact that, as noted earlier, the Suls description is extremely under-specified. Also, if we are considering interpretations of the set-up as a piece of text, then neither of the examples used by Suls (e.g. (18), discussed in Section 7.3) seem to require reinterpretation of the entire set-up text, but they do appear to require some dynamic amending of the contents of nested viewpoints.

The second consequence of adopting this processing description is that it still does not distinguish joke comprehension from more general rectification of misunderstanding. If there are no specific characteristics of the original or the revised interpretations, nor any special relations between them, then the scenario depicted is merely a misunderstanding. Consider the constructed text (23), which is not a joke.

(23) A man jumped into a taxi and said, 'The main railway station, please.' 'OK,' said the driver, 'What time is the train?' 'No train,' said the passenger, 'I'm meeting a friend in the bar there.'

(Constructed non-joke)

In the early stages of this narrative, the driver-character and, presumably, the audience adopt by default the assumption that the passenger-character is going to catch or meet a train. The final sentence reveals that this assumption was incorrect, and provides information that allows an alternative coherent interpretation. Hence, the information flow is exactly as in the FR description of joke structure. Nevertheless, it is hard to argue that (23) is humorous or could be deployed as a joke. (We will say more about this text in Chapter 13.)

It is relatively easy to construct non-humorous mini-narratives like (23), in which there are discrepant viewpoints leading to misunderstandings followed by revisions. This indicates that the FR formal structure alone is not sufficient for humour – there must be some other factor present which causes the humorous effect. (Whether the FR structure is necessary for humour is another matter.)

Some presentations of the FR mechanism address this need for additional factors. One of these is the 'reversal theory' of humour (Apter, 1982; Apter & Desselles, 2012). This presents humour as having two kinds, one of which ('transitional' in Apter (1982), 'disclosure' in Apter and Desselles (2012)) is very similar to that described in FR theories. It also specifies two further requirements: the revised interpretation must not replace the first interpretation but must co-exist with it, and the new interpretation must 'diminish' some aspect of the entities associated with the joke. The first of these conditions, non-replacement, has not been thoroughly tested, but early indications are not positive. An experiment by Vaid et al. (2003) tracked the extent to which different meanings were activated, in the mind of the audience, in the course of comprehension of an FR joke, and found that there is a brief period when both meanings are active, but then the second meaning takes over. Wyer and Collins (1992) carried out a small study in which they modified a joke so as to create two versions, one of which, in their estimation, involved replacement of interpretation, and the other of which did not. Their subjects found the 'replacement' variant at least as funny as the 'non-replacement' version. The second condition, diminishment, will be discussed when we look at superiority accounts of humour (Chapter 11).

Hurley et al. (2011) describe what appears to be an FR model of joke comprehension, with the further stipulations that the information which is revised has been 'covertly entered' into the set of beliefs, and that the audience is 'epistemically committed' to it. These further requirements might tailor the FR configuration to match humorous outcomes, but this remains to be tested.

The SSTH (Raskin, 1985) offers a different suggestion for how to augment the FR model to create a joke; see Section 7.7.

Some of the above discussion also applies to certain other humorous texts in which the text as a whole is ambiguous, but one of the meanings is innocent and mundane, while the other is somehow improper or absurd. Examples are the office notice in (24), the newspaper report quoted in (25), or the headline in (26). (It might be argued that these are originally, by definition, not jokes. However, once they are quoted in a humorous collection like those edited by Parsons, the audience will approach them as texts to be interpreted humorously.)

(24) THE TYPISTS' REPRODUCTION EQUIPMENT IS NOT TO BE INTERFERED WITH WITHOUT THE PRIOR PERMISSION OF THE MANAGER.

(Parsons, 1971, p. 58)

(25) John F—, the celebrated singer, was in a motor-car accident last week. We are happy to state that he was able to appear the following evening in four pieces.

(Parsons, 1971, p. 34)

(26) BRITISH FLY TO DISCUSS PROBLEM PIPELINE

(Parsons, 1969, p. 14)

Some anecdotal observations can be made about these. If the mundane interpretation is the only one perceived, then no humour results. If the abnormal interpretation is the only one perceived, the audience reaction may be puzzlement and/or amusement. The full humorous appreciation of these texts seems to require the perception of both interpretations, although it is not clear whether the order in which these come to light matters. In the case where the mundane reading is encountered first, the scenario is very similar to the FR flow of comprehension, except that there is no punch line which forces a search for re-interpretation. If the abnormal reading is perceived first, the later grasping of the mundane meaning may act as a sort of explanation, thus reflecting in some ways the traditional scheme of 'incongruity followed by resolution'. In either case, it is hard to argue that the interpretation which is perceived later displaces the earlier meaning. Instead, an understanding of the simultaneous validity of both seems to be needed, as in the reversal theory account, above. This could be seen as the audience maintaining two separate joke worlds, one for each possible interpretation.

The term *double entendre* is generally used where one of the two interpretations is risqué or improper (e.g. (24)), but not usually for merely absurd examples like (25) and (26). An ambiguous text with two sensible meanings would not be regarded as humorous, which seems to suggest that one of the interpretations should have particular properties.

Despite the popularity of the FR scheme, or some variant of it, as the central device in jokes, we will not include it as a single primitive construct in our list of potential humour ingredients (Chapter 12). Instead, we view the FR arrangement as a cluster of interacting factors, such as different interpretations being assigned to a portion of text in separate viewpoints, and interpretations varying in how salient they are. This allows us to show how other joke constructions share some of the attributes of FR jokes, by manifesting one or more of these separate components.

It is conceivable that the FR construction is little more than a way of ensuring that a particular interpretation is perceived by the audience only after a cognitive puzzle (an assimilation difficulty).

7.7 Incongruity without temporal sequence

The 'puzzle + answer' arrangements described in Section 7.3 and Section 7.4 depend very much on the temporal sequence of information flow within joke comprehension and on the question-answer relationship between information available at two different stages of the process. There have also been proposals for some sort of incongruity to act as the key ingredient in humour without this crucial dependence on the temporal order of events. In these descriptions of joke mechanisms, a processing sequence is assumed as the overall context of joke comprehension, but the incongruity is seen as occurring once the entire joke has been comprehended (in the 'final' stage), not as a relationship between different stages of comprehension.

We will briefly mention two of the most influential of these non-temporal-sequence approaches to incongruity, from Oring and from Raskin.

Oring (1992a, 2003a) argues that humour is best seen as 'appropriate incongruity'. This is intuitively similar to IR, in that it involves some incongruity which can be viewed as not wholly nonsensical, and Oring cites Beattie, as quoted in Section 7.2, as having essentially the same idea (Hutcheson's conception, quoted in Section 7.1, seems also to be similar). For example, Oring says of example (17) (in Section 7.2) that there is incongruity in the father-character's excuse that he cannot recognise flowers because he is not a milliner, but this incongruity is appropriate because milliners are concerned with women's hats, often florally decorated.

Despite these comparisons, Oring says that his proposal is not an IR theory, partly because '... incongruity resolution theory implies a temporal order such that an incongruity is first recognized and the resolution (or the appropriateness of the incongruity) then follows.' (Oring, 2003b, p. 2). (This view of IR seems to be based on one or both of the variants discussed in Sections 7.3 and 7.4 above.) It is clear that Oring recognises the need for joke comprehension to be described as a dynamic process – see, for example, the analysis of punch lines in Oring (1992b) – but his 'appropriate incongruity' criterion is stated without *requiring* a particular order in which the two aspects must be encountered by the audience. That is, this theory draws no connection between the temporal order of events and the humorous effect. Also, it seems to be the case that the incongruity resides in what we would regard as the final state of joke comprehension.

Because Oring presents his model as not being an IR theory, it includes no explicit mention of 'resolution', but, as Oring implies in one of the quotations above, the notion of 'appropriate' fulfils a resolution-like function: it shows why the incongruity occurs and/or renders it more acceptable. However, Oring does not offer detailed definitions of what it means to be 'appropriate', beyond the everyday meaning of this word.

The Semantic Script Theory of Humour (SSTH) (Raskin, 1985) proposes (p. 99) the following conjecture:

> A text can be characterized as a single-joke-carrying text if both of the text conditions ... are satisfied:
>
> 1. The text is compatible, fully or in part, with two different scripts
> 2. The two scripts with which the text is compatible are opposite in a special sense ...

The 'special sense' of 'opposite' is based on certain '... binary categories which are essential to human life' (Raskin et al., 2009, p. 291), of which Raskin (2017) lists eight examples. This appears to focus on the clash of two concepts, as in the eighteenth-century suggestions of Hutcheson and of Beattie, quoted earlier, rather than a violation of expectations.

Raskin's original presentation asserted that the SSTH was not an incongruity-based theory, but this appears to have been based on a very specific view of incongruity. More recently, proponents of the GTVH have allowed that '... from an epistemological point of view, the SSTH can be classified as an incongruity theory...' (Hempelmann & Attardo, 2011, p. 130).

Although Raskin discusses some aspects of the sequence of joke recognition (for example, 'semantic script-switch triggers' (Raskin, 1985, pp. 114–117)) it appears that such observations establish the environment in which the statement about a 'single-joke-carrying text', above, applies. That is, the critical SSTH criterion for being a joke is statable without obvious procedural or sequential factors. Like Oring's account, it appears that Raskin's script oppositeness is perceived after the punch line is encountered, but as a contrast between two competing interpretations rather than a clash within a single interpretation.

In essence, the SSTH is a particular case of what we called (Section 7.6) the 'forced reinterpretation' model of joke comprehension (see particularly Attardo and Raskin (1991, p. 308)). The account of joke recognition in Raskin (1985) makes it clear that each script comes to prominence at a different stage of the comprehension process, as in the typical FR arrangement. The definition of single-joke-carrying text makes no mention of these sequential aspects, unless we assume that the term 'compatible' is intended to somehow encapsulate this varying salience. In Section 7.6, we noted the need for some further condition, beyond mere FR-style misunderstanding, if humour was to result. The SSTH proposes that this condition is based on an inter-script relation.

Raskin's summary of his theory mentions no construct corresponding to 'resolution', but the widely cited extension of the SSTH, the General Theory of Verbal Humour (GTVH) (Attardo, 1994, 2017; Attardo & Raskin, 1991) identifies Raskin's single-joke-carrying criterion with incongruity, and includes the 'Logical Mechanism' (LM) (or 'pseudo-Logical Mechanism' (pLM)), which is stated to be the resolution (Attardo, 1997; Hempelmann & Attardo, 2011). As briefly mentioned in Section 6.2, the definition of what, formally, constitutes a (p)LM is far from clear (Ritchie, 2004, 2014). Nevertheless, the GTVH is, in its overall conceptual structure, acknowledged to be an 'appropriate incongruity' theory, in Oring's sense (Hempelmann & Attardo, 2011, p. 141).

7.8 Assimilated abnormality

Backgrounded incongruity

So far in this chapter, we have been examining various sorts of incongruity which have been proposed as being the core ingredient that leads, together with resolution, to humour. Hempelmann and Attardo (2011) suggest a three-way classification of the different functions that incongruity can play with respect to the humorous effect of a joke. Incongruity that fulfils the central humorous role in a joke is classed as 'foregrounded' incongruity. On the other hand, a joke may contain incongruity which is not the central humour-creating absurdity or conflict, because jokes, like other kinds of stories, often treat highly unreal situations, such as talking animals, as if they were normal (McGhee, 1972; Oring, 1992a). These oddities can, once established as part of the story setting, be separate from the pivotal incongruity upon which the joke rests, and Hempelmann and Attardo label these as 'backgrounded' incongruity. Such incidental incongruity is then subdivided into plain backgrounded incongruity, which is necessary for the joke to work, even though it is not the core (i.e. foregrounded) incongruity, and 'completely backgrounded' incongruity, which the joke does not rely upon. That is, completely backgrounded incongruities could be edited out without undermining the functioning of the joke. Hempelmann and Attardo (2011) illustrate this with example (27) (which we discuss further in Chapter 13).

(27) A concert pianist traveled to Africa in a bid to prove that music had the power to soothe the savage beast. He set up his grand piano in a small clearing beside a river, and began to play. One by one, animals appeared and soon he was surrounded by lions, giraffes, antelopes, warthogs, and leopards, all sitting peacefully together swaying and tapping their feet. The pianist had just started to play a second piece when a crocodile splashed out of the river, grabbed the man with its jaws, and dragged him into the water. An agitated lion ran over to the water's edge. 'Why in heaven's name did you do that?' he asked. The crocodile cupped a foot to the back of its head and said, 'Eh ?'

(Hempelmann & Attardo, 2011, p. 135)

Here, the incongruities are said to be: the crocodile not being affected by the music (foregrounded), animals behaving like humans (backgrounded), and setting up a grand piano in the jungle (completely backgrounded, because an essentially identical joke could be set in a circus or menagerie).

Backgrounded incongruity is made up of information which is licensed by a non-trivial degree of disbelief-suspension (Section 4.6), just as occurs in some non-humorous fiction (Hempelmann & Attardo, 2011, p. 131) – see the discussion in Section 6.6. Hempelmann and Attardo say that neither of the backgrounded types of incongruity are 'resolved', unlike the foregrounded incongruity which, according to the GTVH, is resolved ('partially', as discussed in Section 7.9 below). By definition, non-completely backgrounded incongruities contribute to the workings of the joke, as they supply information that is necessary to lead to the foregrounded incongruity and/or to its resolution (Hempelmann & Attardo, 2011, p. 134). That is, they form a vital part of the internal logic.

The distributions of the types of incongruity differ: 'Essentially, foregrounded incongruity would occur in the punch line, whereas backgrounded incongruity would occur in the setup phase of the text.' (Hempelmann & Attardo, 2011, p. 136). It is not clear if this is part of the definition of these terms or merely an observation about what is most common, since Hempelmann and Attardo's analysis of (27) locates the foregrounded incongruity as a puzzle in the set-up, much as in the configuration described in Section 7.4. (In some respects, (27) can be seen as having an information flow similar to that of (11), the tap-dancing duck.)

These types of incongruity (foregrounded, backgrounded, completely backgrounded) may differ in the roles they play within the overall workings of the joke, but not in the kind of oddity involved. That is, there is no suggestion that they are qualitatively different sorts of incongruity. In our terminology, they all appear to be anomalies: situations which appear in the joke world, but do not have support in some dominating viewpoint.

Additional punch line incongruity

There is another pattern of incongruity in jokes which, we will argue, has strong formal similarities to backgrounded incongruity, to the extent that the two phenomena are essentially the same.

Various authors have observed that, in some jokes, the punch line, in the course of resolving some previous incongruity, introduces some new incongruity, which is not then resolved. Suls's version of IR, Section 7.3 above, already relies on incongruity being caused by the punch line, but what is being singled out here is incongruity which is not 'foregrounded' in Hempelmann and Attardo's terminology, and which is not resolved by the end of joke comprehension.

(28) Why did the cookie cry?
Because its mother had been a wafer so long.

Rothbart and Pien (1977, p. 37) cite (28), observing '... the answer ... adds the additional incongruity of the cookie having a mother'. Attardo et al. (2002, p. 27) broadly agree with Rothbart and Pien's observations on this matter. Example (15) from Section 6.6 (the diner adding mayonnaise to his hair) is said to involve 'the acceptance of one absurdity to justify another' (Oring, 2003b, p. 18).

Authors are usually careful to make the logical distinction between incongruity introduced in this way and an earlier incongruity, sometimes from the set-up, remaining not fully resolved (which together form 'residual incongruity' (Hempelmann & Ruch, 2005; Samson & Hempelmann, 2011)).

For example, regarding (29), '... the resolution of the incongruity is not a "real" resolution: it does not get rid of the incongruity – it actually introduces more of the same ... ' (Attardo, 1994, p. 144).

(29) How does an elephant hide in a cherry tree?
By painting its toenails red.

(30) Why did the elephant sit on the marshmallow?
Because he didn't want to fall into the hot chocolate.

Similarly, Rothbart and Pien say of the punch line to (30) that it '... partially explains why the elephant is sitting on a marshmallow while adding an even greater incongruity, the idea that the elephant is sitting in a cup of hot chocolate' (Rothbart & Pien, 1977, p. 38). We will say more about examples (29) and (30) in Chapter 13. (Incidentally, all the analyses cited in this subsection locate the crucial incongruity in the set-up, as discussed in Section 7.4.)

The way in which these additional incongruities play a part in the joke has the following characteristics, in our terminology:

(a) They are anomalies, since they are lack support in the audience's view of the real world, but appear within the joke world.
(b) Even within the joke world, no reason is given for them occurring, which is why they are usually said to be 'unresolved'; in our terms, they are apparent anomalies.
(c) In order to make sense of the joke, the audience has to accept these propositions, via disbelief-suspension of a considerable magnitude; if this is unacceptable, then there is an 'unexplained gap' (Section 4.7).
(d) The information conveyed is not redundant, but plays a role within the logical structure of the joke, usually by contributing to the support for some other proposition (also the basis of an anomaly) that is central to the joke.

These are also exactly the characteristics of 'backgrounded' incongruity, as discussed above. The only difference is that backgrounded incongruity, as observed earlier, is viewed as part of the set-up information, whereas these other incongruities arrive with the punch line. From a formal point of view, these are the same phenomenon: information supplied by the joke narrative, which functions within the joke comprehension process in the way outlined in (a)–(d) immediately above. There is no theoretical reason for these two types of 'incongruity', with their very similar formal characteristics, to be classed as completely different simply because one originates in the set-up and the other in the punch line.

We are not saying that all incongruities created by the punch line are to be classed along with backgrounded incongruity. The similarity remarked upon here concerns the particular pattern which has been observed by several authors when discussing examples such as (15), (28), (29) and (30).

Hempelmann and Attardo (2011, p. 143) hypothesise that backgrounded incongruities, with their reliance on disbelief-suspension, add to the 'nonsensical' nature of a joke, which is corroborated by the findings of Samson and Hempelmann (2011). For example, elephant riddles such as (29) and (30) may seem rather absurd because they make sense only if disbelief-suspension is applied to a very large degree – see Section 6.6. Since disbelief-suspension is a general mechanism, not confined either to set-up or to punch line, this covers both 'backgrounded incongruities' and information conveyed in the punch line.

7.9 Partial resolution

Another matter to be considered in exploring the IR model of joke comprehension is this: does resolution completely remove the prior incongruity or merely partially mitigate it? A variety of opinions have been expressed on this question.

Ruch (1992, p. 31) and Hempelmann and Attardo (2011, note 4) regard Suls (1972) as proposing that resolution removes the earlier incongruity, which is a very natural interpretation of Suls's exposition, particularly the passages quoted in Section 7.3 earlier. Similarly, Shultz lists several authors, including Suls, as suggesting that humour requires not just incongruity but 'a second, more subtle aspect of jokes which renders incongruity meaningful or appropriate by resolving or explaining it' (Shultz, 1996, p. 12). This idea has come to be referred to as 'full' or 'complete' resolution.

Rothbart and Pien (1977, pp. 37–38) discuss the distinction between full resolution and 'partial' resolution, which does not completely eliminate incongruity, offering (30) (the elephant on the marshmallow) as an example. Suls, in a later article, agrees that resolution may be partial: '... it is not assumed that the fit must be complete or perfect; in fact joke structure seems to require that some rules are violated' (Suls, 1983, p. 53). Other established authors are equally firm, even where they do not use the term 'partial resolution':

'Resolving the incongruity does not mean eliminating it.' (Forabosco, 1992, p. 59).

'The term "resolution" is somewhat unfortunate insofar as it suggests a "dissolution" of the incongruity ... in fact, the "resolution" of the incongruity is not supposed to get rid of the incongruity...' (Attardo, 1994, pp. 143–144).

'If resolution means finding the correct solution to a problem, incongruity is never completely resolved.' (Oring, 2003b, p. 14)

Ruch (1992, p. 31) supports Suls's model, and distinguishes two classes of incongruity-based jokes. One class is '... characterized by punch lines in which the surprising incongruity can be completely resolved' (Ruch, 1992, p. 32). Regarding the other class, 'nonsense', Ruch offers this description from McGhee, Ruch, and Hehl (1990, p. 124): 'the punch line may (1) provide no resolution at all, (2) provide a partial resolution (leaving an essential part of the incongruity unresolved), or (3) actually create new absurdities or incongruities.' (Ruch, 1992, p. 32)

Within IR theory, it is hard to see how humour could result from full resolution. This is because, if the content of a joke became completely congruous in every way, there would be nothing to distinguish it from non-humorous congruous information arrived at after a temporary puzzle or misunderstanding. Hempelmann and Attardo note this point, and suggest that 'all incongruity resolution in jokes is partial' (Hempelmann & Attardo, 2011, p. 140). However, this dismissal of full resolution is a sound argument only under the assumption that the creation of the humour relies solely on the incongruity and the nature of its resolution, which is essentially the central tenet of IR theory. It is quite conceivable that a workable joke might involve full resolution, if the humorous effect was generated by other aspects of joke comprehension, such as particular subject matter or some aspect of the sequence of cognitive processing. It is arguable that some jokes do involve full resolution (e.g. (14), the squashed hedgehog, (11), the dancing duck, or (27), the deaf crocodile), although it is hard to be sure in the absence of precise definitions.

There are few attempts to define exactly what constitutes partial resolution, and certainly no unanimity on the matter. The presence of backgrounded incongruity has not been taken by previous authors as evidence that resolution is partial. However, the arrangement where new incongruity is introduced by a punch line in the course of resolving some earlier incongruity (Section 7.8) is labelled by Rothbart and Pien (1977, p. 37) as 'partial resolution' (compare option (3) in the quotation above from McGhee et al. (1990)).

On the other hand, the quotations above from Forabosco (1992) and Attardo (1994) suggest that partial resolution leaves some portion of the original incongruity in place (see option (2) in the quotation above from McGhee et al. (1990)).

A third possible defining characteristic of 'partial resolution' is that faulty logic (see Chapter 6) must play a crucial role within the resolution (Hempelmann & Attardo, 2011, p. 140). We will consider this in Section 7.10.

Although there is no single, clear and accepted definition of what is meant by partial resolution, there seems to be a general consensus that partial resolution produces a final interpretation which contains some incongruity. That is, there seems to be a widespread view that the final interpretation of the joke, as an outcome of the comprehension process, should contain some incongruity which has not been fully resolved.

We are not convinced that 'partial resolution' is a helpful construct in describing humorous effects, but it might be possible to define it in terms of our text comprehension mechanisms, as follows. Over Sections 7.7, 7.8 and 7.9, we have seen a recurring pattern within jokes:

(a) There is an anomaly. That is:

  - A situation occurs and/or is treated as normal in a non-audience viewpoint.
  - The logic which would be inherited from a dominating viewpoint (usually the audience's real world) would not provide support for that situation.

(b) Audience inference has devised, within the non-audience viewpoint, some internal logic which leads to the situation in question.
(c) That supporting logic is discrepant (i.e. not the same as the logic in the dominating viewpoint).
(d) Hence, the final stage of comprehension contains a 'relative anomaly'.
(e) The supporting logic requires a significant level of disbelief-suspension to be accepted.

Of these features, (a) seems to correspond to 'incongruity' in the sense used by some of the authors reviewed in this chapter, while (b), (c) and perhaps (e) capture the circumstances in which 'partial resolution' is typically diagnosed. The combination of (b), (c) and (e) embodies, by definition, what we are calling fanciful logic, but it also seems a good match for what has usually been called 'faulty logic'. This would also allow 'full resolution' to label the case in which (a) and (b) (but not (c), (d) or (e)) hold. It may be possible to define the various approaches to IR in these terms, as follows.

In the Suls version (Section 7.3), the initial apparent anomaly (a) occurs at the end of punch line, and this is transformed into a relative anomaly (b) by the post-text audience inference. The situation that lacks support in (a) can be an implicative statement, as in the analysis of (18) in Section 7.3, where '*I'm on a diet* $\Rightarrow$ *four pieces*' temporarily lacks support.

For the set-up puzzle arrangement (Section 7.4), (a) would come about during the set-up, and (b) would result from the post-text inference.

What we referred to as IR without temporal sequence (Section 7.7) would involve the relative anomaly (i.e. the combination of (a) and (b)) being the result of post-text audience inference, present in the final interpretation, without specifying a sequence of how it comes about.

We think that these reformulations capture the essential points of the different versions of IR, but we cannot be sure that they would be accepted by proponents of those variants.

7.10 The incongruity of faulty logic

We have so far followed one particular aspect of the arrangement adopted in most articles on IR, namely that any pseudo-logic (Chapter 6) provides resolution and is distinct from incongruity. However, the distinction is not always as clear as this. In some jokes, one possible source of the feeling of incongruity (at least in the sense of 'absurdity') could be the nature of the faulty logic. That is, the actual line of reasoning, rather than its outcome, could be what seems most odd, so that, when the joke is decomposed into an incongruity with pseudo-logical support, the humour seems to stem as much from the logic as from the incongruity.

McGhee (1972, p. 67), in discussing incongruity humour, sketches three possible 'inconsistencies' which could be the source of the humour in example

(31), one of which is 'buying a dog when you do not like dogs' (which would involve adopting the 'set-up question' variant of IR, Section 7.4).

(31) 'Well, I see you have a new dog. I thought you didn't like dogs.'
'Well, I don't, but my wife bought a lot of dog soap on sale, so we had to get a dog to use it up.

In this example, a relatively mild incongruity (a dog-disliking person acquiring a dog) is 'resolved' by bizarre reasoning, summarised in the punch line, located in the viewpoint of the second speaker-character, and something like:

> *The character has a large quantity of dog soap. Money has been paid for this soap. Economical house-keeping suggests that one should make use of resources in which one has invested money. Hence the dog soap should be used. To use dog soap, one needs a dog. Hence it is necessary to obtain a dog.*

There is no obvious objective way to apportion the humorous effect between the mild incongruity in the set-up and the faulty logic in the punch line, but intuitively it seems to be the reasoning that introduces the humour. We can make this clearer using artificially constructed variants. First, consider (32).

(32) 'Well, I see you have a new dog. I thought you didn't like dogs.'
'Well, I don't, but my wife insisted on getting it.'
(constructed example)

In (32), the same puzzle (in our terms, a justification question) is presented in the initial question, with the answer resolving this puzzle, fully. It is hard to argue that this version functions as a joke in any way. To emphasise how little the initial justification question contributes to the humorous effect in (31), consider (33), in which there is no initial 'incongruity', but the faulty reasoning remains.

(33) 'Well, I see you have a new dog.'
'Well, my wife bought a lot of dog soap on sale, so we had to get a dog to use it up.'
(constructed example)

This variant appears to be a joke, hardly differing from, and not markedly less funny than the (admittedly not hugely amusing) original (31), despite lacking the supposed incongruity of the set-up's justification question.

In (31), the initial justification question seems to be there solely to provide a setting for the faulty logic. The outcome of the character's reasoning (owning a dog) is not incongruous, particularly in (33), but the route to that outcome is odd. (A similar observation could be made about example (18), Ethel and the cake, in Section 7.3, where opting for four pieces is not odd, but the motivation is).

We will say more about these 'dog soap' examples in Chapter 13.

There is a logical connection between discrepant logic and anomaly. If a character in a joke has come to a conclusion *P*, then presumably *P* follows from the rules within that character's viewpoint. In the case where *P* creates an anomaly, this means, by definition, that *P* does not follow from the rules of some higher viewpoint, usually the audience's. In this scenario, it follows that there is a discrepancy between the two sets of rules, which would normally mean that the character's rules are incorrect in comparison to the audience's (Section 6.3). Hence, for the final interpretation of a text to contain an anomaly, there must, almost by definition, be some reasoning which is inaccurate by the audience's standards. In successful joke comprehension, audience inference works out what the pertinent rules (the support) must be, which results in there being a relative anomaly. As outlined in Section 6.6, this working out could fail, if the only discoverable additions to the joke world require excessive disbelief-suspension, as some audiences might find in the case of (15), the mayonnaise in the hair, or (16), ice cream as a vegetable. That scenario would leave an apparent anomaly. In some cases, virtually no audience inference is required to find the support, as the reasoning is spelled out explicitly, as in (31) (the dog soap).

A possible alternative view would be to look upon it the other way: that it is the faulty reasoning that is the core of the humour, with the anomaly being a natural side-effect. That account would mean that humour is generated only if the audience becomes aware of the faulty reasoning, not merely its outcome; this would be comparable to the need for resolution within an IR perspective. As noted in Section 7.9, the use of flawed logic is a candidate to be a defining characteristic of the popular but ill-defined 'partial resolution'.

In view of the above discussion, it should be clear that it may be difficult to tease apart the humorous contributions of differences between rules and differences between the outcomes of those rules.

7.11 Benign violation

A relatively recent theoretical approach to humour, which could be seen as having evolved from IR (and also from Veatch (1998)), is *benign violation theory (BVT)* (McGraw & Warren, 2010; Warren & McGraw, 2016). This proposes that a necessary and sufficient criterion for humour is that a stimulus is appraised simultaneously as being a *violation* (of a norm) and being *benign*. McGraw and Warren define a 'violation' as '... anything that is threatening to one's sense of how the world "ought to be"...' (McGraw & Warren, 2010, p. 1142), explaining that this could include violations of 'personal dignity', 'linguistic norms', 'social norms' or 'moral norms'.

The violation is 'benign' if:

> . . . (a) a salient norm suggests that something is wrong but another salient norm suggests that it is acceptable, (b) one is only weakly committed to the violated norm, or (c) the violation is psychologically distant.
>
> (McGraw & Warren, 2010, p. 1142)

The term 'salient' seems to mean 'relevant to the current circumstances', and not to be a substantive part of the theory. The meaning of 'norm' is treated as self-evident, as is 'weakly committed'. Psychological distance is said to take many forms: 'temporal, social, spatial, likelihood, or hypotheticality' (McGraw & Warren, 2010, p. 1146).

If there are any violations within a joke, they presumably qualify as 'benign' for a few reasons. Since jokes are, by assumption, told in a setting of play (Section 3.3), presumably any violations detected within them are benign, since there is a 'salient norm' (i.e. the conventions of joke-telling) which suggests that it is 'acceptable'. Also, situations recounted in a joke are in a sense 'hypothetical', being fictional, and so could be deemed to be at a psychological distance for the audience. Moreover, where discrepant logic leads to a relative anomaly, as in many cases above, this could qualify as 'benign', under clause (a) in the definition quoted above.

At first, it might seem that what we have termed an 'anomaly' could be seen as a 'violation' in BVT terms. However, Warren and McGraw (2016, p. 409) make a distinction between something which is merely atypical (which they see as one variant of 'incongruity' used in humour research), and a breaking of moral norms. Only the latter counts as a 'violation' in their theory. We will discuss how this relates to our model in Section 10.8.

7.12 Summary

In this chapter, we have reviewed a range of concepts that have been discussed within IR accounts of joke mechanisms. As was observed, a few logically distinct notions of 'incongruity' or 'resolution' have been put forward as the definitive mechanism of jokes. Our position is slightly different. We recognise the informal intuitions (about oddity and about making sense) that have led to the various IR proposals. However, we would argue that once these mini-theories are decomposed into a suitable set of non-humorous text comprehension constructs, such as those in Chapter 4, several aspects are clarified. In particular, we are able to see the relationships between the different perspectives on IR, and observe that some of these supposedly mutually exclusive configurations can occur simultaneously in the same joke. In this way, we obtain an integrated description of the various phenomena that previous work has described in a variety of IR-related terms, and a clarification of how the variants of IR fit together. Compared to these previous accounts, our framework both provides slightly more detail and also makes a better connection to non-humorous concepts. Nevertheless, we would argue that our reformulations remain faithful to the intuitions on which earlier IR expositions were based. In particular, it could be that what we have described as apparent or direct anomalies correspond to 'incongruity', that a relative anomaly is comparable to 'resolved incongruity', the 'resolution' is represented by the support (that is, certain elements of internal logic in a lower viewpoint) which allows an anomaly to be a relative anomaly. This formulation might not be acceptable to all proponents of IR, but it seems to capture most of the essential ideas. However, it does not matter whether these parallels are accepted, as our proposals are not dependent on the terminology of incongruity and resolution.

We have not attempted, in this chapter, to extend the coverage of the IR approach by examining radically new examples. The IR accounts which we are trying to integrate have been justified by various scholars over the years as being helpful in describing certain types of jokes. Where a joke cannot be described by any of those earlier IR concepts, it lies outside the scope of the integration outlined in the current chapter. However, the analyses we have given will form a basis for further investigation in later chapters, where the scope will be widened.

From our perspective, there is no need to use concepts such as backgrounded incongruity or partial resolution if these concepts in themselves play no role in a functional model of the actual workings of joke comprehension. That is, these terms appear to lie between the lower level of our text comprehension constructs and the higher level of 'being humorous' – they are intermediate descriptive concepts, as are our categories of anomaly. They are of use only if they are helpful in framing insightful generalisations about being a joke or being humorous (i.e. at the higher level). It remains to be seen which, if any, of these intermediate constructs are useful in this way. If these concepts are undefined, or defined as a disjunction of very distinct scenarios, then it is not clear how they shed light on the question of humour. If 'partial resolution' or 'pseudo-logic' are defined as being present if and only if humour occurs, then they are uselessly circular.

Perhaps the most fundamental conclusion to be drawn from our review is as follows. All the various configurations of IR that have been proposed as crucial to the creation of humour can be found in the comprehension of non-humorous text, and hence cannot be sufficient conditions for humour; whether any of them are necessary is harder to determine. Consider the following statements about general, non-humorous stories:

> In the course of understanding a text, the audience may be faced with puzzling situations, the explanations for which do not become apparent until much later in the text, perhaps at its end. Or the puzzlement may occur at the end of the text and so must be solved by the audience's mental efforts alone. These various challenges may be because some aspect of the storyworld is abnormal but can be rendered understandable by figuring out some unusual way that the

> storyworld works. In the course of this figuring out, the audience may assess some requirements of the story as highly implausible, even taking into account certain storytelling conventions. After all this is completed, the interpretation of the text may still contain situations which the audience regards as odd.

All the IR descriptions from this chapter appear in this summary of how a non-humorous text is comprehended. This is not a complaint that the IR proposals rely on non-humorous components – as we pointed out in Section 2.3, using non-humorous building blocks is essential. The problem is that specific combinations of these components have been put forward as distinctive of humorous texts, but appear not to be.

Chapter 8

Surprise

8.1 Surprise in jokes

The importance of surprise

An intimate connection between surprise and humour has been asserted by various scholars, including Aristotle and Cicero, over several centuries (Attardo, 1994; Morreall, 1983). In more modern times, Ziv says that 'There is no laughter without surprise' (Ziv, 1984, p. 89), Morreall (1983, p. 84) says that '...what is funny has to surprise us in some way', Morreall (2009, p. 71) notes that humour has an emphasis on surprise, Oring (1992b, p. 90) mentions the importance of 'the surprise element' in a punch line, Attardo (1994) alludes to 'the need for surprise' within joke comprehension (p. 290) and to 'the element of surprise' as 'a basic component of the humorous effect of jokes' (p. 302). Surprise is one of eight types of humour theory in the taxonomy of Keith-Spiegel (1972), and a recent survey remarks that: 'Most psychological theories assume that some degree of surprise is part of the reception of humor' (Hempelmann, 2014, p. 629).

Despite this general consensus about the centrality of surprise in the creation of humour, there is not yet a detailed account of how exactly surprise fits into the general process of joke comprehension. Nor has much hard evidence been put forward in support of the influence of surprise. Interestingly, three wide-ranging and relatively recent works on humour (Martin, 2007; Morreall, 2009; Raskin, 2008) contain no index entries for 'surprise'.

Apter and Desselles (2012) see surprise as an 'enhancer' (Section 3.5) rather than a central component of humour, and Veatch (1998) says that surprise is neither necessary nor sufficient for humour. That surprise is not sufficient is clear, as shown by the plentiful occurrence of non-humorous surprises. Whether it is necessary is a more open question.

Possibly the most persuasive argument to support the idea that surprise is central to the working of jokes is the mundane observation that a joke is usually regarded as funny only when first encountered (Morreall, 1983, p. 50). Subsequent re-hearings or re-readings of the joke will still be understood, and may even evoke admiration, or memories of previous amusement, but the key humorous impact will be much reduced or absent. Similarly, if an audience manages, during the set-up stage of joke comprehension, to figure out how the joke will end, then the final effect may be much less: 'Being shown the solution to a puzzle is qualitatively different from discovering it oneself' (Oring, 1992b, p. 90). This gives the intuitive impression that some form of surprise contributes to the humorous effect.

In terms of the five possible encounters with a joke presented in Section 3.4, the above observations suggest that surprise is a plausible occurrence only in the Natural circumstance, and possibly in the Reencounter case, but not in the other three, where there is nothing unexpected. This would also mean that any contribution which surprise makes to joke comprehension is through joke appreciation in the sense defined in Section 3.6.

Surprise and incongruity

When we examine joke mechanisms, it is natural to compare the concepts of 'incongruity' and 'surprise', given that both could involve the idea of unexpected outcomes (Section 7.1). Brownell et al. (1983), who offer 'surprise' as central to the success of a joke, loosely equate surprise and 'discrepancies from the normal course' (p. 21), which they see as incongruity within a particular kind of incongruity-resolution account (see Section 7.3). Attardo suggests a direct link between surprise and incongruity:

> The concept of incongruity corresponds to that of surprise ... incongruity is a stimulus, and surprise is a response ... surprise and incongruity are conceptualized essentially in the same way. ... The definitions of incongruity used in humor studies do not differ from those of surprise. They can be generalized as divergence from expectations.
>
> (Attardo, 2014b, p. 383)

This would mean that any claims in the research literature about incongruity could be reformulated to make statements involving surprise. However, this may not be completely straightforward. If incongruity is defined in terms of logical or semantic relationships between concepts, as is often done, then this omits any dynamic or temporal aspects, such as suddenness, which might affect whether surprise will occur. Given that several variants of 'incongruity' are used within descriptions of joke mechanisms (see Chapter 7) and more than one definition of 'surprise' (see later in this chapter), it is not at once obvious how these two terms should be made to correspond. We will return to the question of surprise and incongruity in Section 8.2.

Surprise is of interest as a theoretical account of joke humour only if it adds something to the explanation and is not simply a relabelling of some other phenomenon.

We will examine how surprise might form a central part of the humorous effect of a joke. We will tackle this from three angles:

- How can the time course of the experience of surprise be aligned with the process of joke comprehension so that surprise forms a central part of the humorous effect? (Section 8.2)
- How do the mechanisms of surprise proposed within psychology throw light on the processing of jokes? (Section 8.3)
- What conception of surprise seems to be implicitly adopted by humour scholars when they refer to its role in humour? (Section 8.4)

As will become clear, it is hard to see what would be gained by incorporating a notion of 'surprise' in a model of joke comprehension (Section 8.5).

8.2 The timing of surprise

The nature of surprise

Many discussions of surprise focus on a scenario in which some discovery is perceived suddenly, resulting in various immediate, involuntary, physiological reactions: 'Clearly, when people encounter surprising events in the world they often immediately experience the "shock of the surprise" and a certain level of arousal;' (Foster & Keane, 2015, p. 109). Maguire and Maguire (2009) refer to this as 'the more visceral form' of surprise. Darwin wrote of such reactions as an intermediate stage between mere 'attention' and the stronger states of 'astonishment' and 'amazement':

> Attention, if sudden and close, graduates into surprise; and this into astonishment; and this into stupefied amazement . . . Attention is shown by the eyebrows being slightly raised; and as this state increases into surprise, they are raised to a much greater extent, with the eyes and mouth widely open.
>
> (Darwin, 1872)

More recently, the facial correlates of this kind of surprise have been examined more precisely, although there is some dispute about the strength of the association between feelings of surprise and the apparently obvious facial indicators mentioned by Darwin (Reisenzein, Bördgen, Holtbernd, & Matz, 2006). Young et al. (1997, p. 277) observe that surprise is one of '. . . six different emotional facial expressions . . . which have been found to be accurately recognised from forced-choice between these possible emotions in most cultures of the world.' The facial symptoms are short in duration, often lasting less than a second.

Some empirical studies of surprise focus more on these early involuntary stages of surprise, by directly presenting participants with some stimuli and measuring reactions; we will call these *instant reaction* studies. One example comes from Itti and Baldi (2009), who tested a model of surprise based on Bayesian probability, by carrying out various experiments in which the movement of a person's gaze at a screen was recorded while particular visual events occurred on the display (see later in this section for more details). Since this study tracked where a person looked in response to stimuli, this fits well with Darwin's idea of surprise as a more intense form of attention. These trials measured an immediate, probably non-conscious, reaction.

In contrast to this 'visceral' surprise, there is also 'cognitive surprise', in which an individual attempts to find an explanation for a 'discrepant stimulus' (Maguire & Maguire, 2009). Whereas the visceral surprise occurs within a fraction of a second, the cogitation directed to finding an explanation may take much longer. In some cases, there may be little emotional engagement on the part of the person seeking the explanation, as this cognitive quest can be caused by second-hand accounts of situations which have no affectual impact on that particular individual.

A further distinction has been suggested:

> 'The Surprise Experience' can be separated into three phases: (i) noticing the surprise, (ii) an emotional response to the surprise, and (iii) a cognitive response; an attempt to understand why the surprising event occurred.
>
> (Foster et al., 2014)

From that perspective, visceral surprise roughly corresponds to a combination of phases (i) and (ii) in this segmentation, with cognitive surprise corresponding to phase (iii).

Some experiments explore the later, explanation-seeking stage of surprise, usually by asking the participants to consider some fictional scenario and pass judgements explicitly; these we will label *considered assessment* studies. In recent years, there have been several such studies (Foster & Keane, 2015; Maguire & Maguire, 2009; Teigen & Keren, 2003), for which the rationale is stated thus:

> There is some consensus in the literature that asking people to appraise surprising events is a reasonable and ethically more-acceptable paradigm for exploring surprise ... However, ... an important empirical question for future work is to confirm that the resolution of surprise is the same for directly and vicariously experienced events. There are no indications from the current literature that such differences exist, but we know of no studies that have explicitly compared both contexts for surprise at once.
>
> (Foster & Keane, 2015, p. 109)

Both the visceral and cognitive aspects of surprise can occur to varying degrees: something can be slightly surprising, moderately surprising, highly surprising, etc. Also, the degree of surprise can vary greatly between the phases of the experience: intense visceral surprise might be followed by a lower level of cognitive surprise, if an explanation comes readily to mind. For example, imagine someone walking along a quiet city street, when suddenly a large lump of stone crashes to the ground only a couple of metres away, shattering with the impact. This would almost certainly evoke a considerable degree of visceral surprise (and a startle reaction – see next subsection). However, it might be that the cause of the sudden loud noise is immediately apparent: a lump of rock has struck the ground. An explanation for this occurrence could then spring readily to mind: all the surrounding buildings are stone-built, very old, and in a poor state of repair, and so it is natural that a piece of masonry might come loose and fall to the ground. In such circumstances, there might be only moderate cognitive surprise.

The visceral/cognitive distinction will be relevant both when we consider models of surprise (later in this section) and when we relate surprise to joke comprehension (Section 8.3).

The startle response

A visceral surprise might seem to have something in common with the phenomenon of the 'startle reaction' or 'startle response', a deep-seated reflex action caused by sudden, intense (and potentially threatening) stimuli such as loud noises (Lang, Bradley, & Cuthbert, 1990). However, there are a few subtle but important differences between these effects.

> Surprise must be distinguished from the startle reaction elicited by sudden intense stimuli, in particular loud noises ... Whereas surprise is caused by the appraisal of unexpectedness, startle is a reflexlike reaction to intense sensory input.
>
> (Reisenzein et al., 2006, fn. 1)

A genuine startle is not generally suppressed by mere knowledge that the stimulus is about to occur, unlike surprise, which does not occur if the outcome is expected. Also, a startle and a surprise provoke different facial expressions (Ekman, Friesen, & Simons, 1985). Startle is triggered by a high-intensity stimulus, and has distinctive physical and physiological responses, whereas surprise can result from a stimulus merely being unexpected, and is more of a cognitive-emotional response, albeit with some physiological correlates (Rivera, Talone, Boesser, Jentsch, & Yeh, 2014). A sudden, intense, unexpected event might cause both startle and surprise.

Different states of knowledge

As noted by various authors, an event or idea is not surprising in isolation: surprise is a reaction to, or a verdict upon, a relationship between some perception or information and a particular state of belief. Some specific outcome is surprising only relative to a particular view of how the world is or operates.

Adler (2008, pp. 154–155) gives an imaginary example involving two people watching a football match, with widely differing knowledge of the game. He argues that the less expert viewer might find an incident during the game unsurprising initially, but, after being told the relevant technical background, might then be 'poised for surprise'. This emphasises the need for both sides of the relationship: the recently acquired perception or information, and the knowledge base relative to which it is surprising. Adler implies that sometimes the surprising nature of the former may be grasped only after the latter is supplied. This thought experiment involves cognitive surprise.

The stages of the joke

In Section 3.1, we labelled four stages of joke comprehension: 'initial', 'post-set-up', 'post-text', 'final'. The last three of these will be particularly relevant to our discussion of the alignment of surprise with joke comprehension. In particular, the final stage is when audience inference has integrated enough of the meaning of the whole text to trigger amusement. The experience of amusement may persist beyond the final stage, but the final stage is the starting point, where no further information needs to be extracted from the text to achieve joke recognition and, if the conditions are favourable, cause joke appreciation (using the sense of these terms defined earlier, in Section 3.4).

To decide how surprise contributes to joke comprehension, it will be necessary to find a suitable alignment between these temporal stages of joke comprehension and the phases of surprise described earlier: noticing, emotional, cognitive. This will implicitly also align with the corresponding states of knowledge: Prior, Posterior, and Integrated. (Sections 5.2 and 8.3).

Surprise within the comprehension process

In attempting to locate surprise in our joke comprehension framework, we will focus just on those aspects of surprise which mark its beginning and its end: the start of the initial 'noticing' phase, and the finish of the final 'cognitive' phase (in terms of Foster et al.'s three phases of surprise, outlined earlier). We are particularly interested in how the phases of surprise might be related to the important stages of joke comprehension: post-set-up, post-text, and final.

The pre-theoretic notion of 'surprise' is so vaguely defined that it could be seen as occurring, to varying degrees, throughout joke comprehension, including during the processing of the set-up, because any puzzling incidents within the narrative can be so labelled. The audience becoming aware of an abnormality could be the start of a surprise. We will illustrate this with example (34), chosen because it has scope for several abnormalities to be noticed. (This is a British version of a joke discussed by Ritchie (2004). We will analyse it in more detail in Chapter 13.)

(34) The police pull over an old lady in a car. She has a passenger, an old man whose face is frozen in a rictus of fear. The policeman says, 'Madam, I just pulled you off the motorway for driving at 25 miles an hour. Why were

> you driving so slowly?' 'I wasn't,' says the old lady. 'I was doing what the sign told me. It said the "M25", so I drove at 25 miles per hour.' 'That's not how it works, madam,' says the policeman. 'Couldn't your friend have told you that?' He looks at the old man, who's not moved a muscle since they stopped. 'Is he all right?' asks the policeman. 'I'm not sure,' says the old lady. 'He's been like that since we got on the A150.'
>
> (Haskins & Arnott, 2017, p. 320)

It would be possible to propose some form of surprise at various stages of the comprehension of this joke (see Figure 8.1):

(i) The car driving at an unusually slow speed could be the start of a surprise, with the end of the surprise occurring when the audience works out the driver-character's misinterpretation of the road signs. This would be what we earlier classed as a temporary gap. All of this happens before the post-set-up stage, at which point the main humour of the joke has not yet been reached: this surprise both starts and ends before the final amusement reaction.

(ii) It could be that the punch line is not immediately interpretable – see the discussion of relevance questions in Section 4.5. There might therefore be an assimilation difficulty, requiring some post-text inference before it makes sense. This would mean there was a surprise which starts with the completion of the text, and ends when the post-text inference is completed.

(iii) Another possibility (once again, a temporary gap) is that the surprise could start with the fearful state of the passenger-character, which occurs well before the post-set-up stage, and would end with the final stage.

We will use the term *incidental surprise* to refer to any surprise which ends prior to the post-set-up stage, as happens in case (i) above. It is possible that an incidental surprise may have relatively mild visceral stages: the audience may not have much emotional or physiological response. (Here we ignore the

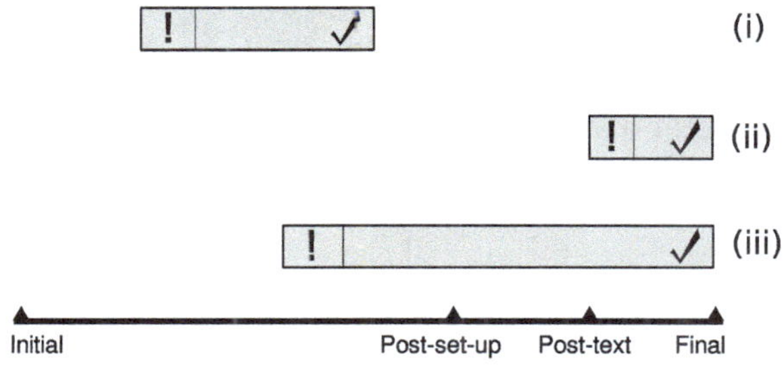

Figure 8.1 Some possible alignments of surprise

possibility of intermediate funny lines in a joke –'jab lines' (Attardo, 2001).) Almost by definition, incidental surprise functions in a rather minor supporting role, rather than being a key component of humour, since this kind of surprise is detached from the amusement reaction. In fact, there can be incidental surprise during the comprehension of a non-humorous text. Hence, it is hard to see how incidental surprise can be the basis of a 'surprise theory of humour'.

Options (ii) and (iii) in this list can be seen as rewordings of the incongruity-resolution analyses we reviewed in Sections 7.3 and 7.4 respectively.

The role of surprise

If there is to be any content in a surprise theory of jokes, then there must be some form of surprise which is an inherent part of the final amusement reaction (in keeping with the various quotations in Section 8.1). This means we have to consider surprise which is not 'incidental' in sense of the previous subsection, but is at least partly simultaneous with the final amusement. Cases (ii) and (iii) above meet this minimal condition. This is not a matter of the substance of the surprise, but simply of its timing within joke comprehension.

It is tempting to link the amusement reaction with the initial phase of surprise, because physiological reactions to that visceral phase (see Section 8.2, particularly the quotation from Darwin) seem intuitively similar to a typical reaction to suddenly grasping a joke. That is, there might appear to be some similarity between the visceral phase of surprise and the feeling of discovery that often coincides with the final understanding of a joke, sometimes accompanied by emotional reactions to particular aspects of the discovered meaning (see Chapters 10 and 11). However, this would have the final cognitive phase of surprise taking place *after* the amusement: the audience would make sense of the surprising information only after they had found it amusing. This extends the cognitive processing beyond the moment of amusement (the final stage), and also suggests that an audience is amused before they have assimilated the relevant information. This is not only intuitively implausible, it very much conflicts with the incongruity-resolution perspective which we examined in Chapter 7. It is therefore highly relevant that none of the three alignments of surprise shown in Figure 8.1, above, have the initial phase of surprise corresponding to the final stage of joke comprehension, where the amusement occurs.

The other natural correspondence would be to equate the cognitive phase of surprise with the post-text audience inference, which seeks to make sense of the punch line. In this case, the visceral phase would be triggered earlier, either by the initial perception of the punch line (case (ii) above) or during the set-up (case (iii) above). Although this alignment may well be an accurate reflection of the sequence of cognitive events, it does not allow the visceral phase of surprise to contribute directly to the amusement at the final stage, since it is now the cognitive phase that overlaps with the final amusement reaction. This would discard a persuasive motivation for a surprise theory – namely, the sudden emotional reaction of surprise being central to the amusement. It would introduce a need to explain why completion of the cognitive phase of surprise should result in humour; that is, labelling it as surprise would not explain much.

It might be possible to make this arrangement seem more plausible by having the surprise commence during the post-text inference. We could speculate that the surprise is initiated (i.e. the noticing phase) by the audience detecting something odd during this stage of inference (e.g. an apparent anomaly), that the cognitive phase is the subsequent inference which finds an explanation (e.g. support) for that oddity, and that the humour derives from the nature of that explanation. This is, in a sense, a rephrasing of the idea of faulty logic as the source of the humour (Section 7.10). Once again, adopting the terminology of surprise adds no additional insight.

8.3 Surprise mechanisms and jokes

Three models of surprise

There is no precise and accepted definition of 'surprise', but various attempts have been made to construct theoretical accounts of how surprise comes about. We will outline some of these, and then consider whether these mechanisms have any particular appropriateness for processing the humorous aspects of jokes. In doing this, we will use the knowledge states Prior, Posterior, Integrated, and Alternative (Section 5.2) to describe different sequences of information change.

Itti and Baldi (Baldi & Itti, 2010; Itti & Baldi, 2009) propose that surprise is based on a difference between the knowledge states Prior and Posterior; that is, before and after the perceived event. More specifically, they regard these knowledge states as associating probabilities with all the propositions within the knowledge base. New information acquired, in the transition from Prior to Posterior, may change these probabilities. The extent of surprise depends on the magnitude of the overall changes in probabilities, sometimes referred to as 'Bayesian surprise'. They hypothesised that humans would attend, by redirection of gaze, to visual stimuli which were surprising by this measure, and tested this empirically, with positive results.

This can be seen as a probability-change model of surprise. The test of the model was, in our terminology, an instant reaction study, focusing (in terms of Foster et al.'s stages) on phase (i), noticing, rather than phase (iii), cognitive response.

Over the past decade, a group of researchers (Foster & Keane, 2015; Maguire & Maguire, 2009; Maguire, Maguire, & Keane, 2011) have proposed an integrative theory, in which the degree of surprise caused by some item of information depends on the cognitive effort required to think of an explanation for that information; that is, to make sense of the outcome. In our list of knowledge states, this would be the transition from Posterior to Integrated.

This hypothesis has been tested in a series of experiments in which participants were asked to rate particular fictional scenarios on a scale of surprise (that is, these were considered assessment studies, in our terms).

Foster and Keane (2015) argue that their results support their explanation-based model over Itti and Baldi's probability-change model, but it is not totally clear that these studies have produced conflicting results, for two reasons. Firstly, Foster and Keane are examining phase (iii) within their own decomposition of the 'surprise experience', whereas Itti and Baldi seem to be investigating the earlier phase (i). Secondly, the term 'surprise' has a different theoretical status in the experiments. Itti and Baldi use a mathematical definition to predict behaviour, possibly involuntary, with the term 'surprise' functioning simply as a way to refer to the phenomenon they are exploring. Foster and Keane, and the others cited above as carrying out considered assessment studies, use their definition as a means to predict the use of the words 'surprise' or 'surprising' to categorise situations. Hence, different phenomena and different kinds of hypothesis are being tested.

This does not mean that the integrative model could not in principle be applied to visceral surprise as well. This would require an appropriate notion of 'stimulus' and of 'explanation' (or 'making sense of').

Teigen and Keren (2003) propose a 'contrast interpretation of surprise', in which the degree of surprise is dependent on the relationship of the actual outcome to alternative but unrealised outcomes. In our terms, this compares Posterior and Alternative knowledge states. More specifically, they hypothesise that greater surprise is associated with a combination of three things: a dominant alternative outcome with high probability; the actual outcome being less familiar, based on past experience; the actual outcome being less similar to the expected outcome. These claims were supported by the results of some experiments (of the considered assessment type). Maguire et al. (2011) argue that this contrast model is less accurate than the integrative model in dealing with how the degree of specificity of a prediction may affect the level of surprise. (The Teigen and Keren model seems to be roughly what Hurley et al. (2011) have in mind in their account of jokes: 'It is the contradiction between an anticipated event or state and a perceived event or state that surprises us' (p.54).)

Failure of prediction

In general, surprise is treated as a reaction to the non-occurrence of something expected: 'Disconfirmation of an explicit or an implicit expectancy has been posited by practically all surprise theorists as the primary, if not the only, cognitive elicitor of surprise and is so regarded in common sense also ...' (Reisenzein et al., 2006, p. 297).

A similar perspective shows up in discussions of surprise and humour. Veatch (1998) suggests that surprise is often present in humour, and that it involves the violation of expectations. Warren and McGraw (2016, p. 408) treat surprise, which they see as one possible meaning of 'incongruity', as a deviation from expectations. Morreall (1983, p. 43) refers to humour deriving from surprise 'based on having part of one's conceptual system violated'. Attardo (1994, pp. 289–290) says that the 'surprise theory of humour' is commonly taken to mean the requirement that the punch line of a joke 'should come unexpectedly'.

In Chapter 5, we set out three different ways in which 'prediction' might be defined: probabilistic, specified outcome and accessibility. The three models of surprise outlined earlier in this section can all be seen as based on violation of prediction if we attribute to each model one of these notions of 'prediction', along with the corresponding definition of 'violation' (Section 5.2), in the following way. Itti and Baldi's probability-change model of surprise would correspond to the probabilistic definition of prediction. Maguire et al.'s integrative model of surprise is consistent with the accessibility definition of prediction. Teigen and Keren's contrasting outcome model is compatible with the specified outcome type of prediction.

As we noted earlier, the expressions 'expectation' and 'prediction' seem to be treated as equivalent by humour analysts, but in Section 4.5 we adopted distinct interpretations for these two terms: predictions are forecasts of outcomes during the process of text comprehension, violations of expectations are situations within viewpoints that do not conform to the internal logic.

In Section 4.5, we adopted definitions of 'anomaly' intended to capture the idea of 'violation of expectation'. These involved something occurring in the storyworld which would not naturally follow in the audience's viewpoint. (This depends on the idea that audience inference may conclude that some situation has taken place or is regarded as normal in a lower viewpoint using evidence other than the currently known internal logic of that viewpoint.) The moment when an audience becomes aware of something with this status could be the start of a surprise, and the search for support for the items causing the apparent anomaly could be the cognitive phase of surprise. (This is regardless of any predictions, in the sense we adopted in Section 4.5.)

There is the further phenomenon of what we will call *non-temporal surprise*; that is, a conscious judgement that something is surprising, separately from any time-sequence of discovery and rationalisation. Where some situation simply does not conform to expected norms, it is sometimes said to be 'surprising' or 'a surprise', even long after it has become known. For example, someone might remark that '*It's surprising that the government has this policy*'. Arguably, this is the type of surprise that is detected by considered assessment studies, in that these experiments present entire scenarios to be judged as being surprising, rather than tracking some temporal sequence of reactions.

Applying surprise models to jokes

We now consider how each of the three models of surprise outlined above can provide a more detailed description of joke comprehension. The possibilities are: the probability-change model (Baldi & Itti, 2010; Itti & Baldi, 2009), the integrative model (Foster & Keane, 2015; Maguire & Maguire, 2009; Maguire et al., 2011) and the contrasting outcome model (Teigen & Keren, 2003).

Attardo (2014a, p. 383) lists several conceptualisations of surprise in humour, all but one of which can be seen as being based on some model from the above set of three. The exception is 'the detection of discrepancies between schemas', which could be seen as what we described above as non-temporal surprise. (In reviewing theories of surprise, Reisenzein et al. (2006, p. 297) use the term 'schema-discrepant' as synonymous with 'unexpected', which still leaves open the precise meaning of 'expected'.)

It is hard to assess where the probability-change notion of surprise, based on the probabilistic version of prediction, may apply in jokes, as there is little evidence about how the variation in probability distributions across options might affect joke comprehension.

The integrative model fits quite naturally into one particular stage of joke comprehension: the puzzlement felt when the punch line does not at first appear to make sense, as in Section 7.3 and case (ii) of Figure 8.1 above. That is, it could well be that the assimilation difficulty experienced at this stage of comprehension arises because the set-up has not made salient the appropriate knowledge for swift and effortless understanding of the punch line. This would be particularly true in the case of 'forced reinterpretation' jokes (Section 7.6) and accords well with the idea, quoted earlier from Attardo (1994), that the punch line should arrive unexpectedly. Similarly, where there is a set-up puzzle, as in Section 7.4 and case (iii) of Figure 8.1 above, it could be argued that there is a shortage of salient knowledge during the set-up, remedied only by the post-text inference (a temporary gap, in the terminology of Section 4.7). Thus the integrative model's phases correspond well to these two variants of IR processing.

An open question is the extent to which the amount of post-text inference corresponds to the degree of amusement, which would presumably be a prediction, in the scientific sense, of adopting the integrative model, aligned in the way we have outlined.

To decide the relevance of the third model of surprise, the contrasting outcome account, it is necessary to determine whether specified outcome predictions occur during joke comprehension and are then violated with humorous consequences. That is, in joke comprehension, does the set-up provide a markedly increased likelihood for a relatively narrow range of continuations, such that the punch line can then violate this prediction by conveying something outside this range of possibilities?

Example (2), the replaceable pilot, is a case where there seems to be a prediction, subsequently not fulfilled, that one of a narrow set of words will follow as the last part of the punch line (Section 5.3). A few more such examples can be found in Ritchie (1999, Section 4.3) and Ritchie (2004, Section 8.4). In (35), the well-known description of Muhammad Ali would tend to cause '*a bee*' to be treated as highly likely at the end of the sentence, and in (36), verbs such as '*perform*' or '*develop*' might have been predicted for the last word.

(35) Floats like a butterfly, stings like one.
Brian Clough, on footballer Trevor Brooking (Tibballs, 2000, p. 578)

(36) With the collapse of vaudeville, new talent has no place to stink.
George Burns (Haskins & Arnott, 2017, p. 171)

Although it is highly plausible to suggest that examples like these involve a degree of surprise, describable using the contrasting outcomes model, it does not follow that this surprise is at the core of the humorous effect. It may be a surprise for the audience to encounter the unexpected word, but a joke is more than simply a sequence of words – the meaning of the text is what gives rise to the amusement. That is, some further processing of the word, in context, is needed, probably involving inference, before the actual humorous effect results. This means that the relatively concrete failed prediction – of the specific word, at a low linguistic level – may happen early in the post-text processing and be only a small early step towards the eventual amusement. This suggests that this surprise probably does not overlap with the final humorous effect, as discussed in Section 8.2.

Some jokes could be seen as involving specified outcome prediction at a higher, more conceptual level, as in (37). (See also (Ritchie, 2004, pp. 96–97 and p. 102).)

(37) The neighborhood borrower approached Mr Smith on Sunday afternoon and inquired: 'Say Smith, are you using your lawnmower this afternoon?'
'Yes, I am,' Smith replied warily.
The neighborhood borrower then answered: 'Fine, then you won't be needing your golf clubs. I'll just borrow them.'
(Brownell et al., 1983, p. 21)

For example, Brownell et al. say of (37):

> Upon hearing the body of the joke, the listener has an expectation of what will follow plausibly: For example, the borrower will be disappointed, or he will ask to borrow the lawnmower on a subsequent occasion. The punch line is surprising at one level precisely because it departs radically from these expectations about the normal course of events.
> (Brownell et al., 1983, p. 21)

For a joke like this, it could be argued both that there is surprise of the contrasting outcome variety and that this surprise involves elements at a higher, more semantic, level. However, it is not entirely clear whether the contrasting elements constitute the humour in themselves or whether further inferences are required. In any case, this example is not typical. For example, most of the jokes quoted in earlier chapters do not lend themselves naturally to descriptions in which there is a strong prediction of some narrow range of possible conclusions to the text. Often there will be no specific prediction beyond the default of 'something conforming with normality'.

Hence, the verdict on the three psychological models of surprise is that there is insufficient evidence regarding the probability-change model; the integrative model could plausibly describe 'surprise' of the types represented by our cases (ii) and (iii) in Figure 8.1 (see also Wyer and Collins (1992)); the contrasting outcome model may match a few jokes, but sometimes at too low a level to embody surprise that is essential to the humour.

As a result of the above arguments, it is not easy to see how surprise, as defined in the three available models, contributes in any general way to the humorous effect of a joke.

8.4 Reconsidering surprise and humour

In this section, we will leave aside the psychological theories of surprise reviewed in Sections 8.2 and 8.3 (i.e. the three phases of surprise and the three processing models of surprise) and simply consider what clues we can glean from joke comprehension about the involvement of some notion of surprise in the humorous climax of a joke. That is, we will try to pin down what conception of surprise can be derived from the remarks of humour scholars on this subject.

As we commented in Section 8.1, it is widely agreed that the effect of a joke can be spoiled by knowledge of the punch line. This suggests that the humorous effect crucially involves final revelations, in the sense described in Section 5.4: propositions which change from unaware to aware status in the final stage. (The discovery of false beliefs, which is the central construct proposed by Hurley et al. (2011), can be seen as a particular case of a final revelation.)

Veatch says that surprise '... functions to create the simultaneous juxtaposition of two understandings of a situation...' (Veatch, 1998, p. 189). Oring (1992d, p. 85) suggests the need for a punch line to contain an 'abrupt and surprising revelation', which brings up another surprise-like ingredient of the final humour effect of a joke: some degree of 'suddenness' (see Section 5.4).

The third aspect of humour-related surprise is the nature of the information that forms the final revelation(s). As we have observed, certain types of what we have defined as 'anomaly' could be seen as a violation of an expectation, hence in some sense a surprise. In some earlier examples (e.g. (13), the Irish Sea Scouts, and (10), the sausage collector), the revelations involved a relative or apparent anomaly: something within the joke world for which there is no support in the audience's viewpoint.

All this would suggest the possibility that, in a joke, humorous surprise requires a *sudden transition from unaware to aware of an anomaly*. The requirement for suddenness means that there is temporal element, but in the discovery of the surprising content, not in the computing of an explanation (which was proposed in the models of surprise that we considered earlier).

This raises the question: are there other kinds of final revelation which, when uncovered suddenly, provide humorous surprise? Some mundane situations might not be surprising, hence it seems likely that not all final revelations of anomaly will result in surprise, and certainly not humour. It may be that the revelations must have some particular content to have these effects. Amongst the possible candidates for this additional ingredient are fanciful logic (Section 6.6), impropriety (Chapter 10), and indications of superiority (Chapter 11). These could, informally, be seen as involving violations of normality, broadly interpreted.

This raises some theoretical questions. Firstly, if the only way to test whether particular circumstances lead to humour-relevant surprise is to ask whether humour is created, then there is a danger of circularity, due to insufficient separation between the question 'what causes surprise at the climax of a joke?' and the related question 'what causes humour at the climax of a joke?'. If the statement that surprise is centrally involved in joke comprehension is to be a useful empirical claim, then we must have an operational definition of surprise which does not rely on the notion of humour. Secondly, if we could specify the combination of features which leads to the kind of surprise that creates humour, what would labelling this as 'surprise' add to our understanding of joke comprehension? We have noted that some surprise-based accounts are simply incongruity-resolution analyses relabelled. If there is a good reason to believe that surprise leads naturally to humour, then framing analyses in terms of surprise may be helpful. Given that many surprises are not humorous, it is far from clear that a reformulation using surprise explains anything. In those circumstances, we would prefer to rely on a description in more basic terms.

8.5 Summary

We have explored how past remarks about surprise in humour could be made more precise, and whether current theories of surprise are useful in characterising the humorous effect of jokes.

If surprise is to be of interest in understanding how jokes work, then it must occur at the end of joke comprehension, as a key part of the humorous effect. This is in contrast to incidental surprise, which can occur at any non-final stage of joke comprehension, with no particular function in the climax.

Some accounts of surprise in jokes seem to rely on the idea of predictions being violated, but it is hard to see how any of the three models of surprise and their allied notions of prediction offer descriptions of humour-creating surprise across a wide range of jokes. Nevertheless, some jokes arguably manifest the contrasting outcome variant of surprise.

Past writings on surprise in jokes seem to assume a concept which has three requirements: final revelation, suddenness, and some further condition on the revealed information, which could very loosely be stated as 'violation of expectations'.

From the perspective of providing useful descriptions of the comprehension of particular jokes, the term 'surprise' is of doubtful value, given the variety of definitions that can be attached to it. In this chapter, we have looked at a number of circumstances within the processing of a joke that could be viewed as causing surprise. Given that these are different eventualities, and that these descriptions convey more than simply saying that there is a surprise, we would prefer to use these separate descriptions, rather than clumping them all together under a pseudo-generalisation as surprise.

The function of surprise in jokes is of theoretical interest only if it is a substantive contribution to the humorous effect of a joke, distinct from other key components. Even if the sequence of cognitive events in joke comprehension were to fit into a model of surprise, it is hard to see how this explains or illuminates the humorous reaction. Simply relabelling existing analyses using concepts of surprise is not an advance, unless we can find, from some independent source, a principled link from surprise to humour.

Chapter 9

The role of language

9.1 The functions of language

In this chapter, we will look at the various contributions that language can make to the operation of jokes, and from there we will examine where, within our framework, we must make allowances for linguistic knowledge. The aim is not to give a detailed description of all the linguistic phenomena which may be involved in creating humour, a topic which is widely documented within the existing literature on jokes. Instead, our narrower goal is to delineate where certain types of linguistic knowledge have to be represented in our text comprehension model. In particular, given that we have structured knowledge into a hierarchy of viewpoints, we will consider to what extent separate viewpoints must contain different linguistic capabilities or knowledge.

Before we start, a brief remark on terminology is in order. In earlier chapters, we have used the term 'rule' informally or semi-formally to denote a logical implication between conceptual items (Section 4.5). We will see (Section 9.3) that there is a need for mechanisms which have a quasi-inferential capability for relating different uses of linguistic elements, and which could perhaps be formulated in a manner similar to logical implications. In addition to these mechanisms, there is also a need for operations which combine linguistic elements, or which map between different types of linguistic structure, for example from syntactic trees to semantic formulae. In this chapter, because we are not going into great detail of how language models might work, we will use the term 'rule' loosely to cover all of these various operations and mappings involved in the processing of linguistic elements. This means that most statements in the next few sections which mention 'rule(s)' can be interpreted much as they would be in any discussion of linguistic mechanisms.

Following on from an earlier review of linguistic factors (Ritchie, 2010), we can identify four broad roles for language within joke comprehension:

Communicative medium: Language is used to convey some set of ideas, and the humour is derived from those ideas. Where this is the only function played by language, the resulting jokes are often described as 'thought-witticisms'

(Freud, 1916), 'conceptual' (Freud, 1966 [1912]) or 'referential' (Attardo, 1994).

Core structure: Linguistic relationships are the key to the status of the text as a joke. The clearest example of this is punning or word play, although more general categories exist, such as 'verbal' humour (Attardo, 1994, Chapter 3; Ritchie, 2004, Chapter 9).

Subject matter: In a small number of jokes, the humour is about the facts of language, so that linguistic knowledge plays a similar role to that of general world knowledge in other jokes (Ritchie, 2010, Section 3).

Style/register: The vocabulary and syntactic constructions chosen to express a particular meaning can also convey nuances of cultural setting, social class, degree of informality, etc. This can be used to humorous effect (Attardo, 1994; Partington, 2006; Venour, Ritchie, & Mellish, 2011).

We will not present extensive examples of any of these here, as they have been discussed elsewhere (see the references cited above). Instead, we will focus on how these different functions of language would fit into the overall joke comprehension scheme that we have been developing.

Since these are different functions of language, not different types of joke, it is possible for more than one function to be present in a single joke. In particular, language acts as a communicative medium in almost all jokes. The interesting distinctions are between those where this is the sole function of language and those where some other linguistic effects are involved.

9.2 Language as the medium

The first of our listed functions is the communication of ideas. In this role, language acts as a mechanism for converting speech sounds or written text into something more abstract and conceptual, which can denote entities in an audience's world and subordinate viewpoints, or convey information about the contents of those viewpoints. It would be a convenient simplification to assume that this mechanism mapping from linguistic input to concepts and propositions is identical in all viewpoints. However, this would make it difficult to capture what happens in many jokes. It is often remarked that many jokes rely on the audience interpreting some initial portion of the text in one way, and subsequently discovering an alternative interpretation (Section 7.6). Often, the alternative interpretation has been adopted, within the joke world, by some character (e.g. example (22), the old man on the highway).

In some cases, the multiplicity of interpretations is made possible by linguistic ambiguity, as in (38).

(38) A woman had just stepped out of the shower when the doorbell went.
'Who is it?' she called through the intercom.
'Blind man,' came the reply.

> She was stark naked but figured that it didn't really matter too much for a blind man, so she released the lock and called out: 'Come on up.'
> Not bothering to cover herself with a towel, she greeted him at the top of the stairs. He said: 'Now where do you want these blinds?'
>
> (Tibballs, 2000, pp. 478–479)

In such jokes, the differing choices of interpretation seem to correspond to variations in the salience of possible readings (Section 4.7) across viewpoints. That is, the language mechanisms of one viewpoint might assign to some linguistic structure, in context, a salience value which is different from the value assigned by another viewpoint. In (38), the salience levels of the two meanings of '*blind man*' must differ between the viewpoints of the woman-character and the man-character.

Variation in the salience allocated to available interpretations may be one pertinent difference between the language models within the viewpoints of a joke. However, viewpoints cannot differ arbitrarily in their language mechanisms. In all jokes where the audience changes from one interpretation to another, it is central to the success of the joke that the audience can understand both of these interpretations, even if the initially more salient one is later downgraded. That is, the audience's language conversion mechanism must be capable of yielding all the interpretations which are germane to the joke, with varying ratings of salience. If the alternative interpretation adopted by a joke-character were to be completely outside the audience's capability, then the audience would not be able to perceive this other interpretation, which would prevent joke recognition or appreciation. (This author has personal experience of this effect, having been, at a very young age, the audience for some basic punning riddles which relied on word-meanings as yet unlearned – only years later did these childhood jokes make sense.)

This emphasises that linguistic knowledge has a similar status to world knowledge in many respects, in that it is localised to particular viewpoints, is subject to deviations from the audience's idea of normality, and is the object of metalevel inference which attempts to ascertain the regularities within this knowledge. That is, audience inference not only has to figure out the internal logic of a joke (Chapter 6), it may have to work out some slightly non-standard language rules used by joke-characters. We argued (Section 6.6) that determining the internal logic was limited by certain constraints of plausibility. For language, the space of possibilities is even more constrained, since inventing arbitrary language rules is not workable. There are only certain non-standard language usages which will allow the text to make sense: see Section 9.3 for discussion of common styles of deviant rule.

There is in principle the possibility that a joke could involve some text, perhaps an utterance by a joke-character, which is completely unintelligible to the audience, even after the post-text inference, but is treated as comprehensible by a joke-character. We have not encountered such an example. Leaving aside this rather marginal case, it appears that a joke-character's idiolect (i.e. personal dialect) must be closely related to that of the audience. A joke displays only a tiny sample of a joke-character's linguistic abilities, and that sample has to be intelligible to the audience. It follows that, for each joke-character, the character's idiolect must overlap with that of the audience (apart from the salience of interpretations, as mentioned above), and any text which that character must interpret has to lie within this overlap.

9.3 Word play and puns

What 'pun' means here

There is not a clear and accepted definition of what counts as a 'pun', in particular whether a pun must be humorous or whether mere use of certain linguistic devices (lexical ambiguity, phonetic similarity, etc.) qualifies as punning. Hempelmann (2003, 2004) distinguishes mere word play from puns which, to be humorous, must involve incongruity. Anecdotally, it seems to be accepted that word play, even when attempted as humour, is often not funny, although, as Hempelmann points out, this can result from mere word play being passed off as humour. Freud (1966 [1912], pp. 45–47) has the opposite terminology: a pun is 'the lowest form of verbal joke', whereas a play on words is a higher form.

In this section, we are considering only the narrow issue of the way in which the various structural patterns and devices fit into our overall framework, and so any potential word play/pun distinction is immaterial, and we will use the term 'pun' for brevity. We will not attempt a full review of the various structures involved in punning; see the references in Section 9.1 for fuller expositions.

Following Ritchie (2010, pp. 38–39), we will not, in this chapter, consider the case of forced reinterpretation (FR) jokes which depend on linguistic ambiguity, particularly lexical ambiguity, in the set-up. Examples (19) (the mouse on vacation) and (38) (the blind man) have roughly this structure, as have some later examples (e.g. (57) and (58) in Section 11.5). We regard these as being a subclass of FR joke, with no additional linguistic requirements beyond those outlined in Sections 7.6 and 9.2 – lexical ambiguity is just one particular type of ambiguity. Whether or not they could be classed as 'puns', as Hempelmann (2003, p. 23) seems to suggest, is a matter of terminology which we leave aside for the moment. For our purposes, the crucial point is that this section examines configurations of elements which operate in a manner which is different from that described in Section 7.6. For simplicity, we will use the term 'pun' for these arrangements, without claiming that this is the definitive use of the term.

Following Ritchie (2004, 2010), we will distinguish two very broad types of puns: *self-contained* and *contextual*. We will now consider how both these types would fit into our framework, and in particular which information must be located in the various viewpoints.

Self-contained puns

In a self-contained pun, there is an entire text containing both the pun and any linguistic context that it requires. This means that it can usually be repeated without requiring some further context for the pun, and so these jokes are a subclass of 'canned jokes' (see Section 2.2).

In this subsection, we will mainly use a particular narrow genre of pun, the punning riddle, to demonstrate the points, but the ideas are of wider application. Some jokes in Chapter 7, such as (28) (the wafer mother), and to a lesser extent the elephant jokes (29) and (30), imitate the form of riddles, in which a question poses a problem to be solved by the audience. The punning riddle is an entire sub-genre of riddle-like jokes, in which the question-answer format is used to deliver a simple, and often rather feeble, pun. Examples are (39), (40), (41) and (42).

(39) What do you get when you cross a choice with a meal?
A pick-nic.

(40) What do you get when you cross a zero with a drink?
A nought chocolate.

(41) What hides in the garden shed and trembles?
A nervous rake.
(Li, 2005)

(42) What knots do undertakers use?
Wreath knots.

In contrast to many of our earlier example jokes, punning riddles do not in any way tell a story, nor do they put forward a world in which characters experience situations (Section 4.3). Their central mechanism is solely concerned with language, manipulating linguistic relations between words and phrases, such as being pronounced in a phonetically similar way or having related meanings. The fact that they depend solely on facts about language, rather than facts about some working replica of the real world in all its complexity, is emphasised by the fact that it is possible to write a computer program to construct riddles of this type, relying only on linguistic data about words and phrases (Binsted, 1996; Manurung et al., 2008). (Examples (39) and (40) were taken from www.abdn.ac.uk/jokingcomputer, accessed 20 February 2015.)

Attardo (1994, Chapter 4) discusses the 'Cratylistic' account of puns, which relies on adopting the notion that '... the relationship between sounds and sense is motivated ...' (p. 152). He observes that 'Puns "fake" a Cratylistic semiotic system in which sound evokes unexpected sense associations ...' (p. 173). Hempelmann formulates this 'false reasoning' thus:

> If meaning motivates sound, and sound is identical (similar), then meaning must be identical (similar).
>
> (Hempelmann, 2003, p. 25)

(See also Hempelmann (2004).) This is a natural way to think about the workings of examples like (39) and (40), by assuming that a similar rule licenses the substitution of homophonic or near-homophonic segments: 'where a phonetically well-formed segment of text *X* sounds very similar to an existing word or phrase *Y*, then *X* also counts as a valid word or phrase'. For (39) to make sense, there might have to be a slight specialisation of Hempelmann's formulation, something like 'where one word contains a shorter word, the denotation of the longer word will include the property denoted by the shorter word'. This is not a wildly ludicrous rule, given the existence of English words such as '*speeddial*' or '*horseshoe*'. Example (40) appears to assume a similar rule about the denotation of compound nouns, which again is not wholly unreasonable, given the existence of '*sofa bed*', '*cafe bar*', '*tuner amp*'.

(There is a well-established precedent within generative linguistics for having formal statements which are of the general form (loosely) 'if a structure of this shape is valid, then so also is a structure of that shape'. For example, there are the 'metarules' of Gazdar, Klein, Pullum, and Sag (1985), or the 'lexical multiplication rules' of Ritchie, Russell, Black, and Pulman (1992).)

We have already adopted the idea that different viewpoints, in particular the viewpoint for the joke world, can contain propositions or logical implications which are empirically incorrect. The Cratylistic sketch here broadens that licence, allowing a viewpoint to contain less than accurate rules about the denotation of words and phrases. That perspective would suggest that when we consider imaginary or hypothetical worlds, as we have been doing, some of the facts and norms which define each world (its belief base) would be about language and linguistic relationships. As Hempelmann (2004, p. 386) points out, adding these non-standard rules of language usage to the joke world involves some suspension of disbelief (Section 4.6), which is comparable to how faulty logic is handled (Section 6.6). Hence, linguistic rules can also be seen as 'fanciful', just as rules about the logic of the world can be. (We will return to this parallel between knowledge about language and knowledge about the world in Section 9.4 below.)

The variety of ways in which there can be deviant rules about the denotation of words is illustrated by (43).

(43) In the 1830s, the artist J. M. W. Turner of the English romantic school painted many views of Margate, but his depictions of unnaturally vivid

> skies has led art critics to suggest that he might have been colour-blind. Living in London, Turner used to arrive here by steamboat from Greenwich, or as he called it, Redwich.
> (*I'm Sorry I Haven't A Clue*, BBC Radio 4, 27 November 2017, recorded in Margate.)

This example involves the adoption of a joke world in which there is a rule of language which says, roughly, '*if two concepts are similar enough to be confused, then the words which denote these concepts will be easily confused, even when not used in a denotative context*'. That is, the rule reasons in the reverse direction from that summarised in the quotation from Hempelmann, above.

Not all texts which would be regarded as punning riddles require the postulation of fictitious rules of word-interpretation as described above. For example, (44) and (45) (again taken from the Joking Computer website), would probably be regarded as punning riddles.

(44) What do you call an inspired pattern?
A divine design.

(45) What is the difference between an arctic hand shovel and a hot assistant?
One is an icy spade, the other is a spicy aide.

In both these examples, the answers could be argued to be semantically valid responses, with no requirement for specious rules of interpretation. The answer texts do have additional linguistic properties: in (44), the answer happens to have two words which sound similar and rhyme; in (45), the answer has been contrived to have a 'spoonerised' structure. These texts express their meaning in a way which may appeal to the recipient, but which does not require any viewpoint-specific language rules. The same is true of the genre of 'story puns' (Binsted & Ritchie, 2001), in which a self-contained pun mimics one of the configurations used in contextual puns (see next subsection).

There can be other varieties of pun which do not require that we posit a dubious rule of language interpretation, Cratylistic or otherwise. A pun may conjure up two senses, either by genuine ambiguity (homonymy) or by phonetic similarity, and in some cases both meanings make sense within the text; for example (46).

(46) A man suffered for months with chronic back pain and was eventually persuaded by his doctor to go and see a chiropractor. But he didn't have much faith in such people and was convinced they wouldn't be able to help him. Yet after a few minutes' treatment, his back felt like new.
'How do you feel about chiropractors now?' asked the doctor.
The man said: 'I stand corrected.'
(Tibballs, 2000, p. 528)

In (46), the punch line '*I stand corrected*' has two distinct meanings, both of which make complete sense both semantically and contextually, without any non-standard rules of language. For the pun to be successful, the audience must realise that two meanings are available, and that both make sense.

Contextual puns

Typically, a contextual pun is made as an impromptu remark in very specific set of circumstances, relying on particular properties of the context for the pun to work (a particular case of what Morreall (2009, Chapter 4) dubs 'wit'). The relevant context may be anything in the surroundings, either textual, visual, physical or abstract. This means that the witticism may not be viable in any other context, and so is distinct from a conventional 'canned' joke. In some cases the pun can, as with other forms of spontaneous wisecrack, be converted into a more portable version, in the form of a report of the utterance with a short description of the context, perhaps fictionalised to some extent, as a preamble to the actual punning remark. We will adopt this latter re-telling strategy to illustrate a real-life contextual pun, (47).

(47) A group of friends have just left the cinema after watching a film about the French king, Louis XIV. They are heading for a local bar, known as 'Sammy Cahn's'. 'Aha!' remarks one of them, 'After Louis Quatorze, Sammy Quinze!'

(Roderick Brodie, personal communication)

This relies on the phonetic similarity between the French word for 'fifteen' and the word '*Cahn's*', but also on a convention that allows a near-homophone to be substituted for a word that would have made sense in context, something like '*if a word/phrase W is related to the context and is phonetically similar to another word/phrase V, then W can be used in place of V within a sentence*'. There then has to be a joke world within which this fake linguistic rule applies – despite the brevity of the pun and the lack of any real narrative, we still posit a joke world, created automatically, unconsciously and on the spot by the audience of the original utterance. We noted in Section 4.3 that joke-telling may often require instantly generated viewpoints.

Simplifying somewhat (see Ritchie (2004, Chapter 9) for a fuller analysis), a contextual pun contains a word or phrase which is either ambiguous or is phonetically similar to some other phrase (e.g. '*Cahn's*' and '*quinze*'). In the case of two similar words/phrases, the two expressions must then meet further constraints regarding how well they fit into the text and how easy it would be for whichever of the expressions does not appear in the text to be 'recovered' (Hempelmann, 2003).

In the same way that there can be a self-contained pun, such as (46), that relies on two equally viable senses, a contextual pun could, in principle, involve two senses which are equally related to the context and either of which would be semantically appropriate within the text. If (46) were an account of a real incident in which the punch line appeared as a spontaneous remark by the patient, that utterance would have been a contextual pun. This emphasises the fact that there is little structural difference between self-contained puns and contextual puns: the former are simply those in which the relevant context is packaged into the joke set-up. In contrast, the contextual pun relies on its environment to provide the necessary connections. This means that self-contained and contextual puns depend on similar linguistic and inferential facilities, with only one consequence for how knowledge is allocated to viewpoints: some puns operate in a joke world in which there are fictitious rules of linguistic usage.

9.4 The world of language

In the two previous sections, we have highlighted linguistic knowledge, and some of the ways in which this knowledge could vary between viewpoints, in a way comparable to the variation of factual knowledge discussed in earlier chapters. This touches on the issue of whether facts about language are somehow qualitatively different from facts about the external world. Ritchie (2010) argued that jokes sometimes treat language as the subject matter of the joke, rather than simply the communicative medium or the source of connections from which to construct the text. For this reason, it is hard to make a clear distinction, in terms of the role played within jokes, between these two types of knowledge. This is the third function of language listed in Section 9.1 above.

For example, (48) is humorous relative to the knowledge of how to spell the names of days of the week (in English).

(48) I never take exercise on a day of the week with a 'd' in its name.

(This wording would also work relative to knowledge of French, but would need a change from '*d*' to '*t*' for a German-based version, for example.)

Similarly, (49) (perhaps more a whimsical remark than a conventional joke) depends upon the audience being familiar with the stereotype of the German language as having inordinately long sentences with the verb at the end.

(49) Whenever the literary German dives into a sentence, that is the last you are going to see of him till he emerges on the other side of his Atlantic with his verb in his mouth.

(Twain, 2006 [1889])

Jokes which make crucial use of this function do not rely on false assumptions about language. Instead, these jokes take the facts of the language as it is, and then build on that. These rather rare jokes are usually not classed as puns, but they do rely crucially on knowledge of the specific language. In examples like these, language knowledge is treated as just another form of general world knowledge, and hence we can take it to be part of the belief base of the viewpoints involved, but the jokes themselves do not rely on variation of knowledge across the viewpoints.

9.5 Style and register

So far we have considered language as a means of conveying ideas, as a complex medium which has its own internal relationships (e.g. phonetic similarity), and as possible subject matter for jokes. A further facet of language use could be described as 'style' or 'register': a segment of text can, by the choice of words and constructions, convey various subtle nuances such as social standing, cultural setting, or relationship between speaker and hearer. For example, a school pupil may talk to his peer group in a different register from that used to talk to a school teacher; a political statesman will adopt a different style for a public speech from that which he uses with his spouse. Regional dialect can be seen as a vivid case of this phenomenon.

Jokes can make use of language style or register in various ways:

- Telling an entire joke in a particular style may enhance the impact of the humour (Section 3.5), for example where a idiosyncratically regional joke is told in a dialect associated with the region in question.
- A joke-character's reported speech may be in a particular register in order to convey various social aspects of that character (Davies, 2010).
- It is possible to create humorous effects by mixing registers within a text (Attardo, 1994; Partington, 2006; Venour et al., 2011; Venour, 2013). These authors quote examples from film scripts, comic novels, cartoon captions, etc., but this phenomenon rarely occurs as the central humour of a self-contained textual joke.
- Adopting a particular register, particularly a dialect, may introduce pronunciations which then license word play or misunderstandings which would not be possible in another (perhaps more standard) register; that is, the speech idiosyncrasy is there to enable outcomes which are more directly involved with the humour.

(50) What do you call a pigeon enjoying winter sports in the Scottish mountains?
A ski-in' doo.

For example, (50) puns across two different language systems. In Scots dialect, a '*doo*' is (loosely) a pigeon, and there is a Scots Gaelic term '*sgian-dubh*' (a small ceremonial dagger), pronounced roughly '*skee-en-doo*'.

Since non-humorous narrative also needs support for variations in style and/or register, joke comprehension does not require any special humour-inspired mechanisms. At the least, lexical items and grammatical constructions need to be available for alternative registers, and there must be rules which relate utterances in specific registers to any inferences which can be derived, for example about the social class or geographical origin of a character.

As far as variations across viewpoints is concerned, register rules have to follow the same idiolect pattern as rules of language interpretation (Section 9.2): where a joke-character is depicted as understanding an utterance in a particular register and that utterance must also be intelligible to the audience, then the relevant rules of register must be common to the viewpoints of both the character and the audience. Where a joke-character is shown as failing to understand such an utterance, then this can be accounted for by an absence of the relevant register rules.

9.6 Summary

We have looked for evidence, from the various ways language can be used within jokes, about possible differences of linguistic skills across viewpoints, and we have come to the following conclusions:

- The language mechanisms within the joke world, including subordinate viewpoints, can be inherited from the audience's linguistic knowledge and capabilities, much as factual knowledge and rules are inherited (Section 4.3).
- In particular, all aspects of language within the joke world, including subordinate viewpoints, are initially the same as the audience's until contrary evidence appears.
- Each joke-character can, in general, have an idiosyncratic set of language interpretation rules, including lexicon and register, and the language-understanding demonstrated by a character is evidence of an overlap with the language-understanding capabilities of the audience. The relevant parts of the text must fall within the appropriate overlap.
- Each viewpoint may have its own measure of salience (the relative prominence of different interpretations). In particular, there may be differences between a joke-character and the audience.
- There is, in principle, the marginal case of the joke containing textual material which is treated as comprehensible by a joke-character but is never understood by the audience; we have no real example of this.

- Some puns require the joke world to have special rules which license the use of linguistic forms based on specious relationships between linguistic properties such as semantic and phonetic similarity.
- Not all jokes which might be classed as puns require non-standard rules of language.

This means that, despite the prominent role that language has played within the tradition of joke analysis, the needs of verbal humour do not make a great difference to the overall architecture of our framework.

Chapter 10

Impropriety

10.1 The Freudian view

The idea that there is an important relationship between humour and socially unacceptable ideas is far from new, and is often associated with the writings of Freud (1966 [1912]). The central idea is that certain situations would be socially unacceptable if mentioned directly, but can nevertheless be mentioned indirectly by means of a joke. Freud also allowed that humour might be generated by direct mentions of these topics, but treated this as a slightly different, and apparently less interesting, phenomenon. (Freud saw this as related to social class, with lower classes indulging in more direct forms of impropriety, while more refined people used jokes for the same function.)

The topic has been complicated by the way in which his terminology has been translated. Freud posits a subtype of joke which is, in German, 'tendenziös':

> Der Witz ist das eine Mal Selbstzweck und dient keiner besonderen Absicht, das andere Mal stellt er sich in den Dienst einer solchen Absicht; er wird tendenziös.
>
> (Freud, 1940 [1905], pp. 97–98)

An early translation treats this as 'having a purpose':

> Sometimes wit is wit for its own sake and serves no other particular purpose; then again, it places itself at the service of such a purpose, i.e., it becomes purposive.
>
> (Freud, 1916, p. 128)

However, a later, highly influential, translation (Freud, 1966 [1912], p. 90) adopts the term 'tendentious', a word which nowadays has a connotation of confrontation: 'having or showing an intentional tendency or bias, esp. a controversial one' (Makins, 1994, p. 1558). Freud seems to anticipate – or perhaps initiate – this semantic trend, as he immediately adds: 'Only jokes that have a purpose run the risk of meeting with people who do not want to listen to them' (Freud, 1966 [1912], p. 90). That is, although tendentious jokes are defined as purposeful, they are then the only kind of joke that can be controversial. (Like many of Freud's steps in reasoning, this is simply asserted without evidence or even informal argument.) Freud reinforces this interpretation by his choice of label for other jokes: 'Non-tendentious jokes were described by Vischer as "abstract" jokes. I prefer to call them "innocent" jokes.' (p. 90) (The earlier translation uses the term 'harmless' jokes.) We will return to the matter of 'innocent' or 'harmless' jokes in Section 11.4.

Tendentious jokes are initially partitioned into two subtypes: 'obscenity' or 'hostility' (Freud, 1966 [1912], p. 97). Further subtypes are then introduced (pp. 115–116): 'cynical' jokes, a subclass of hostile jokes which attack organisations rather than people, and 'sceptical' jokes, 'attacking... the certainty of our knowledge itself'. We see no reason to treat 'sceptical' jokes as primarily hostile, despite Freud's use of the word 'attacking', since they seem to be more related to pseudo-logic or absurdity (Chapter 6). Also, we will consider, in Chapter 11, hostility as a whole, without making the distinction between people or organisations as targets.

Despite being grouped under the heading of 'tendentious', the topics of obscenity and hostility are often dealt with separately by other authors. Even Legman (1972), who develops the Freudian theme at great length, indicates both in his title and his introduction (pp. 9–10) that he is analysing only a particular type of joke: 'erotic' and/or 'scatological'.

In the current chapter, our deliberations are probably general enough to cover both obscenity and hostility, or indeed any notion which is taken as being offensive in society, but our focus will be more on potentially distasteful concepts such as those singled out by Legman, as should become clearer in later sections; see Section 10.2 for an informal sketch of the types of material we have in mind.

Hostility and aggression will be covered in more detail in Chapter 11.

10.2 What we mean by impropriety

Taboo and impropriety

Before we start to explore the ways in which joke comprehension may involve some notion of socio-cultural unacceptability, we need to sort out some terminology. Legman (1972) uses the term 'taboo' to denote the kind of topic (sexual, scatological, etc.) that he examines. In his discussion of taboo, Freud (2012 [1919]) starts with an extract from the 11th edition of the *Encyclopædia Britannica*. The most recent edition of that work describes taboo thus:

> ...the prohibition of an action based on the belief that such behaviour is either too sacred and consecrated or too dangerous and accursed for ordinary individuals to undertake.
>
> (*Encyclopædia Britannica*, 2017)

Frazer (1922) sees taboo as related to magical thinking and superstition.

These notions are narrower and more intense than the more general concept of unacceptability that we wish to explore, and hence we will avoid the term 'taboo', instead adopting the weaker terms *impropriety* and *improper* to refer to actions or situations which might violate social and/or cultural conventions of acceptable behaviour. This does not exclude the possibility that some of these situations may also be taboo in some stronger anthropological sense.

Social and other origins

Although we will continue to use locutions such as 'socio-cultural acceptability', we may be grouping together, for humour purposes, phenomena which are conventional (i.e. wholly socio-cultural) and those which are more deeply based. It could be that humans have evolved to have negative feelings, such as disgust, about certain phenomena for good reasons: '... faeces, urine, sweat, spittle, and semen are all seen as "filth", treated with revulsion and generally avoided, even to the extent of being taboo in conversation' (Apter, 1982, p. 148). For the purposes of theorising about humour, we will treat the origins of any aversion as immaterial: if these ideas cause discomfort to those encountering them, our analyses of jokes do not take account of whether this emotion is socially conditioned embarrassment or innate disgust. Also, because we are interested only in how impropriety can affect joke comprehension, we need consider only verbal expressions of improper concepts, without taking account of other forms of confrontation with impropriety, such as visual or tactile interactions within any of the phenomena described as 'filth' in the above quotation from Apter.

A rough draft

We are not attempting to characterise exactly how impropriety, in any of its subtypes, determines whether or not a text is a joke. The more limited aim here is to set out some distinctions and terminology which will be useful for describing the interplay between different factors within a joke. If impropriety were to form part of a full theory of jokes, there would have to be a firm definition. (This is perhaps less critical if impropriety is regarded as merely an enhancer (Section 3.5), as suggested by Hurley et al. (2011, p. 214) in the case of sexual content.) Even with our more limited aim of describing joke comprehension, it would be helpful to try to narrow down the notion.

We cannot offer a definitive statement of what is improper in all joke encounters, partly because the concept will vary between people (Section 10.3), and partly because we do not have any clear evidence. To allow us to comment, when analysing specific jokes, upon circumstances where impropriety might be relevant to joke comprehension, we will take at least the following as being potentially improper topics: sexual or lavatorial matters, particularly where unconventional; bodily fluids, as in the quotation from Apter in the previous subsection; gruesome violence, particularly when fatal;

rough or disrespectful treatment of the sick, injured or deceased. Subjects such as racism or homophobia could also be considered improper in modern society, which emphasises that impropriety and hostility may be related categories, as in Freud's classification.

Intuitively, impropriety seems not to be an all-or-nothing category, but a property which can be present to varying degrees. Hence, some jokes may involve impropriety which is quite mild, while in others it may be stronger.

10.3 Impropriety and the audience

Because at least some factors determining impropriety are social or cultural, impropriety is relative to a particular socio-cultural group, in the sense that some topics might be wholly acceptable in one section of society but might meet with strong disapproval in another. Even individual people may have different views on what is an example of impropriety. Since we are interested in describing the process whereby a single audience comprehends a joke, standards of impropriety fall within our general assumption (Section 4.2) that we need to consider only factors that are in some way embodied in the mental and emotional aspects of that idealised audience. That is, in understanding a joke, the only relevant standards of impropriety are those which are known to the audience.

Although an individual may have particular views about what is improper, each person in a society will usually have some grasp of wider social norms, in much the same way that they will have cultural knowledge about matters such as ordering a meal in a restaurant or using public transport. A person can usually recognise, and often appreciate, jokes in which the potential impropriety is not something that he would find uncomfortable if mentioned directly. This could be explained if the audience assesses the joke relative not to his own social norms, but to those of wider society (a conjecture which could be checked only by proper sociological study). Any beliefs about impropriety, whether personal or societal, which might affect joke recognition or appreciation would have to be represented as part of the belief base of the audience's view of the real world. We will refer to the audience's beliefs about impropriety, both his own preferences and society's, as *social standards*. These are not a further formal mechanism, but simply further content that must be represented in the belief base (just as there might be rules about normality or causation, as observed in Chapter 4).

We have to consider two slightly different functions for social standards. Firstly, they may affect the audience's own reaction to a joke, something which we will explore further later in this chapter. Secondly, they provide information upon which a joke may depend, since stories or jokes may depict characters behaving in ways which are best explicable by attributing opinions about impropriety to them; for example (51) (and Ritchie (2004, example (79)).

(51) Once there was a little boy in church. He had to go to the bathroom so he told his mother, 'Mommy, I have to piss.' The mother said, 'Son, don't say "piss" in church. Next time you have to piss, say, "whisper" because it is more polite.' The next Sunday, the little boy was sitting next to his father this time, and once again, he had to go to the bathroom. He told his father, 'Daddy, I have to whisper.' The father said, 'OK. Here, whisper in my ear.'

(Hurley et al., 2011, p. 171)

To understand (51), the audience must understand the mother-character's concerns about impropriety, but need not share these opinions. For our framework, this separation of judgements can be achieved naturally by allowing any viewpoint associated with a joke-character to include its own social standards.

Although in (51), the social standards of the embedded viewpoint are revealed by a judgement that something is improper, there can also be jokes where a situation that might be deemed improper in wider society is treated as acceptable by a joke-character. For example, in (52), the concept of adultery is treated as acceptable by the woman-character, and in (53), group sex is treated as normal by the narrator.

(52) A woman goes to the doctor. He examines her and tells her she has a strained groin. 'How frequently do you have sex?' asks the doctor. 'Five times every week,' says the woman.'On Monday, Tuesday, Wednesday, Friday and Sunday.' 'I would suggest,' says the doctor, 'that you cut that down a little and perhaps leave out the Tuesday session.' 'I can't do that,' says the woman, 'that's the only night my husband's home.'

(Haskins & Arnott, 2017, p. 402)

(53) I believe that sex is a beautiful thing between two people. Between five it's fantastic.

(Woody Allen, quoted by Tibballs, 2000, p. 286)

In earlier chapters, we examined how there can be differences between viewpoints regarding the outcome of rules about the world. The above discussion has indicated that these mismatches across viewpoints can involve judgements in the area of impropriety.

10.4 The use of impropriety in jokes

Fictional impropriety

It is possible that the boundaries of what can be mentioned has become stylised with the development of jokes. Many readers may not regard the topics in the jokes in this chapter ((51), (52), (53)) as particularly unacceptable, but it could be that the activity of joke-telling has its own conventions about which ideas are to be treated as improper for the purposes of joke construction. That is, the categorisation of something as unacceptable to mention may have to balance the origin in social custom with the way in which joke-telling culture has somehow preserved this function, even as the ideas become less shocking in normal discourse. Jokes may continue to be based on final revelations of situations which are deemed much less improper than they would have been some decades ago.

It could be that impropriety in a fictional world operates slightly differently from impropriety in discourse about the real world. Just as the audience can put up with all manner of implausible or frightening situations in a story or joke, fictional transgressions of social standards may matter less: the audience's assessment of the impropriety is, in a way, hypothetical. If joke recognition depends on the impropriety, the audience must be able to sense the indirectly conveyed impropriety, by applying, perhaps unconsciously, some social standards in a way that detects the violation, but he must then treat the resulting violation as not real (see related ideas in Section 10.8). This cannot, however, be the sole mechanism involved in humour, as it would still leave some unanswered questions. For example, why do some fictional improprieties arouse amusement while some do not? Why are some audiences simply amused while others are shocked or offended, even though the impropriety is equally fictional for both?

Impropriety without effect

We mentioned in Section 4.7 that a text might allude to a concept in very oblique ways, prompting the audience to make inferences which somehow touch upon the image in question. This is particularly pertinent in the case of impropriety, where the text may not state or imply that the socially awkward situation actually occurs in the joke world. For example, in example (51), the situation where the small boy urinates into his father's ear is conjured up as a possible outcome of what happens in the joke world, but is not stated as happening.

In Freud's proposals (Section 10.1), indirect reference to improper concepts is central to the humorous effect. It would follow that a joke's indirect allusion to impropriety would have to be what we have called a 'final revelation', since that is the stage at which amusement results. Making an indirect allusion to impropriety in the set-up could not be the key to the humorous effect.

Nevertheless, a potentially improper topic can appear, directly or indirectly, in the set-up of a joke. This happens, for example, in those jokes where the set-up establishes a situation involving some unconventional sexual activity. In (54), adulterous liaison is both depicted in the set-up and implied as a final revelation.

(54) A woman was in bed with her husband's best friend when the phone rang. After hanging up, she turned to her lover and said: 'That was Jim, but don't worry, he won't be home for a while. He's playing cards with you.'
(Tibballs, 2000, p. 126)

It is not clear how this conforms to Freud's suggestions. If a topic can be mentioned in the set-up of a joke without creating humour, it is hard to see why an indirect mention should be the cause of amusement.

(55) Serenissimus was making a tour through his provinces and noticed a man in the crowd who bore a striking resemblance to his own exalted person. He beckoned to him and asked 'Was your mother at one time in service at the Palace?' – 'No, your Highness,' was the reply, 'but my father was.'
(Freud, 1966 [1912], pp. 68–69)

Freud (1966 [1912], p. 104) admits that the set-up in (55) contains a question which could be seen as having 'the character of a joke with the technique of allusion'. However, he says that the effect of the punch line is such that 'we are inclined to forget' this (sexual and potentially hostile) allusion.

Similarly, in (14) (the squashed hedgehog) and (27) (the deaf crocodile), it could be argued that the distasteful mishaps constitute impropriety, but these situations are conveyed explicitly in the set-up. This goriness has to be accepted by the audience, even if evaluated as a form of impropriety relative to the audience's social standards. We discussed earlier (Section 7.8) the way in which abnormal information might appear in an incidental supporting role within a joke, without being part of the final humorous message. The occurrence within a set-up of information that might constitute impropriety is comparable, and perhaps could be seen as a form of 'backgrounded impropriety', by analogy with 'backgrounded incongruity'.

10.5 Expressions of impropriety

In order to be more precise about different possible functions of impropriety within jokes, we need to make some finer distinctions between different ways in which impropriety may be expressed.

Being improper is a property of some topic or idea in general. When such a topic/idea is embedded in a segment of discourse, this creates a mention of the idea, which will be termed *discourse impropriety*. There are two subcases of this: when the topic is mentioned explicitly, this is an instance of *blatant* discourse impropriety; where there is an indirect mention (that is, relying on significant inference), this is *oblique* discourse impropriety.

Another possible property of a discourse is what we will call *linguistic impropriety*. This happens where the way of expressing a topic is socially deviant, owing to the choice of language (such as swear words), regardless of whether or not the topic itself has any attributes relevant to impropriety. That is, being a case of linguistic impropriety is quite independent of displaying discourse impropriety: one, both or neither of these might be present. This judgement is relative to the viewpoint in question, as opinions on language forms vary (Section 9.5). In example (51), whispering in church, the mother-character could be reacting to perceived linguistic impropriety.

A further distinction we wish to make is related to the context, or type of discourse, in which an improper topic is mentioned. For some people, a topic can be freely mentioned in non-humorous text, but joking about this topic is socially unacceptable. In a setting where joke comprehension is occurring, the audience is usually aware, or becomes aware, that the text is being proffered as something light-hearted and potentially amusing (see Section 3.3). Hence, it may be the placing of the idea within a joke that creates an adverse reaction from an audience, rather than the topic itself or the mentioning of the topic. This has been observed regarding 'disaster jokes': '... one is not *supposed to* talk about human suffering and disaster graphically or flippantly' (Oring, 1992c, p. 39). After a major tragic event, comedians may find that audiences are not ready for jokes about the recent calamity, although this unease tends to fade with the passage of time (Kuipers, 2005; Steir-Livny, 2016). Such socially unacceptable uses of humour we will refer to as *levity impropriety*.

Although there has been a proliferation of categories within this section, these distinctions are necessary if we are to document what occurs when a joke is comprehended, particularly the process of joke appreciation.

10.6 Specifying impropriety

Given the various phenomena and classifications from the previous section, the question arises: how does this fit into our overall descriptive model of texts and jokes?

Linguistic impropriety is caused by the use in a text of certain words, phrases, idioms, etc. This can be represented by having properties, possibly graded, attached to lexical items, including phrases and idioms, with one such property indicating its status with respect to impropriety (much as conventional dictionaries attach labels such as 'coarse slang' to particular entries). This assumes that linguistic knowledge, including lexical information, is specific to viewpoints, so that an audience will have a personal lexicon; this is compatible with what we said earlier about linguistic knowledge (Chapter 9). A text whose interpretation involves one of these items then manifests linguistic impropriety to a certain extent.

This allows a joke to depend upon some segment of the text manifesting impropriety for a particular joke-character, independently of the impropriety experienced by the audience. Also, it allows the description of word play involving the relation between a linguistically improper item and some other lexical entry such as a homophone. There might have to be some way of combining ratings of linguistic impropriety, to cater for the scenario in which several improper items appear within a text.

The more general notion of impropriety can be handled, as indicated earlier in this chapter, by the rules which we are calling 'social standards'. This category does not apply to specific linguistic items, nor even to atomic propositions, but rather to whole situations (configurations of elements), which could be expressed in any one of a very large number of language forms. Hence, any general labelling of impropriety will have to be based on patterns or formulae, rather than the simple tagging of basic items which we suggested for the lexical case. This can be done by having the social standards in a viewpoint provide ratings for any situation, indicating to what extent it is improper.

A topic which can give rise to levity impropriety (see Section 10.5) might be much more acceptable in non-humorous discourse. Thus there is a distinction between broad impropriety and subjects which are not available for joking. We will use the term *unmentionable with levity* for topics/ideas which should not be introduced in a joking context, and which would lead to levity impropriety if made the subject of a joke. This can also be assigned to situations by social standards.

Other categories required to describe joke comprehension, or to characterise jokehood, will depend on how Freudian a position we adopt. There might be a need for 'impropriety' to have subcategories of *unmentionable directly* and *unmentionable indirectly*. Whatever mention-related categories are used, it would be useful to have a default that situations are freely mentionable unless some social standard indicates otherwise.

There is a widespread idea (Eco, 1984; Veatch, 1998) that humour is intimately bound up with the violation of norms (see Section 10.8). We have already explored the idea of violation of expectation and its relevance to 'incongruity' (Chapter 7). It may also be possible to arrange the formulation of impropriety so that it shows up as the violation of (social) norms. We have suggested that social standards could be rules which assign ratings for the categories relevant to impropriety, but it might be equally workable to state these ratings more as prohibitions. That is, where we could formulate a rule which says '*Any situation which matches pattern P is rated as unmentionable directly*', there could instead be a rule which says something like '*Any situation which matches pattern P should not be expressed directly in discourse*'. Then impropriety would result from the violation of such prohibitions. As remarked in passing earlier, impropriety is a matter of degree, hence any encoding in terms of norm-violation would have to allow for degrees of violation.

10.7 Amusement or offence

The outline above of how impropriety can be involved in joke appreciation can be contrasted with the scenario where a joke indirectly mentions a particular concept and an audience is offended by the presence of that concept in the joke. If the audience has been offended by the indirect mention, it follows that he must have made whatever inferences were required to reach that concept. In the case where the offending concept is crucial to the working of the joke, it seems likely that our hypothetical offended audience has fully comprehended the joke: joke recognition has occurred, but with a zero level of joke appreciation. This could be described by having this audience treat the key content as being improper, perhaps unmentionable indirectly; hence, the indirect mention gives rise to discourse impropriety, for this audience. Alternatively, it could simply be that the offended audience classed the particular topic as unmentionable with levity. If the development of a fuller theory of joke comprehension depended upon a choice between these accounts, a suitably subtle empirical study would be needed to choose between them.

We might also consider the possibility that different individuals attach different weights to their various personal social standards, with the amused audience not assigning much weight to the particular discourse impropriety manifested by the joke, while the offended audience attaches much greater weight to this violated convention.

There is another possible scenario: an audience is amused by a joke but suppresses his reaction or indicates that he is guilty or apologetic. This might indicate that the audience's own social standards are compatible with joke appreciation, but the audience's knowledge of wider social conventions states that some crucial concept is unmentionable indirectly and/or unmentionable with levity. These particular behaviours would only occur if, additionally, the audience cares sufficiently about social disapproval to modify his reaction in this way.

10.8 Benign violation

We briefly mentioned (Section 7.11) the 'benign violation' theory (McGraw & Warren, 2010; Warren & McGraw, 2016), which offers this hypothesis:

> ... three conditions are jointly necessary and sufficient for eliciting humor: A situation must be appraised as a violation, a situation must be appraised as benign, and these two appraisals must occur simultaneously.
>
> (McGraw & Warren, 2010, p. 1142)

Although this is intended as a general theory, covering all forms of humour, it is particularly relevant in the current chapter because McGraw and Warren (2010) present five small studies which focus specifically on violations which could be viewed as impropriety.

In the studies, the researchers presented very short narratives to the participants, and observed their reactions and/or asked follow-up questions. McGraw and Warren describe the content of the narratives as potential 'moral violations'. In practice, the participants were asked if they regarded the described situations as 'wrong' or not, which appears to be the defining test for the presence of a violation. In some studies, the participants were offered the gloss '(i.e. immoral)' for 'wrong'. A few of the studies also asked participants whether they felt 'disgusted', but the reporting of results suggests that being judged as 'wrong' was treated as a potential cause for disgust and/or amusement. That is, disgust was treated as a possible consequence of violation, rather than a diagnostic for violation. (The published account does not explicitly state which are the dependent and independent variables.)

These studies did not set out to study joke comprehension as such, but aimed to judge how amusement arose from the combination of certain factors: being simultaneously wrong and benign. Hence, the materials used in these studies were not collected or constructed so as to be jokes. This shows up in their lack of typical joke characteristics: they had no set-up/punch line structure, there was no problem-solving required at the end, and all information was described directly, including the potentially improper situations. The authors argue that their hypothesis was supported; the studies '... show that moral violations that simultaneously seem benign elicit laughter and amusement in addition to disgust' (McGraw & Warren, 2010, p. 1141).

The materials used in these five studies seem to assume a notion of violation which is wide enough to include, and perhaps is typified by, the breaking of moral norms. As McGraw and Warren's studies did not investigate the phenomenon of potential impropriety being conveyed indirectly, they did not address the Freudian approach (Section 10.1). Also, their definition of 'benign' (see Section 7.11) seems to cover any case where a violation occurs in a fictional context, which would mean that all violations conveyed in jokes, whether directly or indirectly, are benign.

10.9 Summary

We have reviewed the general idea of impropriety, particularly with respect to discourse and jokes, and made a number of conceptual distinctions which we believe are pertinent to giving a detailed analysis of various jokes. This is particularly relevant if we are to see how Freud's ideas in this area might connect to other factors within jokes. It is also pertinent to any theories, such as McGraw and Warren's, which include violations of morality or good taste alongside the breaking of more logical norms discussed in earlier chapters.

A potential criticism is that we have over-simplified the whole complex issue of impropriety and related matters, such as taboo, social conventions, etc. However, we again appeal to the methodological precept outlined in Section 2.3: that we are simply summarising, at a very abstract level, the information or affordances that we require from other areas in order to describe joke comprehension. It may well be that some of our terms, such as 'unmentionable with levity', are labels for the outcome of very complicated socio-cultural systems of conventions, but this does not matter for our purposes. If a topic is treated as not appropriate to mention humorously, that is the property we will refer to in describing joke comprehension, but we do not need to include a full theory of how that topic came to have that status.

In terms of developing our model of how an audience comprehends a joke, we have introduced certain further content that should be in the belief bases of viewpoints. The lexicon should have markings to indicate possible linguistic impropriety, and there should be, in each viewpoint, 'social standards': rules which categorise situations as to their impropriety-related properties.

Chapter 11

Superiority and aggression

11.1 Background

When considering the causes of humour, notions such as 'hostility', 'aggression' or 'superiority' tend to be grouped together as a single factor. The argument that humour is closely related to these concepts has a long history, traceable as far back as Aristotle, Plato and Cicero (Martin, 2007; Morreall, 1983, 1987), and it continued to be prominent for some time: 'It is the superiority theory that dominates the philosophical tradition until the eighteenth century ...' (Critchley, 2002, p. 3). Perhaps the most widely cited exposition is that offered in the seventeenth century by Hobbes (1840 [1650]). In spite of a fairly cogent critique of Hobbes's views by Hutcheson (1987 [1750]), some philosophers still took it very seriously:

> The oldest, and probably still the most widespread theory of laughter is that laughter is an expression of a person's feeling of superiority over other people.
> (Morreall, 1983, p. 4)

Freud (1966 [1912]) suggested that hostility was one of the two main purposes of 'tendentious' humour (see Section 10.1). Both Morreall (1983) and Raskin (1985) discuss advocacy of an aggression-based (and evolutionary) approach by Rapp (1951), and the 'reversal theory of humour' (Apter, 1982; Apter & Desselles, 2012) includes a condition for humour that can be seen as related to the superiority perspective (see Section 11.6). Veale (2004) argues that incongruity-resolution is less central to humour than a desire to discover insulting content (see Section 11.7).

Within mainstream humour research of the past half-century, perhaps the most extensive and detailed exposition of the superiority perspective is provided by Gruner (1978, 1997). Gruner's supposed theory is unsatisfactory in several respects (Section 11.2), but it provides a useful starting point for devising a brief taxonomy of humour-as-superiority constructs (Section 11.3), from which we will distill a few key elements (Section 11.9) for use in our integrated framework (Chapter 12).

11.2 Superiority as 'winning'

Gruner (1997) suggests that humorous experiences are very similar to 'games', such as everyday sports, and that humour is caused by 'winning', in the sense that the person experiencing amusement gets what he/she wants. The pleasure of amusement is directly analogous to the elation and joy felt by sports spectators or participants when they encounter a turn of events which is favourable, but unexpected. In particular, the perception of winning in humour must occur *suddenly* (see Sections 5.4 and 8.4).

He argues that this notion of humour as winning can manifest itself in a variety of ways:

- Even a very young baby will smile when she 'gets what she wants'.
- In many funny stories, there is competition between characters in some way, and at the end, some character(s) 'win' while others 'lose'.
- In many funny stories, some character is shown to have some personality flaw such as greed or stupidity; that is, this character 'loses', then the audience feels superior to the character, and so 'wins'.
- When someone tells a joke, even an apparently victimless pun, that person is displaying their cleverness, and hence winning.
- When someone manages to understand a joke after slight effort (e.g. a clever but obscure pun), that person feels a sense of achievement (winning).

Gruner offers other illustrative examples, including allusions to topics, such as death, which are unpleasant or taboo (see Chapter 10), for which Gruner does not explicitly indicate a 'winner', but which he offers as obvious corroborating examples. Also put forward in support are cases in which people use humour to put down other people, and cases in which the audience 'loses' by discovering the joke is not very good after all, which makes the joke teller a 'winner',

The first major objection to Gruner's proposal, if assessed as a theory of humour, is that the central concept of winning is excessively elastic. In the various scenarios listed above, there are certain quite different concepts demonstrated, including: simple gratification of basic desires, viewing – but not personally experiencing – a competition which has a winner, feeling superior to a fictional character, showing intellectual skills in a social setting, gaining a sense of achievement through cognitive effort. In this way, Gruner conflates some very different concepts, with the vagueness and flexibility of the English language allowing him to pull together many disparate notions. There is no objective or operational definition of winning, the ultimate arbiter on this being Gruner himself.

The next complication is that some of Gruner's supposedly supporting examples concern how humour is used, socially or culturally, such as the use of sarcasm to insult or to assert authority over another person. Such instances concern the social function of the humorous act, but do not illuminate the question of what makes the utterance or action humorous, as opposed to a non-humorous insult or scolding. (In the terminology of Chapter 1, this might contribute to a 'theory about humour', but does not constitute a 'theory of humour'.) Even the idea that a pun acts as humour because it allows the teller to display verbal ingenuity is largely a comment about the social function of the witticism, rather than an analysis of the mechanism of the actual joke.

This leads to the third, but definitely not the least, objection to this supposedly 'comprehensive theory'. Gruner (1997, p. 10) sets down various methodological desiderata for a theory of humour, one of which is the need to provide both necessary and sufficient conditions for something to be humorous. Two and a half centuries earlier, a central component of Hutcheson's critique of Hobbes's proposals was the complete lack of evidence that a feeling of superiority is sufficient for laughter. Despite this, Gruner puts all his effort into trying to demonstrate that instances of humour invariably involve winning, in his extended sense; that is, if there is humour, then there is winning. Hence, he is attempting to show that this ingredient is necessary, but he offers little or no evidence to show that winning is sufficient. This is a serious shortcoming of a proposed explanation of 'why we laugh'. Gruner's notion of a competition with 'winners' and 'losers' is, as argued above, so broad that it can be found in many non-humorous eventualities or artefacts. Indeed, Gruner at one stage argues for the ubiquity of this ingredient in things which interest us in everyday life, such as news stories. He suggests that this concept of 'getting what one wants', or failing to, would show up in many different circumstances, either in real life or in fiction. Hence, even the argument that this competitive element is an necessary component of humour becomes less interesting if this ingredient is also an essential part of almost all eventualities.

Nevertheless, the wide-ranging nature of Gruner's review of the superiority aspects of joking means that it offers a useful catalogue of concepts within this subarea. In the next section, we will try to arrange these concepts into a systematic picture, with a view to using some of them in our framework.

11.3 Collating the concepts

We will now, starting from Gruner's discussion, organise a set of concepts potentially useful for a superiority/aggression account of jokes. Some of the scenarios which Gruner uses to flesh out his notion of winning are not relevant to our particular focus, as they do not involve deliberate joke-telling. For example, we will omit the basic gratification which can cause laughter in very young babies. (Gruner does not make a clear distinction between humour and laughter.) Since there is, as far as we know, no suggestion that feelings of inferiority lead to amusement in the sufferer, we will phrase everything in terms of outcomes involving the feeling of superiority in its intuitive sense. We will limit our attention to cases in which there is an identification of superiority, or similar feelings, on the part of some individual directly involved in the encounter with the joke, thereby omitting cases where Gruner points only to a negative feeling – inferiority or similar – without specifying a corresponding winner. As we are focusing on how the audience's inner cogitations and feelings may affect the perception of humour in a joke, we will ignore cases where feelings of superiority might be attributed to the joke teller (but we will return to the question of teller superiority in Section 11.5). The abstractions in our list are not mutually exclusive, in the sense that more than one of these effects could occur in the same joke comprehension.

(The labels we attach here are merely for convenience of reference, and the words used in these labels have no theoretical content or significance.)

The audience feels:

Fictional insult: superiority to a person, organisation or group within the world of the joke, because of that entity losing out in some way or revealing flaw(s) such as stupidity, greed, or corruption.

Real-world insult: superiority to a person, organisation or group within the real world, because of that entity losing out in some way or revealing flaw(s) such as stupidity, greed, or corruption.

Self-improvement: superiority to his/her own past self, who used to have the flaws implied by the joke, although the present self no longer has these shortcomings.

Joke-getting: superiority to his/her own past self, who was initially fooled by the joke, whereas the present self understands the joke.

Self-congratulation: superiority in a general way, having been clever enough to grasp the joke.

This rough taxonomy allows us to compare how different theorists draw the definition of superiority. Some writers allow for several of the notions listed above as possible manifestations of superiority. Gruner uses all these concepts and more, whereas Hobbes's proposals can be seen as comprising Fictional insult, Real-world insult and Self-improvement. Real-world insult together with Fictional insult give at least a close approximation to Veale's notion of 'insulting others' (Section 11.7).

Normally, the route to a Real-world insult will involve a Fictional insult, where the insulted entity in the joke world will have a direct counterpart in the real world, such as a prominent politician, and the Fictional insult is taken to apply to that real-world person. Hence it will be unusual to find a case where there is a Real-world insult without a corresponding Fictional insult.

11.4 Harmlessness and aggression

We mentioned, in Section 10.1, that Freud saw jokes as divided into 'tendentious' and 'innocent/harmless', with 'hostile' jokes as a subset of 'tendentious'. Hence, 'innocent' is not, for Freud, the exact complement of 'hostile'.

Gruner is highly critical of the idea that there can be 'harmless' or 'innocent' humour, arguing that no one has ever put forward an instance of humour that is entirely harmless, in the sense that Gruner can always find at least a small trace of competition therein. He quotes Koestler (1970) as likening the aggression in humour to salt in food, being essential but sometimes very hard to detect. As argued in Section 11.2, Gruner's notion of 'aggressive' is very wide and elastic, so his claim that no joke is harmless is hardly surprising. His conclusion seems to be based on the argument that every joke involves superiority of some sort, hence there must be some entity to which superiority is felt, and this constitutes a harmful attitude to that entity, even in cases where the predication of superiority derives from Joke-getting and/or Self-congratulation.

Strain (2014) defines humour as 'harmless' depending on its use within society or culture. Harmless humour is either 'benign' – 'does not target a certain person or individual' – or 'affiliative' – 'used to relate to others and build relationships'. This is in contrast to 'aggressive' humour, which 'is used to ridicule or mock a target, which is most often a person or group'. This definition of 'harmless' is slightly unclear: is it possible to use a joke with a target in order to relate to others, and if so, is that harmless or aggressive humour?

Aggression can result from the way that a joke is used, including the manner or the context in which it is told. Since we are focusing narrowly on joke comprehension, we will consider only aggression which results from the content of a joke and the way that this is processed by the audience. In our terminology, a plausible way of delineating harmless joke-tellings would be to single out those in which no negative implications are made about any real-world entities, such as real people, social or cultural groups, organisations, etc. This would rule out any joke-tellings which created the effects which we have classed above as Real-world insult. There are then the Fictional insult instances, where the criticism, disrespect or unmasking of vice is confined to the storyworld, with no implications for the real world. While this is conceptually a different case, it is not totally certain that it could be called 'harmless'. However, any joke instance which leads to neither of these effects – Real-world insult and Fictional insult – could perhaps be argued to be relatively 'harmless'.

In the next section, we will explore some jokes which fall slightly outside the remit of this chapter, as they could be seen as aggressive towards the audience, perhaps displaying superiority on the part of the teller.

11.5 Fooling the audience

Many of the ways in which jokes can be used in a hostile manner lie within the territory of a 'theory about humour' in the sense of Section 1.3: a theoretical account of how humour is used in social contexts. We speculate that in such cases, the internal mechanisms of the jokes are similar or identical to those mechanisms which are used when the social purpose is less aggressive; that is, it is the use of the joke that varies, including its content, but most of the ways that jokes can be created are used in both aggressive and benign applications of humour. In this section, we consider some jokes which might be more suited to a mildly hostile use.

We have already seen that many jokes involve the audience having to alter their interpretation of the information from an earlier part of the joke, usually because the viewpoint of a joke-character has to be amended (Section 7.6). There is a sense in which this type of joke makes a fool of the audience, who is temporarily misled. However, it is not entirely clear whether the audience will feel they have 'lost' (in Gruner's terminology), and whether the joke teller will feel particularly superior as a result of this playful storytelling, as opposed to more general feelings such as displaying ability by telling a joke. Arguably, the audience may experience Self-congratulation rather than inferiority.

There are some jokes where the deception is slightly deeper, as the teller misleads the audience about the status of the verbal interaction, sometimes quite blatantly, as in (56).

(56) What's the difference between an elephant and a post box?
(I don't know.)
I wouldn't send you to post a letter.

We will assume that this example is intended to be delivered interactively, rather than read in a book, so that the ritualised confession of ignorance is supplied by someone to whom the question has been addressed. In this arrangement, what the audience is lured into adopting, and forced into revising, is the view of the real world, in particular the nature of the interaction with the questioner. (It might seem that this involves the reversal of a judgement about joke detection, in the sense of Section 3.4, but there is not a revision from 'joke' to 'non-joke'. Instead, the joke mechanism is relocated to a different level – there is semantic-pragmatic ambiguity (Ritchie, 2004).)

In other cases, the trickery may be more embedded in the text, where the audience is likely to take on trust the reliability of the narrator. For example, there may be exploitation of an ambiguity, as in (57) (aquarium *vs.* military vehicle) or (58) (brand of ice cream *vs.* type of handgun). (See comments in Section 7.6 about the presence of joke-critical ambiguities in sections of text which are not attributable to the narrator.)

(57) Two goldfish were in their tank.
One turns to the other and says, 'You man the guns, I'll drive.'
(Hurley et al., 2011, p. 42)

(58) Nobby's little boy keeps begging him for an ice cream. In the end Nobby gives in and hands the little lad a Magnum. 'I'll show you how to take the safety catch off,' he tells him, 'then you can use it to hold-up an ice-cream van.'

(Haskins & Arnott, 2017, p. 242)

This need to revise the view of reality is to some extent what makes this kind of joke a form of 'practical joke', which Marsh (2014, p. 592) describes as '. . . a play activity in which one party . . . arranges things so that another party . . . is led to have a false idea about what is currently going on' and in which the '. . . targets eventually find out they have been made fools of. . .'. Marsh (2015) offers a classification of practical jokes into four broad categories: the 'put-on/leg-pull', in which something factually incorrect is conveyed, but no action is required from the target; the 'fool's errand', in which the target is lured into acting on a false belief, following a 'behavioural script' devised by the perpetrator; the 'booby trap', in which the environment is rearranged to cause a surprise to the target; and the 'stunt/hoax/spoof', in which some group demonstrates creative skill in creating a false appearance of some event, state of affairs, or artefact.

As Marsh (2014, p. 593) makes clear, practical jokes are '. . . enacted rather than being told.' However, in the case of jokes such as (56), the telling of the joke constitutes the 'enacting' – the audience experiences the deception rather than hearing/reading about it happening within a narrative. The comprehension of these jokes could be seen as a very transient form of (mental) 'fool's errand', in Marsh's taxonomy: the audience is tricked into adopting an interpretation which subsequently proves to be incorrect.

In many practical jokes, the primary recipient may not find the experience funny, with the humorous reaction being confined to the joker and possibly some other viewers: '. . .some jokes are not meant to be funny to all' (Smith, 2009, p. 162).

There is a relatively plausible argument that jokes such as (56), (57) or (58) could result in a frisson of superiority for the joke teller rather than for the audience. This could arise not just from the teller showing ability to tell a joke, which presumably applies to every successful joke-telling, but more specifically from having fooled the audience. In contrast, it is less obvious that the audience/victim would share these feelings, although a committed superiority theorist might argue that Joke-getting and Self-congratulation would apply. A more radical position would be to argue that some jokes are told for the benefit of the teller rather than the audience, which again draws a parallel with practical jokes.

Apter and Desselles (2012, p. 430) point out that jokes which trick the audience undermine the case for a simple Hobbes-style explanation of humour. In this class of jokes they include 'shaggy dog stories' (i.e. long rambling set-ups with anti-climactic punch lines), and also, surprisingly, 'puns and witticisms'.

11.6 Diminishment

The reversal theory of humour covers various aspects of humour (Apter (1982), updated slightly by Apter and Desselles (2012)). One of the conditions that it proposes as necessary for humour to occur is 'diminishment'. That is, some entity involved in the humorous stimulus is perceived, as a result of the comprehension of the humour, as being less, or lower on some dimension, than it was before the stimulus (or, in the case of a joke, during the set-up). Examples of possible dimensions along which diminishment might occur include importance, dignity, worthiness of respect, and seriousness (Martin, 2007, p. 77). The range of entities to which this could apply is very wide, since it includes not only characters or situations in the joke world, but the very communicative act of the joke, which may be viewed in a different way as a result of getting the point of the joke. Apter and Desselles (2012) list three ways in which diminishment may occur in humour: 'content' – something in the joke world is downgraded; 'presenter' – the joke teller is diminished in some way; 'observer' – the audience is diminished, typically by finding they have been fooled (as in Section 11.5).

This has clear echoes of the superiority account of humour, particularly the type of superiority which we labelled Fictional insult. However, since Apter's diminishment can include the realisation that something is more mundane or trivial than it first appeared, this concept can extend slightly beyond the types of superiority which we listed earlier. Since the very joke itself, as a communicative act, may be perceived as diminished, Apter's classification includes, as 'observer' diminishment, cases where the audience is misled about the nature of the joke, as in Section 11.5.

11.7 Collaborating to insult

Veale (2004) gives a brief critique of the idea that incongruity-resolution (Chapter 7) might be the essential cause of the humorous effect in jokes, and offers an alternative perspective. He argues that the joke teller provides the audience with an opportunity to find an interpretation which is pleasing because it has certain properties, typified by '...narratives where pomposity is deflated, excessive authority is thwarted, modesty is rewarded and arrogance is punished' (p. 425). One of the jokes Veale examines is (55), Serenissimus and the possible half-brother, and it is interesting that this expansion of the notion of 'insulting' allows for a distinction between the two utterances in that narrative (which puzzled Freud – see Section 10.4).

Of (59), Veale remarks that '...we choose the insulting non-sexual interpretation precisely because it is enjoyably insulting...' (p. 424).

(59) Woman are always using me to advance their careers. Damned anthropologists.

Such remarks are very reminiscent of the superiority theory of humour as normally understood. Veale's concept is much more focused and narrowly defined than the catch-all 'winning' of Gruner, but he also emphasises the need for the cause(s) of amusement to connect to the wider context, arguing that a theory of humour must '...provide a social explanation for why we enjoy insulting others and why a feeling of social intimacy can arise when this insult is licensed by the cooperative principle of joke-telling' (p. 424). For Veale, insult is not a simple ingredient that causes humour, but is a class of idea that the joke audience prefers when seeking out possible interpretations, and which also directs human interest in other activities such as gossip. He argues that humour research needs a social account of the kinds of interpretation which are deemed rewarding in this way,

As well as emphasising insults and the deflation of the pompous, Veale also says that his perspective is '...consistent with the Freudian view...' (p. 423) and, in passing, hints at a more general range of topics which may render an interpretation attractive to a listener: 'Even when a joke does not have a victim as such, it may, following Freud, serve as a collaborative means to engage a titillating or taboo topic' (p. 426). This apparent extension from 'insulting' to 'taboo' is a relatively radical shift, which Veale does not discuss in detail, but it does seem to echo Freud's position, in which 'hostility' and 'obscenity' are grouped together as 'tendentious' (Section 10.1). Perhaps we should see Veale's proposal as 'collaborating to find tendentiousness'.

This is not only one of the most recent variants of the superiority approach, it is one of the more subtle, in that it tries to connect superiority both to incongruity-resolution (as an 'epiphenomenon') and to social and cultural aspects. However, it is still very underdeveloped.

11.8 Separating the effects

When investigating the role, within jokes, of superiority and/or insults, it can be hard to separate out some of the factors in this area. For example, we remarked in Chapter 6 that some jokes portray an instance of faulty logic by depicting a character or group of characters as having some beliefs, or carrying out some action, which would indicate stupidity on their part (as in examples (13), the Irish Sea Scouts, and (18), Ethel and the cake). Arguably, the demonstration of stupidity allows the audience a feeling of superiority to that story-character. The question then arises: which of these attributes is primary, and which is there merely as support or simply as an accidental side-effect? That is, does the joke depict a stupid character in order to trigger a superiority effect, and the faulty logic is merely a means to that end? Or is the faulty logic the key to the amusement (see Section 7.10), and the stupid character is there solely in order to have a viewpoint within which dubious reasoning can occur, and any superiority is an accidental side-effect? (This is like Veale's suggestion, Section 11.7, that incongruity is present only as an 'epiphenomenon'.) There is no obvious answer to this, so we have, in our list of humour-relevant factors (Chapter 12) included both superiority-based items and flawed reasoning.

11.9 Superiority more precisely

For our purposes, we need some constructs which can be used to describe the influences on the comprehension of a joke. We will start from the list of five categories in Section 11.3, some of which we can eliminate as not relevant to our purposes. We can omit Joke-getting and Self-congratulation as these throw no light on the process of joke comprehension, being stated not as mechanisms, but as inevitable *consequences* of successful joke recognition. They also apply to any type of joke and any means of comprehending whatsoever.

As we are modelling the audience's comprehension and reaction, there would seem to be no need for any categories referring to the feelings of the joke teller. However, if we omit these completely, we will have no way to express the hypothesis that some jokes are motivated solely by their effect on the teller, with no inherent amusement for the audience, as discussed in Section 11.5. For that reason, we will include a single category *Teller-benefit* to cover this eventuality, although it is only tenously linked to the source of amusement for the audience.

This pruning leaves us with four categories: Fictional insult, Real-world insult, Self-improvement, Teller-benefit. (The first three of these more or less capture Hobbes's proposal.)

This then raises the question: what does it mean for propositions (in the belief base of a viewpoint) to constitute an insult, or any of the other categories? We can devise a definition by adapting the 'diminishment' concept from Apter's reversal theory (Section 11.6). To match our specific constructs more exactly, we require a narrower version of 'diminishment', which applies to entities within the representation of the joke, but does not cover the act of joke-telling itself. This appears to be the 'content' subtype identified by Apter and Desselles (2012), but since we are not adopting the full synergy-based analysis of reversal theory, we will call our variant something else: *deflation* (echoing Veale's usage). This will be something that can befall, within the joke world, any entity, where the entity is typically a person, an organisation or an anthropomorphised creature, perhaps represented figuratively. We will assume that there are certain socially defined *worth scales* within the real world and the joke world, represented in the belief bases of viewpoints. The values on these scales are potentially associated, via audience inference, with conceptual items, such as those representing individual characters. As mentioned in Section 11.6, there could be scales representing importance, dignity, etc. A reduction in value on a worth scale is deemed to be negative for the entity involved, is said to have *happened to* the entity in question, and constitutes 'deflation'. This occurrence is an event within the incremental joke comprehension process and involves two stages of that process, with some entity having a noticeably lower value on a worth scale in the later stage than in the earlier stage. Usually within joke comprehension, the two stages will be post-set-up and final. Such scales may result from from complex social or cultural mechanisms, such as hierarchies of social status, but – as elsewhere in this framework – we have abstracted away from these more complex phenomena in an attempt to identify how these contextual aspects influence joke comprehension.

(The introduction of such scales may seem to require conceptual items to have a set of attributes to record their ratings, which would be a further apparatus within the internal logic. This is not necessarily the case. These assignments of values can be treated as further propositions, for example that concept *C* has rating *R* on scale *S*. This allows ratings to be the result of, or to feed into, reasoning involving propositions and rules within the belief base.)

We are not suggesting that our 'deflation' should take the place of Apter's 'diminishment' in his theoretical statement of the causes of humour. We simply require a concept which is both more restricted (applying only within the joke world) and not dependent upon adoption of reversal theory. This 'deflation' can be used to express the details of our two insult constructs, as follows. A deflation constitutes a 'Real-world insult' if the joke world entity involved has a counterpart in the audience's view of the real-world, and a 'Fictional insult' if there is no such real-world counterpart. Both types of insult will be associated with the interpretation in the later stage of the deflation, which in a joke will usually be the final state.

The Self-improvement construct is hard to make precise, given the published accounts from which we have abstracted it and the fact that it is difficult to find jokes where Self-improvement is a plausible and helpful part of the analysis. A possible approximation might be that the comprehension of a particular joke manifests Self-improvement if, in the final interpretation, it associates a relatively low value on a worth scale with some entity, and, in the audience's real-world viewpoint, the audience also had a low value on this scale at some past time in the real world, but now has a much higher value on that scale. This means that almost any joke involving a 'deflation' has the potential for Self-improvement, depending solely on the audience's view of himself, with no joke-internal factors affecting this.

11.10 Summary

The case for aggression or superiority as the single factor which is necessary and sufficient for humour is very feeble (and has been since Hutcheson's dismantling, three centuries ago, of Hobbes's pronouncements). However, the idea that humour mechanisms involve superiority or insults has never completely gone away, and a more complex formulation of jokehood or funniness might be possible which incorporates superiority as an ingredient. It is therefore prudent to include in our framework some facility to document humour-related superiority. The comprehension model will have, in each viewpoint, 'worth scales', and a substantial decrease in value on a worth scale will be termed a 'deflation'. Joke comprehension may result in any of the four categories listed in Section 11.9: Real-world insult, Fictional insult, Self-improvement, Teller-benefit. We believe that these constructs allow us to capture the key intuitions expressed by several authors.

Chapter 12

What's in a joke?

12.1 Integrating the miscellaneous factors

Much past work on humour has been based on a proposal that some specific factor, such as faulty logic or superiority, is crucial in humour. However, such accounts relying on a single cause of humour are hard to defend. It is easy to construct texts which manifest just one of these ingredients, such as impropriety, but which are in no way humorous. There is, as yet, no real case for any one of these factors being necessary and sufficient for jokehood or funniness. Also, we have argued that some of the incongruity-resolution configurations are not mutually exclusive, and that some of the superiority constructs can occur together. Similar remarks can be made about the possibility of combining the different ingredients, such as impropriety, superiority and incongruity.

One of the aims of this book is to bring together these separate strands within research on joke mechanisms. The hope is that this may serve as a sketch for future development. This integration does not have the immediate goal of determining exactly what constitutes the essence of humour. Instead, we aim, as discussed in Chapter 2, to develop a framework in which the comprehension of jokes can be documented more accurately and in more detail using non-humorous constructs.

In Chapter 4, we presented the structures and processes that we would assume are necessary to support text comprehension, and which are therefore available as building blocks in describing the comprehension of any joke. In other chapters, we reviewed, and in some cases made more precise, a number of aspects of texts which have been proposed as having some relationship either to the status of a text as a joke or to the extent of its humorous effect. These two strands of development – basic elements of text comprehension and humour-related concepts proposed by previous authors – have provided us with a broad collection of raw material, which we will now organise into an overall picture.

12.2 A review of the factors

The required environment

There is some degree of agreement that humour generally, and jokes in particular, can operate only in a suitable setting; see Section 3.3. The two attributes of this setting which are usually mentioned are 'security' (freedom from negative emotions or urgent tasks) and 'playfulness' (treating the material as being for enjoyment rather than for some functional purpose). Although this aspect is not discussed by every author, there appears to be no argument against it. As observed earlier, we have not looked at this condition in detail, as it appears to be a general facilitating aspect of the overall environment, rather than an internal detail that might interact with other factors to create the humorous effect.

Process conditions

Within the various information elements that have been discussed in earlier chapters, it is possible to see a subclass of factors which we will call *process conditions*. These are attributes of the dynamic processing of the text of a joke, focusing on the sequence of events and how these events are handled cognitively. Examples of this are assimilation difficulty and surprise. We see the following process conditions as particularly important:

Salience: The salience of various concepts is likely to change during comprehension. In particular, some concepts may shift from the unaware to the aware level (Section 4.7), often leading to final revelations (Section 5.4). Salience is mainly of interest insofar as it leads to final revelations or to temporary differences in perceived interpretations of a text.

Post-text assimilation difficulty: By the nature of text comprehension, there is almost certain to be some inference at the post-text stage, and hence this is hardly worth remarking upon. However, there may also be an assimilation difficulty, which leads to some additional cognitive effort (Section 4.7) by the audience. (Some authors mention this prominently, others assume it, but no one disputes it.) It has been suggested that, for joke comprehension to be successful, both the amount of cognitive effort and the temporal duration of this inference should lie within some optimal ranges, as yet undetermined (Section 5.4).

Final revelations: The post-text inference leads to material which is new, in the sense that the audience was not aware of it until the completion of this inferential work. That is, there is a significant change in the salience of items in the audience's viewpoint (Section 5.4).

Failed prediction: We have made a distinction between 'prediction' (of events during audience inference) and '(violation of) expectation' (of situations in internal logic). As discussed in Chapter 5, we found that a failure of prediction could occasionally occur at a humour-related moment, although we argued that there was little evidence that it was centrally involved in the amusement reaction. Violation of expectation is not a dynamic aspect of the processing, but can constitute an anomaly (Section 4.5).

Knowledge conditions: final state

In contrast to process conditions, some other components are *knowledge conditions*: properties that describe some aspect of the belief bases in the various interpretation states of the comprehension. Some criteria apply to the final state, usually as final revelations:

Linguistic: It may be necessary for some embedded viewpoint to contain language-interpretation rules which are slightly different from those normally used by the audience (Section 9.3). Where this occurs, these rules may contribute to the humour in various ways: a source of linguistic impropriety (Section 10.5), the creation of a form of anomaly (Section 9.3), or a device to allow an alternative interpretation which manifests one of the other types of knowledge conditions.

Logical: Some viewpoint will have an internal logic which is discrepant (i.e. distinct from that of a higher viewpoint), often resulting in a relative anomaly (Section 4.5). In many cases, this discrepant logic will also be fanciful (Section 6.6).

Improper: Some concept constitutes an impropriety according to social standards in some relevant viewpoint (Chapter 10).

Knowledge conditions: state comparison

Many authors have suggested knowledge conditions which involve a relationship between two particular interpretations in the sequence of interpretations. The relationship between the corresponding knowledge states is usually one of the following:

Post-text puzzle: The post-text state presents some form of justification question (often a relevance question) and the final state contains the support which answers this question (Section 7.3).

QA: The post-set-up state contains a justification question and the final state holds the corresponding answer (Section 7.4).

Revision: The post-set-up state includes a viewpoint containing some beliefs or norms (inferred, often by default) while the final state has these beliefs/norms overridden in that viewpoint (Section 7.6).

Contrast: There is some contrastive or conflicting relationship between the post-set-up and the final versions of the content of some viewpoint

(Section 7.7). Some theoretical proposals combine this with 'Revision' (Section 7.6).

Insulting: The information causes a 'deflation' for some agent depicted or referred to in the joke (a 'Fictional insult', Chapter 11).

Combinations of factors

There is little agreement amongst past authors about which of the conditions listed above, if any, are necessary or sufficient for jokehood. Both process and knowledge conditions can act as building blocks when formulating hypotheses about what might be necessary or sufficient for the creation of humour. Conjunctions and disjunctions of these conditions can be combined into conjectures about joke recognition or joke appreciation.

On the basis of current findings, it is hard to dismiss any of the factors listed above as definitely being irrelevant to joke recognition and/or joke appreciation. For each of these potential ingredients, there are specific jokes for which it seems particularly plausible to suggest that factor as being pertinent to the humour.

Some properties of the comprehension process may act as enhancers (Section 3.5), rather than being centrally involved in joke recognition or in establishing the pre-conditions for joke appreciation. As noted in Section 3.6, making this distinction is properly part of what we called, in Section 2.3, the characterisation phase of research, in which some hypothesis is put forward regarding the underlying causes of humour in jokes.

12.3 Some deliberate omissions

There are some aspects of jokes which might be thought to be important enough to be candidates for our list of relevant factors, but which have not appeared so far in this chapter. These include:

Incongruity and resolution: As argued in Chapter 7, we prefer to see these traditional but ill-defined terms replaced by more precise and fine-grained constructs which are related to general text comprehension. (See Section 7.12 for a brief sketch of how IR terms might be expressed using our constructs.)

Narrative structure: As discussed in Section 4.8, there is no sign that having a plot, in the traditional storytelling sense, is a crucial to the workings of jokes. A story can result in various factors, such as an inference of deflation for a character, and a joke text is expected to manifest some degree of coherence (as noted in Chapters 4 and 7), but there seem to be no interesting generalisations relating plot structure itself to the workings of jokes.

Forced reinterpretation: As outlined in Section 7.6, we include various building blocks with which forced reinterpretation jokes can be described, but that particular cluster of factors does not appear as a single unit. Nevertheless, it can be a convenient label to refer to exactly that cluster of factors, instead of having to spell out the details each time.

Surprise: As we discussed in Chapter 8, it is hard to see how exactly a well-defined notion of surprise should contribute to joke appreciation, and in what way the concept of surprise offers a useful generalisation.

12.4 Summary

The possible aspects of a joke which we have catalogued in this chapter can, from a formal point of view, be seen as conditions which may apply to the comprehension history: a record of the comprehension process over time, including all intermediate states of knowledge (Section 4.9). The application of these conditions is dependent on the details of the audience, which we treat as being, from an abstract point of view, a text comprehension model as outlined in Chapter 4, with the relevant belief bases containing the mechanisms proposed in Chapter 10 (social standards and lexical labellings of linguistic impropriety) and in Chapter 11 (worth scales).

The intention is that an integrated framework like this should allow the construction of fuller and more precise analyses of jokes, in order to illuminate more clearly what is going on in any specific joke. In this way, better empirical evidence can be gathered to support (or to undermine) particular hypotheses about the role played by certain factors in causing a text to be regarded as a joke.

Chapter 13

Applying the framework

13.1 Some preliminaries

Ease of description

In this chapter, we demonstrate how the various constructs we have proposed can be used to describe the comprehension of some jokes. First, however, we must make a small disclaimer. Although we emphasise the importance of describing in detail what occurs during joke comprehension, the collection of mechanisms we have proposed may not be convenient for certain common styles of description. Some articles on humour need, as part of some larger project, to summarise briefly the characteristics of particular jokes or other verbally expressed humour. For this, they typically deploy some small set of category labels, often borrowed from existing humour theories; see, for example, Popescu (2011), Tsakona (2013). Such informal summaries of the properties of a joke are usually sufficient for the purpose at hand, without the need to go into great detail about the internal workings of the joke. This is closely related to a point made in Section 2.2: theoretical frameworks which are worked out to a useful level of technical detail may be too complicated to lend themselves to neat informal summaries. Our framework is intended as a rough draft of a fuller cognitive/affective model of the process of joke comprehension, with the result that it may not be ideal for the construction of quick informal outlines of jokes. Working through a joke using our constructs in full detail could be time-consuming and tiresomely fiddly, and hence would not be a task that someone would embark upon if their primary interest in humour lay elsewhere.

Despite that difficulty, we will, in this chapter, try to give *brief* outlines of how we envisage joke comprehension proceeding, for a few illustrative example jokes. These sketches were originally made as part of the process of developing our ideas, and they are included here in order to convey more fully the content of our proposals.

Making statements about conditions

In Section 3.6, we suggested that when analysing a joke (one of the five encounter scenarios from Section 3.4), the analyst is imagining the course of events in some hypothetical joke comprehension, a Natural encounter. Hence, where a description alludes to process conditions such as post-text assimilation difficulty (Section 12.2), this is largely speculative. It would be possible to put such claims on a firmer footing by carrying out careful experimental work with human subjects and a suitable test set of jokes, but this is not the way that informal analyses have typically been conducted in past research, and we have not yet reached that stage of sophistication (see Section 14.2 for remarks on possible future developments).

Some authors attribute amusement solely to some set of what we have called 'knowledge conditions' (Section 7.7), whereas others make prominent mention of certain 'process conditions' (Section 7.3). This is part of a general trend: humour analysts usually emphasise those factors which they believe are centrally involved in the humour, while omitting or mentioning only briefly any other aspects. Consequently, when an analyst is silent about some construct, we should not interpret this as a denial of the presence of that phenomenon in the comprehension of jokes. We can instead interpret it as a tacit claim that this factor is not critical to the humorous effect.

Our illustrative analyses

The commentaries we provide in this chapter are slightly different in purpose from the joke analyses from which we have taken inspiration in developing our framework. Our aim is to illustrate, for expository purposes, the ways in which our various constructs could provide a suitably rich account of joke comprehension. We are not proposing a theory (or proto-theory) regarding exactly which factors within a joke lead to humour. Hence, we are not in a position to omit certain factors on the grounds that they should not feature in a theory of humour and we will be unable to make firm statements about which elements are merely 'enhancers' (Section 3.5).

Nevertheless, there are many parts of our framework which it would be clumsy, tedious and obfuscating to mention repeatedly. In particular, we have adopted a general infrastructure of comprehension (Chapter 4), which provides many mechanisms which will be present in the comprehension of any joke, simply because they are inherently part of text comprehension. These include, for example, the hierarchy of knowledge viewpoints and the process of audience inference. These will be mentioned only where necessary to make some point related to humour.

There are also factors which are potentially highly relevant to joke recognition and/or joke appreciation, but for which there are no clear indicators of their presence when we are simply inspecting a joke text and imagining a comprehension process for it. For one of these, namely the availability of a playful/secure environment, we will simply assume that this is present for all the hypothetical joke comprehensions that we are dissecting. For others, such as post-text inference, we will mention these if they seem particularly relevant, but otherwise we will assume that they may well arise in joke comprehension in a Natural encounter.

As we have noted already (e.g. Section 11.8), sometimes the presence of one factor can be enmeshed with the presence of another, with the dependence perhaps being wholly predictable. We may sometimes omit mentioning a factor where it is clearly predictable from an already-mentioned condition.

The content of the analyses

For each text, we will sketch the principal viewpoints involved, which will usually include the audience's view of the real world (AUD), which is the root for the hierarchical arrangement of viewpoints, and the joke world (JW), directly subordinate to the audience's viewpoint. There may also be one or more viewpoints associated with fictional characters within the joke. These will be subordinate to the joke world, and not subordinate to each other.

There will be an approximate sketch in English of some conceptual material that is conveyed, directly or indirectly, during the comprehension of the text. More precisely, these items are amongst all the ideas produced by audience inference. They do not represent everything that might be inferred by the audience, only a few interesting propositions we believe to be potentially pertinent to the comprehension of the text as a joke. As noted in Section 12.2, these conceptual items will usually be in the belief base states corresponding to the post-set-up and/or final stages of comprehension.

13.2 Some illustrative descriptions

Previously quoted examples

We will start with items from earlier chapters before introducing some additional example jokes. Our first example, (30), was mentioned in Section 7.8.

(30) Why did the elephant sit on the marshmallow?
Because he didn't want to fall into the hot chocolate.

There are no character viewpoints, just AUD and JW. The first sentence presupposes that, in JW, an elephant-character has sat on a marshmallow, which the audience should be able to accommodate, with a relatively small degree of disbelief-suspension. This sentence also raises a explicit justification question, about the reason for the elephant-character's act of sitting. The second sentence raises a momentary relevance question and a slight assimilation difficulty, but post-text inference constructs the internal logic of the JW, in the form of propositions which must hold for the text to make sense. This contains material inherited from AUD: '*marshmallows conventionally float on top of hot chocolate*', '*something can, subject to certain constraints of weight, be supported by being on top of a floating object*'. It also contains some propositions which the text treats as completely normal but which might not seem so in AUD and for which the support is not known (that is, apparent anomalies): '*the elephant-character could have been in danger of falling into hot chocolate*', '*the elephant-character would not want this to happen*', '*the elephant-character could float on a single marshmallow*', '*the elephant-character would work out the consequences of these propositions*'. Accepting these as part of the internal logic will probably require a large amount of disbelief-suspension (see Section 6.6). If all these propositions are accepted into the internal logic, it follows that, in JW, sitting on a marshmallow would prevent the elephant-character from being immersed in hot chocolate, thereby answering the set-up justification question. The very large degree of disbelief-suspension needed to construct this internal logic adds an air of absurdity to the joke, as well as making the logic highly fanciful.

Unsurprisingly, a broadly similar analysis can be constructed for (29), the elephant hiding in the cherry tree, with even more unsupported premises requiring to be added, with considerable disbelief-suspension.

A textually very different joke, (15) from Section 6.6, has some very similar elements.

(15) A man at the dinner table who was being handed fish dipped his two hands twice in the mayonnaise and then ran them through his hair. When his neighbour looked at him in astonishment, he seemed to notice his mistake and apologized: 'I'm so sorry, I thought it was spinach.'

In addition to AUD and JW, there are two characters, man and neighbour, with their own viewpoints. The set-up shows JW to contain a situation (applying mayonnaise to hair) which is treated as normal in the viewpoint of the man-character, but for which no support is readily available in any viewpoint. This is an apparent anomaly, creating a justification question. The punch line supplies another oddity (mistaking mayonnaise for spinach), which results in another apparent anomaly. Audience inference then leads, abductively, to some internal logic within the viewpoint of the man-character which requires a high degree of disbelief-suspension, as discussed in Section 6.6. Thus (15) has the same broad logical structure as some other jokes, such as (14) (the squashed hedgehog) and (34) (the road numbers as speed limits), but with a much greater demand for disbelief-suspension. Like the elephant jokes (29) and (30), (15) has a high level of absurdity, owing to its very fanciful logic.

The next example, repeated from Section 7.8, shows how an anomaly may be present in JW without the judgement of normality coming from some higher viewpoint; this is a definite anomaly, in our terms.

(27) A concert pianist traveled to Africa in a bid to prove that music had the power to soothe the savage beast. He set up his grand piano in a small clearing beside a river, and began to play. One by one, animals appeared and soon he was surrounded by lions, giraffes, antelopes, warthogs, and leopards, all sitting peacefully together swaying and tapping their feet. The pianist had just started to play a second piece when a crocodile splashed out of the river, grabbed the man with its jaws, and dragged him into the water. An agitated lion ran over to the water's edge. 'Why in heaven's name did you do that?' he asked. The crocodile cupped a foot to the back of its head and said, 'Eh ?'

This requires a few character viewpoints: pianist-character, lion-character, crocodile-character. A moderate degree of disbelief-suspension is required for: the animals being pacified by the music, the animals speaking, the crocodile using the paw-cupping gesture. The first two sentences establish a norm within the JW: '*music soothes animals*'. The mauling of the pianist-character (third sentence) is therefore a definite anomaly in the JW, and raises a justification question. The penultimate sentence, with the lion's utterance, makes this justification question explicit, while introducing some more anomalies which can be supported only subject to some disbelief-suspension, such as the animals communicating in human language. The final sentence raises a transient relevance question, but then post-text inference works back from this information thus: '*crocodile has not heard the lion*', '*crocodile has hearing problems*', '*crocodile cannot hear the music*', '*crocodile is not affected by the music*', '*crocodile retains natural aggression*'. This reveals that the internal logic within the viewpoint of the pianist-character contained the argument '*music removes aggression therefore animals exposed to music will not be aggressive*', instead of the slightly more rigorous argument '*music removes aggression therefore animals which hear music will not be aggressive*'. With the internal logic revised in this way, the earlier definite anomaly (the crocodile's attack) is not present in the final state. That is, the revision between post-set-up and final states involves the rules of JW, relative to which the abnormality was defined. (For those concerned with the distinction between full and partial resolution, Section 7.9, this example could be argued to involve full resolution of the incongruity of the attack.)

In this example, the role played by discrepant logic is similar to that in example (14) (the squashed hedgehog) in Section 6.5, in that the reasoning contributes to the occurrence of the anomaly in the set-up. In (27), as in (14), a character in the joke world has adopted a line of reasoning which is only slightly different from a rule which more accurately accounts for the situation in the joke world, and this lures the character into a particular situation which leads, during the set-up phase, to an unfortunate outcome.

The story reveals the pianist-character to have been mistaken, which may provide a relatively mild Fictional insult. The bloodshed may, for some audiences, constitute blatant discourse impropriety, as the mention of the fate of this character is direct. The difference between the rules in the various viewpoints means there is discrepant logic, but as this fragment of logic does not rely on significant disbelief-suspension, there does not appear to be fanciful logic, in the sense we are using this term (Section 6.6). There is some need for disbelief-suspension in the narrative, although not a marked amount by the usual standard of jokes, and not involved with any final revelations. An anomaly in the set-up becomes supported as a result of post-text inference. The support, the discrepant nature of the logic and the Fictional insult are all final revelations.

Example (27) might be seen as a forced reinterpretation (FR) joke. For comparison, in Section 7.6 we looked at a constructed non-joke, (23), which seemed to be an instance of the FR structure with no humorous effect. We will now dissect that example in more detail.

(23) A man jumped into a taxi and said, 'The main railway station, please.' 'OK,' said the driver, 'What time is the train?' 'No train,' said the passenger, 'I'm meeting a friend in the bar there.'

There are two story-character viewpoints, for the driver-character and the passenger-character. After the initial text, up to '*what time is the train?*', the audience can infer that in JW, the passenger-character wishes to go to the railway station and the driver-character is willing to take on this fare. The driver-character's viewpoint appears to contain internal logic which says that when a person sets out for the railway station, they are most likely going to catch or meet a train, leading to that viewpoint also containing the proposition that the passenger-character wishes to catch or meet a train. The audience may also accommodate these propositions into the viewpoints of JW and the passenger-character, where the same internal logic may hold, by default. The driver-character has raised an explicit question, although it is not strictly a justification question, as it requests further information rather than seeking the reasons for some situation. The rest of the text then contradicts the earlier default inference about the passenger-character's wishes, in whatever viewpoints it may have been placed. This reveals the supposed norm about the reasons for going to a rail station to be inaccurate, in any of the viewpoints that it may have been assumed. (In some ways this is comparable to the inferences in (14) and (27).)

Hence, there is discrepant logic, primarily in the viewpoint of the driver-character, giving rise to a relative anomaly. The driver-character has been shown to have been mistaken, which in principle could give rise to a Fictional insult. Both of these are final revelations.

As we observed in Section 7.6, (23) is not only not funny, it does not, intuitively, qualify as a joke. This indicates that the mere presence of the observed components – final revelations of discrepant logic and Fictional insult – is not sufficient to give rise to either joke recognition or joke appreciation. This could be because some further component is required, such as the presence of fanciful logic rather than merely discrepant logic, or perhaps there is some notion of 'extent' or 'degree' for these aspects, which does not reach a sufficient level in (23), or possibly some adjustment is needed to the definitions of these components.

Another example we looked at, in Section 7.10, is (31).

(31) 'Well, I see you have a new dog. I thought you didn't like dogs.'
'Well, I don't, but my wife bought a lot of dog soap on sale, so we had to get a dog to use it up.'

In (31), there are three character viewpoints: character-1, character-2, wife-character. The audience can infer from the first sentence that the character-1 viewpoint includes the propositions: '*character-2 dislikes dogs*', '*character-2 owns a (new) dog*', '*character-2 possesses something he dislikes*', '*if you dislike something, you should not obtain it*'. A further inference may be that some or all of these propositions also figure in JW. This creates an apparent anomaly (deliberately acquiring a disliked object) in JW. By the end of the punch line, the audience can infer the following contents of the wife-character viewpoint: '*if something is on sale, a lot should be purchased, even if it is not immediately useful*'. Also, the character-2 viewpoint contains: '*character-2 and wife-character own a lot of dog soap*', '*if you have a large amount of a consumable it should be used*', '*to consume dog soap you need a dog*'. This means that the anomaly-creating proposition is supported in the viewpoint of character-2, even though it may still lack support in AUD. Thus it forms a relative anomaly.

The fragments of internal logic attributed to the wife-character and to character-2 involve a point made in Section 6.6: an apparently general rule may have exceptions which are brought to light when the rule is applied in a way that feels odd. Here, the rule about opportunistic purchases and the rule about using up a resource should both have a condition along the lines of: '...*unless it will entail considerable inconvenience and/or expense to make use of it*'. It is the disbelief-suspension necessary to accept that the characters would ignore these pre-conditions that renders the logic fanciful (it is already discrepant relative to AUD). Also, the JW situation of character-2 adopting and acting upon this logic may be taken as evidence of that character not being wise, thus creating a Fictional insult. This results in a few final revelations: a relative anomaly, some fanciful logic and a Fictional insult.

When (31) was discussed earlier, we compared it with the constructed non-joke (32), to demonstrate certain points.

(32) 'Well, I see you have a new dog. I thought you didn't like dogs.'
'Well, I don't, but my wife insisted on getting it.'

We can expand this comparison by analysing this non-joke text in a similar manner to that used for (31) above. The initial portion of the analysis, up to the punch line, is identical to that for (31). After the punch line, the audience can infer that the wife-character strongly wishes to own a dog, and that the viewpoint of character-2 contains the logic: '*if your wife insists on something then you should concur even if it conflicts with your wishes*'. The situation established by the punch line is then supported. If AUD also contains the rule about meeting one's wife's wishes, then there is no longer an anomaly. It is hard to see any reason for the internal logic being fanciful. Some might argue that the situation described in the text depicts character-2 as weak, thereby supplying a Fictional insult.

The main difference between the two analyses is that (31) contains two instances of clearly fanciful logic, whereas (32) contains a single instance of internal logic which might be discrepant (depending on the audience's views of marital life), but which seems to require very little disbelief-suspension. This tends to support the speculation (Section 7.10) that the humorous effect in (31) may be caused by the fanciful nature of the internal logic. This also highlights the distinction between internal logic which is merely discrepant (different from that in a dominating viewpoint) and that which is also fanciful (requires significant disbelief-suspension). As in (23) (the non-humorous taxi story), merely discrepant logic has not led to jokehood, and certainly not funniness.

We have already, in Section 7.5, examined some aspects of (21). Now we can add more detail to this account.

(21) A couple from Seattle were talking about their holiday to their friend. 'Sounds as if you had a great time in California,' said the friend, 'but I didn't know you were planning to take in Florida as well.'
'We weren't,' said the wife, 'but Ted simply will not ask for directions.'

In this joke, there are at least two character viewpoints: wife-character and friend-character. The text up to the phrase '*as well*' results in these two belief bases (and JW and AUD) sharing various situations: '*the couple went on holiday*', '*the couple were in California*', '*the couple were in Florida*'. The friend-character's viewpoint also includes the belief that the couple planned to visit Florida, derived as a presupposition from the sentence starting '*I didn't know* …'. (This could be seen as a belief in the friend-character's view of the wife-character's beliefs, in the sort of arrangement depicted in Figure 4.3, in Section 4.3.) After the phrase '*said the wife*', this belief is amended, resulting in a definite anomaly: in JW, the couple planned to go to California but not Florida, and yet visited Florida. The final clause (the punch line) triggers audience inference which reconstructs the internal logic of JW, which runs roughly as follows:

The driver refuses to ask for directions. Hence, he may lack sufficient knowledge to navigate accurately. Ignorance of this sort can cause a driver to reach the wrong destination. Invoking a device of exaggeration, the destination could be hugely incorrect. Hence, starting out for California could result in reaching Florida.

This then supports the otherwise abnormal Florida visit, but there is discrepant logic (and a relative anomaly) if the audience does not accept the entire sequence of internal logic reasoning. In particular, the exaggeration step may require a high degree of disbelief-suspension, rendering the logic fanciful. In addition, the esteem of the husband-character is subject to deflation. There are thus three final revelations: a relative anomaly, a Fictional insult and fanciful logic.

Example (34), from Section 8.2, illustrates a more extended sequence.

(34) The police pull over an old lady in a car. She has a passenger, an old man whose face is frozen in a rictus of fear. The policeman says, 'Madam, I just pulled you off the motorway for driving at 25 miles an hour. Why were you driving so slowly?' 'I wasn't,' says the old lady. 'I was doing what the sign told me. It said the "M25", so I drove at 25 miles per hour.' 'That's not how it works, madam,' says the policeman. 'Couldn't your friend have told you that?' He looks at the old man, who's not moved a muscle since they stopped. 'Is he all right?' asks the policeman. 'I'm not sure,' says the old lady. 'He's been like that since we got on the A150.'

The first speech by the policeman-character raises an explicit justification question ('*Why were you ...?*'). The reply by the driver-character, up to '*... miles an hour*', answers this question, subject to internal logic within the viewpoint of the driver-character, sketched by the content of this speech. If the text were to terminate here, then this might work as a rather weak joke, but since the text continues, we have to treat this as at most an intermediate 'jab line' (Attardo, 2001). The fact that the passenger-character is terrified might raise a justification question, which is explicitly established by the policeman-character's '*Is he all right?*' The final sentence may transiently raise a relevance question, perhaps with some assimilation difficulty, but audience inference makes the connections whereby the route number together with the driver-character's misconceptions will lead to hugely fast driving, which in turn could induce fear. This not only solves the relevance question, it answers the most recent justification question.

It is not immediately obvious which of the usual ingredients of joke humour occur as final revelations. During the set-up, the driver-character is depicted as ignorant (a deflation), and there is logic which is both discrepant and fanciful, namely the idea that the route signs specify an ideal speed. The post-text inference merely works out the consequences (by valid reasoning) of combining this flawed belief with driving on a road marked '*A150*'. The main final revelation that emerges from this is that the car has been driving at an extremely high speed. This might constitute a relative anomaly, since ultra-fast driving, particularly by an elderly couple, is probably not a normal situation in AUD. It is possible that the revelation of high-speed driving increases the audience's estimation of how misguided the driver-character's belief about road signs is, perhaps increasing how fanciful it seems. Or it could be that some disbelief-suspension might be required for the idea that the driver-character would be so committed to this mistaken belief that she would try to drive at 150 mph on a normal road. Overall, although the information flow seems relatively clear, it is hard to be sure which factors are leading to the text acting as a joke.

Some further examples

We now look at a few jokes which have not appeared in earlier chapters.

(60) The chef flew into a rage at his new assistant. 'Didn't I tell you to notice when the soup boiled over?' he yelled. 'I did,' said the assistant. 'It was half past eleven.'

(Tibballs, 2000, p. 276)

In (60), there are two character viewpoints: chef-character, assistant-character. After the utterance by the chef-character, the audience infers that, in the joke world, the assistant-character did not intervene when the soup boiled over. This is initially an apparent anomaly (in JW, relative to AUD), raising a justification question. When the assistant-character reports the time, this may briefly raise a relevance question, resulting in assimilation difficulty. Post-text inference leads to attributing to the assistant-character the reasoning, as part of the internal logic for this viewpoint, that if the chef-character has asked to notice when soup boils, this concerns timing, not a need for action. The justification question about the lack of intervention is thus answered, based on this internal logic. This reasoning may also require an idiosyncratic notion of normal kitchen procedure in the assistant-character viewpoint, which would require a degree of disbelief-suspension; that is, this would be fanciful logic, to some extent. The apparent anomaly of the assistant-character's lack of action becomes, as a result of this reasoning, a relative anomaly. The two possible interpretations of the chef-character's original instruction (which is not shown verbatim, but indirectly quoted) must have different salience ratings in the assistant-character's viewpoint from those in the chef-character's viewpoint or in the audience's. (This use of ambiguity to allow adverse consequences is reminiscent of the suggestion by Oring (1992a) that ambiguity can provide the 'appropriateness' to counter the incongruity between two readings.) The final interpretation may contain the inferred proposition, in JW, that the assistant-character is not too smart, a deflation from some assumed default level of commonsense, and hence a Fictional insult.

Hence, this example manifests a difference in language models, a relative anomaly, potential Fictional insult and probably fanciful logic. All of these are final revelations (and hence some of them might, under suitable circumstances, constitute surprises – see Section 12.3). There is also a revision of interpretation, inside the assistant-character viewpoint.

Impropriety has been absent from most of the jokes examined so far in this chapter, but is prominent in (61).

(61) What do you give an elephant with diarrhoea?
Plenty of room.

(Tibballs, 2000, p. 122)

The first sentence, in its more salient interpretation, raises a question involving medication. The second sentence may temporarily raise a relevance question, resulting in assimilation difficulty. The post-text inference discovers, in the JW viewpoint, a less salient interpretation of the first sentence, which means that JW has a slightly different language model from AUD. This results in the following internal logic in that viewpoint: '*there is no remedy for elephantine diarrhoea*' (requires only mild disbelief-suspension), '*an elephant with diarrhoea will generate a torrent of excrement*' (inherited from AUD, perhaps with some exaggeration), '*it is best to avoid a torrent of excrement*' (inherited from AUD), '*hence one should stand clear of any such ailing animal*'. All of these are final revelations, but are barely discrepant and certainly not fanciful. The development of this internal logic is enabled by the ambiguity of the first sentence, which involves a degree of disbelief-suspension over the rules of English, since the idiom '*give (plenty of) room*' cannot usually be split in this way. The audience may, depending upon his social standards, regard the inferred torrent of excrement as oblique discourse impropriety. Also, the audience may see this as levity impropriety if copious excrement is treated as unmentionable with levity.

Example (62) appears to use a surprisingly small number of humour-related factors.

(62) After a long day on the course, an exasperated golfer turned to his caddie and said: 'You must be the worst caddie in the world.'
'I don't think so,' replied the caddie. 'That would be too much of a coincidence.'

(Tibballs, 2000, p. 141)

There are two character viewpoints, and the caddie-character's view of the golfer-character's viewpoint is also involved. Nothing of interest occurs until the post-text stage, when the final utterance is likely to give rise to a relevance question and assimilation difficulty. Audience inference then attributes various propositions to the caddie-character viewpoint: '*the utterance by the golfer-character can be taken as a literal assertion, not merely an exaggerated insult*', '*in the golfer-character viewpoint, the caddie-character is the worst caddie in the world*', '*the golfer-character is the worst golfer in the world*', '*if the caddie-character were also the worst caddie in the world, that would be a great coincidence*'. Most of these steps seem relatively sound and not in need of disbelief-suspension, with the possible exception of the interpretation of the golfer-character's remark as factual rather than as an exaggerated insult (which would be an indication of a different language model in the caddie-character viewpoint). The golfer-character is, in the JW, portrayed as the recipient of a witty put-down, and possibly also a poor golfer, which provides a Fictional insult. There are two insults: explicit from the golfer-character, implicit from the caddie-character. If the audience deems it improper to draw attention to someone's shortcomings, then these might count as discourse impropriety, but this would involve conflating aggression (in a joke) with the range of topics we are treating as improper – see Section 10.1. The final revelations include the internal logic sketched above, with one possibly slightly fanciful step leading to a relative anomaly over language, and also the Fictional insult. There may also be the attribution of wittiness to the caddie-character, but it is not clear which humour component this would manifest; it might be an enhancer.

We will turn now to an example of a simple (but typical) self-contained pun (computer-generated – see Section 9.3).

(63) What kind of tree is nauseated? A sick-amore.

There are no character viewpoints in this example, only JW, which has rules about word-meaning which are not shared with the dominating audience viewpoint (see Section 9.3). The set-up raises an explicit question, but also presupposes that a tree can be nauseated, an apparent anomaly. For the audience to accept the set-up, this counter-factual assumption has to be accommodated into the joke world, subject to a fair degree of disbelief-suspension, hence the joke is seen to be slightly absurd even during the set-up. The punch line may cause assimilation difficulty owing to a justification question, 'why should this particular kind of tree be nauseated?'; temporarily, there is an unsupported proposition. Audience inference uncovers the pertinent part of the internal logic of JW: '*if two words sound similar, their meanings are similar*' ('*syc*', '*sick*'), '*phonetic string subsequence implies meaning inclusion*' ('*sick-amore*', '*sick*'). This provides support for the proposition that this invented word is an answer to the question. The final interpretation therefore contains no final revelation anomalies about non-linguistic entities, but it does show an apparent anomaly transformed into a relative anomaly, and includes some internal linguistic rules which are fanciful (see Sections 6.6, 7.10 and 9.3). In overall form, it is relatively similar to the 'elephant' pseudo-riddles (29) and (30) earlier in this section.

The pseudo-rules of English word-meaning used in (63) are also used in many other similar puns in this genre, which means that the possibility of such rules can hardly be much of a surprise after the audience has experienced a few of these riddles. However, each new joke reveals the potential semantic consequences of these pseudo-rules when applied to another set of words. This is analogous to the arrangement in our description of (34) (the misunderstood road signs), where the final revelation was primarily about the consequences of an already established flawed rule.

13.3 Reflecting on the illustrations

Some general observations

The analyses in this chapter were useful in the development of the ideas within our analysis framework, as it is difficult to know exactly which constructs are appropriate without testing them on actual texts. It is interesting to consider which factors seem to recur in most of the jokes we have examined in this chapter and earlier chapters.

One extremely common feature is some degree of fanciful internal logic. Sometimes the logic is not conveyed initially to the audience, but is adopted by some character, resulting in actions (in JW) which seem abnormal relative to more conventional reasoning. This is the case, for example, in (12) (the woman and the psychiatrist), (13) (Irish Sea Scouts), (31) (buying dog soap) and (60) (letting soup boil over). The internal logic is then uncovered as a result of post-text inference; that is, it is a final revelation (although the uncovering takes little effort in (31), since the text spells out the logic).

A slightly different arrangement has the internal logic conveyed during the set-up, perhaps quite explicitly, with its faultiness unnoticed or accommodated, thus establishing a fictional norm. The faultiness comes to light later as a result of post-text inference. This is the arrangement in (27), the deaf crocodile, and in (14), the squashed hedgehog. Hence, the substance of the internal logic is not a final revelation, but its faultiness is.

In still other examples, the internal logic and its faultiness are both exposed before the punch line, but the final revelations include some outcome of that logic (as in (34), the misinterpreted road signs). Arguably, some puns follow this pattern too, in that some Cratylistic rules of language are shown as applied to words not previously considered.

Many of the jokes include some form of relative anomaly in the final revelations, which is hardly surprising in view of the close relationship between discrepant logic and anomaly (Section 4.5).

There seem to be very few humour-related aspects to (61) (elephant diarrhoea): an oblique discourse impropriety seems to be the principal (and perhaps only) factor, apart from a possibly fanciful manipulation of an English idiom. Another joke with few apparent humour ingredients is (62) (the worst caddie). In particular, it is hard to find any trace of anomaly and the internal logic is only very slightly faulty. The joke seems to rely primarily on a Fictional insult (together with the usual post-text cognitive effort).

A tentative generalisation

Our hope is that the descriptive framework presented in the preceding chapters provides a suitable repertoire of concepts for framing precise hypotheses about the root causes of humour in jokes. This book does not have the purpose of presenting a theory of jokes, but the outline in Chapter 12 might be seen as providing the building blocks for making theoretical statements about what constitutes a joke, or, to be more precise, what results in joke recognition and joke appreciation. Moving in this way from description to characterisation (in the terminology of Section 2.1 earlier) would require the development of some hypotheses about which combination(s) of the listed factors are necessary and/or sufficient for the recognition and appreciation processes. The sooner the framework can realistically be used in that way, the better, since description, although a worthy aim, has to be seen as a precursor to the more significant stage of characterisation (and, eventually, explanation).

The analyses presented in this chapter are intended to serve two functions: they illustrate how our framework can be used to document the details of joke comprehension, and they make a step, admittedly very small, along the path of understanding how joke comprehension works. We have presented analyses of only a small number of texts, which is a flimsy basis for attempting any strong hypotheses about joke recognition and joke appreciation. Nevertheless, we have, as remarked in the preceding subsection, noticed a few recurring patterns. We will therefore, in a slightly speculative way, set out what we have so far learned from using our framework to analyse simple jokes. This can be seen as a descriptive generalisation about the circumstances in which, for a particular audience, joke recognition will take place and the basic pre-requisites for joke appreciation will be established; that is, the audience will 'get the joke'.

As we noted in Section 13.1, there may be some conditions which cannot be discerned simply by examining the text of a joke, as they depend entirely on the cognitive events which take place during a Natural encounter. For example, remarks about the occurrence of optimal amounts of cognitive effort at the post-text stage are, while very plausible, wholly speculative without proper experimental results. However, certain ideas have appeared in the humour research literature without being seriously contested and are also compatible with our analyses of jokes:

- As the end of the text is encountered, there is an assimilation difficulty.
- The assimilation difficulty is overcome (i.e. the puzzle is solved).
- The amount of cognitive effort required and the time taken to overcome the assimilation difficulty lie within some optimal ranges, as yet undetermined.
- As a result of the post-text inference, there are final revelations.

More concretely, our own analyses and studies elsewhere seem to indicate that, at the end of joke comprehension, the final revelations will include

(a) discrepant logic, resulting in a relative anomaly (in beliefs either about the world or about language);

(b) at least one of the following:

(i) fanciful logic;
(ii) an improper concept, resulting in oblique discourse impropriety;
(iii) a Fictional insult.

Although several of the jokes analysed earlier in this chapter show more than one of the items listed here as (i) – (iii), examples (61) and (62) appear to manifest just (ii) and (iii) respectively.

We believe this describes the jokes we have examined so far, both those in this chapter as well as others. Also, it is compatible with many of the observations of previous writers. Nevertheless, we have no principled basis for arguing for any greater generality.

13.4 Summary

We have shown how our descriptive framework could be applied to some illustrative example jokes, in order to convey more clearly what we mean by some of our constructs. We have also drawn attention to some recurring patterns within these descriptions, which could potentially give clues about a future theory of jokes.

Chapter 14

The way forward

14.1 A summary of our programme

In this final chapter, it may be helpful to recapitulate how we have addressed some of the principal points of our guiding strategy in this work.

Most previous proposals about joke mechanisms are intended as theories of humour. That is, they set out to offer conditions under which a text (or other stimulus) will be a joke/humorous. Although we very much hope that our work will be helpful in moving towards a fuller theory of jokes or of humour (see Sections 1.3 and 2.1), we have not presented a set of necessary and/or sufficient conditions for jokehood or funniness.

This does not mean that our proposals have no theoretical content, or are in some way neutral between all possible theories (see Section 2.3). The constructs we have put forward in earlier chapters can be seen as hypotheses about the mechanisms which are involved in joke comprehension. Hence, these proposals can be seen as conjectures about the workings of jokes, even if we have not offered a full statement of exactly what makes something humorous.

Attempts to construct theories of humour have usually involved a quest for a specific property of jokes (or other humorous items) which acts as the essential cause of humour (Ritchie, 2004, Section 2.4). Although some scholars have considered several facets of humour, many 'theories' are based on one particular aspect. In contrast, we have brought together aspects of joke comprehension which have typically been treated in isolation within humour theorising, such as incongruity-resolution, superiority, impropriety and surprise.

As noted by many authors, jokes are by no means the only form of humour, and other varieties of humour may have different properties from those found in jokes. Nevertheless, for reasons set out in Section 2.2, we have focused narrowly on the mechanisms of jokes, a working strategy that is widespread within humour research.

As we have argued throughout, any account of joke comprehension must be closely tied to more general notions of text comprehension, reasoning, etc., with as few specialised humour mechanisms as possible (Section 2.3).

We believe we have made useful contributions in this respect, by presenting an abstract model of text comprehension and related processes (Chapter 4) and framing our observations about jokes in terms of this model as much as possible.

Our framework shows some progress in increasing the level of detail in cognitive models of joke comprehension (Section 2.1). We have also endeavoured to make explicit certain aspects of joke comprehension which previous accounts either ignored or tacitly took for granted.

As well as putting forward a range of constructs for use in describing joke comprehension, we have also tried to show how the various components connect to each other to form a working system, rather than simply presenting a list of labels which can be attached to jokes.

14.2 Areas to develop

What needs more work

The descriptive framework developed in the preceding chapters is still very sketchy and is at best a preliminary step towards understanding jokes. There are several ways in which these ideas could be developed, including the following:

- defining the basic concepts
- expanding descriptive coverage
- developing hypotheses about jokes
- empirical testing
- generalising beyond jokes

In this section, we will indicate some ways in which these directions might be pursued.

Improving the components

All of the abstract constructs we have proposed could be sharpened up. For example, the ways in which disbelief-suspension operates is as yet unclear (Chapters 4 and 6), and the idea of 'impropriety' (Chapter 10) would benefit from further clarification. There is a need to continue to refine the intuitive notions of the basic concepts, in order to ensure that they are appropriate for the function of characterising joke mechanisms. Also, it would be desirable to formulate more precise definitions. Ideally, such clarifications of the primitive components would, for reasons set out in Chapter 2, provide definitions which were

- stated in a way which does not assume any notion of 'humour' or 'funniness';

- framed in terms of independently established concepts from some other area of research, such as psychology or sociology;
- operational, in the sense of making clear how a researcher could determine whether something qualifies as an instance of the construct.

Examining more jokes

In order to achieve the aim of improving our constructs, we need to find out more about the ways in which the basic elements can be combined within a joke. This means finding out which configurations occur in the comprehension of real jokes. Hence, a useful way to move forward would be to attempt to apply the framework to a wide variety of jokes. If this is done thoroughly, with no licence to skip over difficulties or to stretch concepts unreasonably, then it will quickly reveal shortcomings of the latest version of the descriptive framework. This can then feed into a cycle of revision of the framework, followed by further descriptive work and more cycles of revision. If the approach is on the right lines, the framework will, in due course, stabilise, and there will be an integrated and comprehensive framework. If the approach is seriously flawed, then corrective revisions either will not be possible, or the amendments will build gradually into an incoherent and badly structured account, whose very messiness will count against it.

Characterising jokes

One rather obvious – but difficult – further step is to move from describing jokes to characterising jokehood; that is, formulating a hypothesis about which attributes of joke comprehension are necessary and sufficient for joke recognition to occur and joke appreciation to be possible. We hope that the ideas in this book help to clear the ground for this to happen.

Psychological testing

All of the proposals we have made consist of 'armchair theorising', based on the study of past literature and the analysis of example jokes. The correctness of these proposals can be informally checked by this kind of rational cogitation, but ultimately there is a need for some carefully designed psychological experiments.

If semi-formal descriptive testing, as advocated earlier in this section, is at least moderately successful, it will then be worthwhile investing some effort in evaluating the psychological reality of some of the proposed mechanisms. The framework is intended as a step towards a cognitive model and hence psychological evidence will be crucial in testing its validity. It may require some ingenuity to design experiments which will probe all the aspects of the model, but experimental psycholinguists are often highly inventive in this respect. Fully rigorous testing, although critical in the long term, may have to wait until the framework becomes more articulated, in the ways we have indicated above.

Even more important is the testing of any hypotheses about jokehood/funniness that might emerge as a result of further work. The intention of this whole line of work is that if we can develop a descriptive framework which is precise, detailed and operational, then any hypotheses which are stated using the framework will be amenable to rigorous empirical testing.

Going beyond jokes

We have argued (Section 2.2) that, although there are methodological advantages to studying jokes, particularly textual jokes, care must be taken that other forms of humour are not ignored. Hence we must not mistake a description of joke mechanisms, however detailed and formal, for a theory of humour. We believe that understanding jokes will help us on the way to a fuller theory of humour in general. The viability of this approach will depend on how jokes are taken as fitting into the broader picture, and what can be exported from joke descriptions into a more general theory of humour. Decisions on such matters may have to wait until we have a well-supported description of exactly how joke mechanisms operate. At present, it is hard to guess how a comprehensive and substantiated account of jokes will relate to the wider question of humour.

14.3 In conclusion

We have argued for a particular approach to understanding the workings of jokes and have developed a set of mechanisms within that approach, based on ideas from existing research into humour. We have also illustrated how these mechanisms might provide illuminating descriptions of joke comprehension. The framework presented in this book is at best an interim version with many gaps and imperfections, but we have set out some ways in which this line of enquiry might be further developed. Even if this development does take place, there is still a long road ahead to an eventual theory of humour.

Appendix A

Example items

This is a list of all the numbered items, both jokes and constructed texts, from the main body of the book.

(1) Two grand Southern ladies are taking the air on the veranda of a fine mansion. One says, 'You see that there Rolls-Royce? Well, my husband gave that to me on our fifth wedding anniversary.' Her friend says, 'Well, isn't that fine.' The woman points to some horses in a paddock. 'And on our tenth wedding anniversary he bought me a string of race horses.' Her friend says, 'Well, isn't that fine.' The woman points to huge swimming pool at the side of the house. 'And for our fifteenth anniversary, he built me this beautiful pool and spa, all for me.' Her friend says, 'Well, isn't that fine.' 'So tell me,' says the woman. 'Does your husband buy you nice things?' 'Why, yes,' says the friend. 'Only last year he sent me to a charm school to improve my vocabulary.' 'Your vocabulary?' says the woman. 'Yes,' says the friend. 'I used to say "I don't give a rat's ass". But now I say "Well, isn't that fine."'

(2) A plane was delayed nearly an hour on take-off. When it eventually took to the air, the passengers asked the stewardess the reason for the late departure.
'Well,' she explained, 'the pilot was worried about a noise he heard coming from one of the engines and it took us a while to get a new pilot.'

(3) Last night I went to see the worst faith healer I've ever seen. He was so bad a guy in a wheelchair got up and walked out.

(4) A husband and wife were sitting watching a TV program about psychology explaining the phenomenon of mixed emotions. The husband turned to his wife and said, 'Honey that's a bunch of crap. I bet you can't tell me anything that will make me both happy and sad at the same time.' She replied, 'Out of all your friends, you have the biggest penis.'

(5) A gentleman entered a pastry-cook's shop and ordered a cake; but he soon brought it back and asked for a glass of liqueur instead. He drank it and began to leave without having paid. The proprietor detained him. 'What do you want?' asked the customer. – 'You've not paid for the liqueur.' – 'But I gave you the cake in exchange for it.' – 'But you didn't pay for that either.' – 'But I hadn't eaten it.'

(6) How many Poles does it take to screw in a light bulb? Five. One to hold the light bulb and four to turn the table he's standing on.

(7) A couple woke up in the morning. 'Did you hear the storm last night?' asked the husband.
'No,' said his wife. 'Was there thunder?'
'Yes, it was terrible. It sounded like the end of the world.'
'Why didn't you wake me? You know I can never sleep when it thunders.'

(8) Farmer Giles goes out and ploughs one of his fields with a steamroller. 'What are you doing?' asks his wife. 'Isn't it obvious?' he says. 'I'm growing mashed potatoes.'

(9) I woke up at six o'clock this morning and lay there with a terrible hangover. Already my next-door neighbour was out mowing his front garden. At first I thought I'd smack him in the mouth. But then I thought, 'No! Blow it! He'll just have to mow round me.'

(10) Patient: 'My wife thinks I'm crazy because I like sausages.'
Psychiatrist: 'Nonsense, I like sausages too.'
Patient: 'Great – you should come and see my collection. I've got hundreds of them.'

(11) A circus owner walked into a bar and found everyone gathered around a table. On the table was a duck tap dancing on an upturned flower pot. The circus owner was so impressed he immediately bought the duck and the flower pot for 1,500 dollars. Hundreds flocked to see the duck's first performance in the Big Top but, to everyone's disappointment, the duck didn't dance a step. The angry circus owner went back to the bar to seek out the man who had sold it to him.
'That duck is a fraud,' raged the circus owner. 'He hasn't danced a step for me.'
'That's odd. Did you remember to light the candle under the pot?'

(12) A woman sat down in a psychiatrist's office. 'I think I may be a nymphomaniac,' she said.
'I see. Well, I can help you, but I ought to tell you in advance that my fee

is 75 dollars an hour.'
'Hmmm,' she said. 'How much for all night?'

(13) Did you hear what happened to the Irish Sea Scouts? Their tent sank.

(14) Some rabbits are explaining to a hedgehog the safest way to cross a busy road at night. One says 'If you see some headlights coming, just line up between the two headlights, roll yourself up, and you'll be fine.' The hedgehog nervously sets out across the dark highway. Then, some headlights appear, approaching fast. He lines up between the beams, rolls up, and waits. Splat! He gets completely squashed. One rabbit turns to the other and says 'It's rotten luck to get a Reliant Robin on your first time.'

(15) A man at the dinner table who was being handed fish dipped his two hands twice in the mayonnaise and then ran them through his hair. When his neighbour looked at him in astonishment, he seemed to notice his mistake and apologized: 'I'm so sorry, I thought it was spinach.'

(16) He's so perverse, he likes meat better than any vegetable, except ice cream.

(17) A guy in the garment industry has a son who asks him, 'Daddy, what kind of flower is that?'
He says, 'What am I, a milliner?'

(18) Fat Ethel sat down at the lunch counter and ordered a whole fruit cake. 'Shall I cut it into four or eight pieces?' asked the waitress. 'Four,' said Ethel, 'I'm on a diet.'

(19) What is grey, has four legs, and a trunk? A mouse on vacation.

(20) Woman walks into bar with duck on leash. Bartender says, 'Where'd you get the pig?' Woman says, 'This is not a pig, it's a duck.' Bartender says, 'I was talking to the duck.'

(21) A couple from Seattle were talking about their holiday to their friend. 'Sounds as if you had a great time in California,' said the friend, 'but I didn't know you were planning to take in Florida as well.'
'We weren't,' said the wife, 'but Ted simply will not ask for directions.'

(22) A senior citizen is driving on the highway. His wife calls him on his cell phone and in a worried voice says, 'Herman, be careful! I just heard on the radio that there was a madman driving the wrong way on Route 280'. Herman says, 'Not just one, there are hundreds!'

(23) A man jumped into a taxi and said, 'The main railway station, please.' 'OK,' said the driver, 'What time is the train?' 'No train,' said the passenger, 'I'm meeting a friend in the bar there.'

(24) THE TYPISTS' REPRODUCTION EQUIPMENT IS NOT TO BE INTERFERED WITH WITHOUT THE PRIOR PERMISSION OF THE MANAGER.

(25) John F—, the celebrated singer, was in a motor-car accident last week. We are happy to state that he was able to appear the following evening in four pieces.

(26) BRITISH FLY TO DISCUSS PROBLEM PIPELINE

(27) A concert pianist traveled to Africa in a bid to prove that music had the power to soothe the savage beast. He set up his grand piano in a small clearing beside a river, and began to play. One by one, animals appeared and soon he was surrounded by lions, giraffes, antelopes, warthogs, and leopards, all sitting peacefully together swaying and tapping their feet. The pianist had just started to play a second piece when a crocodile splashed out of the river, grabbed the man with its jaws, and dragged him into the water. An agitated lion ran over to the water's edge. 'Why in heaven's name did you do that?' he asked. The crocodile cupped a foot to the back of its head and said, 'Eh?'

(28) Why did the cookie cry?
Because its mother had been a wafer so long.

(29) How does an elephant hide in a cherry tree?
By painting its toenails red.

(30) Why did the elephant sit on the marshmallow?
Because he didn't want to fall into the hot chocolate.

(31) 'Well, I see you have a new dog. I thought you didn't like dogs.'
'Well, I don't, but my wife bought a lot of dog soap on sale, so we had to get a dog to use it up.'

(32) 'Well, I see you have a new dog. I thought you didn't like dogs.'
'Well, I don't, but my wife insisted on getting it.'

(33) 'Well, I see you have a new dog.'
'Well, my wife bought a lot of dog soap on sale, so we had to get a dog to use it up.'

(34) The police pull over an old lady in a car. She has a passenger, an old man whose face is frozen in a rictus of fear. The policeman says, 'Madam, I just pulled you off the motorway for driving at 25 miles an hour. Why were you driving so slowly?' 'I wasn't,' says the old lady. 'I was doing what the sign told me. It said the "M25", so I drove at 25 miles per hour.' 'That's not how it works, madam,' says the policeman. 'Couldn't your friend have told you that?' He looks at the old man, who's not moved a muscle since they stopped. 'Is he all right?' asks the policeman. 'I'm not sure,' says the old lady. 'He's been like that since we got on the A150.'

(35) Floats like a butterfly, stings like one.

(36) With the collapse of vaudeville, new talent has no place to stink.

(37) The neighborhood borrower approached Mr Smith on Sunday afternoon and inquired: 'Say Smith, are you using your lawnmower this afternoon?'
'Yes, I am,' Smith replied warily.
The neighborhood borrower then answered: 'Fine, then you won't be needing your golf clubs. I'll just borrow them.'

(38) A woman had just stepped out of the shower when the doorbell went.
'Who is it?' she called through the intercom.
'Blind man,' came the reply.
She was stark naked but figured that it didn't really matter too much for a blind man, so she released the lock and called out: 'Come on up.'
Not bothering to cover herself with a towel, she greeted him at the top of the stairs. He said: 'Now where do you want these blinds?'

(39) What do you get when you cross a choice with a meal?
A pick-nic.

(40) What do you get when you cross a zero with a drink?
A nought chocolate.

(41) What hides in the garden shed and trembles?
A nervous rake.

(42) What knots do undertakers use?
Wreath knots.

(43) In the 1830s, the artist J. M. W. Turner of the English romantic school painted many views of Margate, but his depictions of unnaturally vivid skies has led art critics to suggest that he might have been colour-blind.

Living in London, Turner used to arrive here by steamboat from Greenwich, or as he called it, Redwich.

(44) What do you call an inspired pattern?
A divine design.

(45) What is the difference between an arctic hand shovel and a hot assistant?
One is an icy spade, the other is a spicy aide.

(46) A man suffered for months with chronic back pain and was eventually persuaded by his doctor to go and see a chiropractor. But he didn't have much faith in such people and was convinced they wouldn't be able to help him. Yet after a few minutes' treatment, his back felt like new.
'How do you feel about chiropractors now?' asked the doctor.
The man said: 'I stand corrected.'

(47) A group of friends have just left the cinema after watching a film about the French king, Louis XIV. They are heading for a local bar, known as 'Sammy Cahn's'. 'Aha!' remarks one of them, 'After Louis Quatorze, Sammy Quinze!'

(48) I never take exercise on a day of the week with a 'd' in its name.

(49) Whenever the literary German dives into a sentence, that is the last you are going to see of him till he emerges on the other side of his Atlantic with his verb in his mouth.

(50) What do you call a pigeon enjoying winter sports in the Scottish mountains?
A ski-in' doo.

(51) Once there was a little boy in church. He had to go to the bathroom so he told his mother, 'Mommy, I have to piss.' The mother said, 'Son, don't say "piss" in church. Next time you have to piss, say, "whisper" because it is more polite.' The next Sunday, the little boy was sitting next to his father this time, and once again, he had to go to the bathroom. He told his father, 'Daddy, I have to whisper.' The father said, 'OK. Here, whisper in my ear.'

(52) A woman goes to the doctor. He examines her and tells her she has a strained groin. 'How frequently do you have sex?' asks the doctor. 'Five times every week,' says the woman.'On Monday, Tuesday, Wednesday, Friday and Sunday.' 'I would suggest,' says the doctor, 'that you cut that

down a little and perhaps leave out the Tuesday session.' 'I can't do that,' says the woman, 'that's the only night my husband's home.'

(53) I believe that sex is a beautiful thing between two people. Between five it's fantastic.

(54) A woman was in bed with her husband's best friend when the phone rang. After hanging up, she turned to her lover and said: 'That was Jim, but don't worry, he won't be home for a while. He's playing cards with you.'

(55) Serenissimus was making a tour through his provinces and noticed a man in the crowd who bore a striking resemblance to his own exalted person. He beckoned to him and asked 'Was your mother at one time in service at the Palace?' – 'No, your Highness,' was the reply, 'but my father was.'

(56) What's the difference between an elephant and a post box?
(I don't know.)
I wouldn't send you to post a letter.

(57) Two goldfish were in their tank.
One turns to the other and says, 'You man the guns, I'll drive.'

(58) Nobby's little boy keeps begging him for an ice cream. In the end Nobby gives in and hands the little lad a Magnum. 'I'll show you how to take the safety catch off,' he tells him, 'then you can use it to hold-up an ice-cream van.'

(59) Woman are always using me to advance their careers. Damned anthropologists.

(60) The chef flew into a rage at his new assistant. 'Didn't I tell you to notice when the soup boiled over?' he yelled. 'I did,' said the assistant. 'It was half past eleven.'

(61) What do you give an elephant with diarrhoea?
Plenty of room.

(62) After a long day on the course, an exasperated golfer turned to his caddie and said: 'You must be the worst caddie in the world.'
'I don't think so,' replied the caddie. 'That would be too much of a coincidence.'

(63) What kind of tree is nauseated? A sick-amore.

Appendix B

Terminology

The framework presented in this book is still not highly developed, and we will therefore not attempt to specify its constructs in full mathematical detail. Instead, this glossary lists some of the abbreviations and technical terms used in the main chapters, with definitions in English which are relatively precise. This should serve both as a reference guide to terminology and a clarification of the meaning of some of the technicalities we have introduced.

This appendix does not include terms which are used only in the immediate vicinity of where they are introduced or which are standard terms from disciplines such as linguistics. The head words/phrases in entries are marked to indicate whether they are peculiar to this text: '(∗)' indicates a specialised term introduced within this book; '(†)' indicates a term of wider currency to which we have assigned a slightly specialised meaning; and '(‡)' shows that the term originates wholly outside this text. Terms in THIS FONT indicate entries elsewhere in the glossary.

accessibility prediction(∗) A form of PREDICTION in which items of knowledge (in the BELIEF BASE of the AUDIENCE) have varying levels of SALIENCE, with the result that different outcomes result in varying degrees of COGNITIVE EFFORT, owing to the differing accessibility of necessary knowledge. (Section 5.1).

accommodation(†) The process whereby some PROPOSITION(S) which have not been mentioned explicitly are added by default to a BELIEF BASE in order to SUPPORT some stated or inferred information, when there is no good reason not to adopt these assumptions. (Section 4.6).

anomaly(∗) A state of affairs in which there is a SITUATION S in a VIEWPOINT V_1, such that there is a viewpoint V_2, and S (or the COUNTERPART of S in V_2) has no SUPPORT in V_2. If $V1 = V2$, this is a 'definite anomaly'. If V_2 DOMINATES V_1, then if there is support in $V1$ for S, this is a 'relative anomaly', otherwise it is an 'apparent anomaly'. (Section 4.5).

assimilation difficulty(∗) This describes one of the circumstances where the AUDIENCE becomes AWARE of the need for COGNITIVE EFFORT in order to absorb the most recently encountered segment of text. If the content of the most recent segment of text cannot be immediately integrated into the current interpretation, but can be absorbed with additional COGNITIVE EFFORT without further information from the input text, this is an 'assimilation difficulty'. See also TEMPORARY GAP, UNEXPLAINED GAP. (Section 4.7).

audience(†) The idealised individual recipient of a text, particularly a joke, whose internal cognitive and emotional states and processes provide the resources for the comprehension of the text. (Section 3.1).

audience inference(*) Cognitive processing undertaken by the AUDIENCE in order to make sense of input during text comprehension, going beyond syntactic parsing or simple compositional semantics, and including reasoning of various forms. (Section 4.4).

aware(†) During text comprehension, many data items and processes are involved without the audience being conscious of this involvement. When the audience does take notice of data (typically some SITUATION) or some process (see COGNITIVE EFFORT), the entity in question is said to have reached the 'aware' level, and the audience is 'aware' of it. The contrary term is 'unaware'. (Section 4.7).

backgrounded incongruity(‡) A term used by proponents of the GTVH for an INCONGRUITY which is not resolved, but must be accepted in order for the joke to make sense. If it could be easily removed from the narrative while preserving the essential characteristics of the joke, then this is known as 'completely backgrounded incongruity'. (Section 7.8).

belief base(*) The collection of CONCEPTUAL ITEMS, including both PROPOSITIONS and RULES, which form the knowledge content of a VIEWPOINT. (Section 4.4).

broad brush theory(*) A theoretical account, usually at an early stage of development, which is stated in imprecise, informal terms, and, even if potentially accurate, lacks detail. (Section 2.1).

BVT(‡) Benign Violation Theory. A general theory of humour put forward by McGraw, Warren, and collaborators. (Sections 3.3, 7.11 and 10.8).

characterisation(†) An account of some phenomenon is a 'characterisation' if it puts forward hypotheses which make non-trivial predictions about how the phenomenon will or will not occur (but does not offer an EXPLANATION in terms of wider independently accepted principles). See also DESCRIPTION. (Section 2.3).

cognitive effort(‡) Mental work expended by the AUDIENCE during comprehension; mainly of interest where it is at a particularly high level, especially when it reaches the AWARE level. (Section 4.7).

comprehension history(*) An abstract representation of what the AUDIENCE experiences during joke comprehension, containing: the ordered sequence of all COMPREHENSION STATES through which the comprehension process has passed; the amount of COGNITIVE EFFORT expended in passing between consecutive states; the time expended in passing between consecutive states. (Section 4.9).

comprehension state(*) An abstract representation of a state of knowledge (including all VIEWPOINTS) which the AUDIENCE experiences during joke comprehension. (Section 4.9).

conceptual item(*) A basic building block of the knowledge and beliefs of the AUDIENCE, consisting of any type of concept, including PROPOSITIONS and RULES. (Section 4.4).

considered assessment study(*) A type of investigation of surprise in which participants are asked to rate hypothetical scenarios for how surprising they are. (Section 8.2).

contextual pun(*) A PUN in which the punning text is delivered in a specific setting (social, cultural, etc.), and relies crucially on aspects of that context in order to achieve its effect. (Section 9.3).

contrasting outcome model of surprise(*) A theoretical account of surprise compatible with SPECIFIED OUTCOME PREDICTION. (Section 8.2).

counterpart(†) By virtue of the way that INHERITANCE operates between VIEWPOINTS, one viewpoint may initially be a replica of another, containing the same conceptual material. This implicitly sets up a correspondence between each CONCEPTUAL ITEM in the originating viewpoint and an item in the lower viewpoint. These are treated as separate entities, but each one is a 'counterpart' of the other. (Section 4.3).

Cratylistic(‡) A description of the mechanisms of punning, in which the relationship between sound and meaning (of a word or phrase) is treated as non-arbitrary. (Section 9.3).

data abstraction(‡) A technique in computer science in which a process, program or set of facilities is described abstractly in terms of what it provides to the surrounding environment, with no statement of how this is achieved within the process or program. (Section 2.3).

defeasible(‡) An inference which is 'defeasible' may be overridden by other information, and so has only a tentative or provisional status. (Section 4.5).

deflation(†) When there are two COMPREHENSION STATES, S_1 and S_2, such that S_2 is later than S_1, some CONCEPTUAL ITEM X has an attribute A which has values v_1 in S_1, v_2 in S_2 for some WORTH SCALE E, and $v_2 < v_1$, then X is said to have suffered a 'deflation', or been deflated. (Section 11.9).

description(†) An account of some phenomenon is a 'description' if it documents, at some level of detail and abstraction, the theoretically important features of the phenomenon, without purporting to give a CHARACTERISATION of the phenomenon or an EXPLANATION in terms of wider principles. (Section 2.1).

directly mention(*) A text is said to 'directly mention' a concept C if C appears in the LITERAL MEANING of the text. See also INDIRECTLY MENTION. (Section 4.2).

disbelief-suspension(†) (i) The mechanism by which the AUDIENCE may assess the plausibility of the content of a story, particularly material which has to be added to the STORYWORLD to achieve coherence. (ii) The rating that this mechanism assigns to an item, indicating its degree of implausibility. (Section 4.6).

discrepant(∗) The INTERNAL LOGIC of a VIEWPOINT is 'discrepant' if it differs from the logic of a dominating viewpoint. (Section 4.5).

dominate(‡) The VIEWPOINTS associated with the comprehension of a text are arranged in a hierarchical (tree-shaped) structure, and V_1 is said to 'dominate' V_2 if there is a path from V_1 to V_2 in this graph. (Section 4.3).

encounter(∗) An AUDIENCE may meet a joke in a number of different ways, which we can categorise as types of 'encounter'. Of these, the 'Natural' case is what is usually considered when analysing jokes. (Section 3.4).

enhancer(‡) An 'enhancer' is some aspect of the COMPREHENSION HISTORY which is not central to the core amusement effect in a joke, but which increases the strength of this effect (FUNNINESS) for the AUDIENCE, by influencing JOKE APPRECIATION. (Section 3.5).

explanation(‡) An account of some phenomenon is an 'explanation' if shows how the details of the phenomenon follow from wider independently accepted principles, for example from another field of enquiry. See also DESCRIPTION, CHARACTERISATION. (Section 2.3).

fanciful(∗) When AUDIENCE INFERENCE devises CONCEPTUAL ITEMS to add to the INTERNAL LOGIC of a VIEWPOINT in order to construct a coherent interpretation of a text, these items are 'fanciful' to the extent that they require some degree of DISBELIEF-SUSPENSION. (Section 6.6).

Fictional insult(∗) One of the attributes of the comprehension of a joke which could be relevant to an analysis based on some form of SUPERIORITY. It is defined in terms of DEFLATION. (Section 11.3).

final revelation(∗) A 'final revelation' is any PROPOSITION which is at AWARE level for the AUDIENCE in the FINAL STATE, but is at the unaware level at the POST-TEXT STAGE. (Section 5.4).

final stage(∗) There are various stages during joke comprehension, with the 'final stage' occurring after the completion of all AUDIENCE INFERENCE necessary to the comprehension of the text as a joke. (Section 3.1).

final state(∗) The state of the AUDIENCE's knowledge at the FINAL STAGE of comprehension. (Section 4.9).

forced reinterpretation(∗) A joke arrangement in which AUDIENCE INFERENCE at or after the POST-TEXT STAGE results in some aspects of the original (POST-SET-UP STAGE) interpretation of the SET-UP having to be revised, at an AWARE level, in order to achieve coherent comprehension. Abbreviated FR. (Section 7.6).

FR(∗) Abbreviation for FORCED REINTERPRETATION.

funniness(†) An informal term for the degree of amusement felt about a joke. The assessment of 'funniness' is what the process of JOKE APPRECIATION addresses.

GTVH(‡) The General Theory of Verbal Humour. (Section 7.7).

impropriety(†) A general term referring to any concepts which are deemed offensive (known as 'improper'). 'Discourse impropriety' is where there is a MENTION in the text of some improper concept: if an improper concept is DIRECTLY MENTIONED, this is 'blatant discourse impropriety'; if an improper concept is INDIRECTLY MENTIONED, this is 'oblique discourse impropriety'. If a concept which is UNMENTIONABLE WITH LEVITY is mentioned in a joking context, this is 'levity impropriety'. 'Linguistic impropriety' is where certain words, phrases, or constructions which are deemed to be socio-culturally unacceptable are used in the text. (Section 10.5).

incongruity(‡) A term widely used in theorising about jokes, with the rough meaning of 'oddity' or 'inconsistency'. Several distinct usages occur in the literature. See also RESOLUTION. (Chapter 7).

indirectly mention(*) A text is said to 'indirectly mention' a concept *C* if *C* does not appear in the LITERAL MEANING of the text, but appears in content inferred from the text. See also DIRECTLY MENTION. (Section 4.2).

inheritance(‡) The process whereby information (elements of the BELIEF BASE) in one VIEWPOINT is automatically treated as also appearing in a subordinate viewpoint. (Section 4.3).

initial stage(*) This is the stage of joke comprehension when no text has yet been encountered. (Section 3.1).

instant reaction study(*) A type of investigation of surprise in which participants react involuntarily to stimuli which are directly presented. (Section 8.2).

insult(‡) See FICTIONAL INSULT, REAL-WORLD INSULT.

integrative model of surprise(*) A theoretical account of surprise compatible with ACCESSIBILITY PREDICTION. (Section 8.3).

internal logic(*) The system of knowledge structuring within the BELIEF BASE of a VIEWPOINT, including rules of consequence. (Section 4.4).

joke appreciation(†) The process by which a joke yields amusement to the AUDIENCE, to some degree. It can occur only if JOKE RECOGNITION also occurs. (Section 3.4).

joke detection(*) The process by which the audience determines that a joke-telling is taking place. It must be distinguished from JOKE RECOGNITION. (Section 3.4).

joke recognition(†) The process by which the audience understands a text and as a result concludes that the text is genuinely a joke. It must be distinguished from JOKE DETECTION and from JOKE APPRECIATION. (Section 3.4).

joke world(*) The STORYWORLD of a joke text. (Section 4.3).

jokehood(†) An informal term for the status of a text as either a joke or not a joke. A decision about 'jokehood' is what the process of JOKE RECOGNITION addresses.

justification question(∗) A question perceived by the AUDIENCE when AUDIENCE INFERENCE results in a SITUATION which is not SUPPORTED within some VIEWPOINT. (Section 4.5).

knowledge conditions(∗) These are conditions which are imposed upon interpretations at various stages of comprehension and which might be used to specify when a text is comprehended as a joke. (Section 12.2).

literal meaning(‡) The semantic content of a piece of text, prior to any expansion using inference or contextual effects. (Section 4.2).

logical mechanism(‡) A technical term within the GTVH, abbreviated LM. Sometimes known as a 'pseudo-logical mechanism (pLM)'. Closely related to RESOLUTION. (Chapter 6).

mention(†) If a text segment *T* either DIRECTLY MENTIONS or INDIRECTLY MENTIONS some CONCEPTUAL ITEM *C*, then *T* is said to 'mention' *C*. (Section 4.2).

non-temporal surprise(∗) A form of surprise not crucially based on the time sequence of events. (Section 8.3).

normality(‡) An informal notion which seems to underlie various intuitive judgements about the usual way that a world operates. (Section 4.5).

post-set-up stage(∗) This is the stage of joke comprehension when the SET-UP has been completely absorbed, including inferences, but the PUNCH LINE has not yet been processed. (Section 3.1).

post-text stage(∗) This is the stage of joke comprehension which is located immediately after the LITERAL MEANING has been determined for the last segment of the text (which in a joke would usually be the PUNCH LINE), but before inferences have been made from that meaning. (Section 3.1).

prediction(‡) In general, this refers to the anticipation of the occurrence of an event at some stage in the future. In the context of the process of text comprehension, it is taken to denote predictions about events that might occur within that process, as opposed to the 'events' within the STORYWORLD that might appear as part of the narrative. (Section 4.5).

probabilistic prediction(∗) A form of prediction in which all possible outcomes are assigned some level of probability. (Section 5.1).

probability-change model of surprise(∗) A theoretical account of surprise compatible with PROBABILISTIC PREDICTION. (Section 8.3).

process conditions(∗) These are conditions which are imposed upon the way that the text is processed and which might be used to specify when a text is comprehended as a joke. (Section 12.2).

proposition(‡) A CONCEPTUAL ITEM which, intuitively, represents a statement which can be true or false. (Section 4.4).

pun(‡) A widely used term, with various shades of meaning. In this book, taken to mean certain classes of joke which rely on similarity of sound (or spelling) between words or phrases. It can be seen as the humorous subset of WORD PLAY. (Section 9.3).

punch line(‡) The final part of a joke, which creates the humorous effect. See also SET-UP. (Section 2.2).

Real-world insult(∗) One of the attributes of the comprehension of a joke which could be relevant to an analysis based on some form of SUPERIORITY. It happens to an entity E in the AUDIENCE's real-world VIEWPOINT when there is, in some VIEWPOINT, a FICTIONAL INSULT which applies to a fictional entity E' which has E as a COUNTERPART. (Section 11.3).

recoverable(‡) In a PUN, there is usually some textual item which is not explicitly part of the actual text, but bears a relationship to part of the text in a way that is central to the punning effect. It must be possible for the AUDIENCE to work out what this textual item is, i.e. to 'recover' it. (Section 9.3).

register(‡) The style or tone of language, usually indicative of some social or cultural aspects of the writer/speaker, or of the particular context in which the text is delivered. (Section 9.5).

relevance question(∗) A question perceived by the AUDIENCE when a SITUATION S is conveyed by the text relatively directly but the AUDIENCE is not immediately AWARE of any PROPOSITIONS related to the current interpretation of the text which use S as SUPPORT. (Section 4.5).

resolution(‡) A term widely used in theorising about jokes, with the rough meaning of 'making sense' or 'reducing incongruity'. Often regarded as having two subtypes: 'full' resolution (the INCONGRUITY is eliminated, resulting in complete sense), and 'partial' resolution (the incongruity is reduced but not eliminated). (Chapter 7).

reversal theory(‡) A theory developed by Apter and colleagues which includes an account of joke comprehension which is in some ways similar to FORCED REINTERPRETATION. (Sections 3.3, 7.6 and 11.6).

rule(†) (i) An element of the BELIEF BASE of a VIEWPOINT, which defines how PROPOSITIONS are related to each other via some form of consequence; (ii) an operation which can have various effects on linguistic structures, including combining items or defining the validity of a structure; (iii) informally, a usage covering both senses (i) and (ii).

salience(†) A property that any element of a BELIEF BASE has, indicating its level of prominence to the AUDIENCE or to any joke-character. (Section 4.7).

script(‡) A complex knowledge structure embodying what is known about some familiar event or set of circumstances. Prominent versions are due to Schank and Abelson and to Raskin, the latter as part of the SSTH. (Section 4.5).

self-contained pun(∗) A PUN in which the text contains all the necessary contextual material, so that the pun can act as a canned joke, able to be told in a variety of settings. (Section 9.3).

Self-improvement(∗) A variety of superiority that may be felt by an AUDIENCE who feels that he/she would now be rated higher on an WORTH SCALE than at some previous time. (Section 11.3).

set-up(‡) The initial part of a joke, which prepares the way for the PUNCH LINE. (Section 2.2).

situation(∗) A set of PROPOSITIONS within a BELIEF BASE. Usually, these will be linked in some way, so that the set represents some intuitively coherent abstract object, a 'situation' in the informal, everyday sense. (Section 4.4).

social standard(∗) An element of a BELIEF BASE which assigns ratings to other CONCEPTUAL ITEMS, representing social attitudes towards the rated elements. (Section 10.3).

specified outcome prediction(∗) A PREDICTION in which some relatively narrow set of outcomes is treated as being much more likely than all other possible outcomes. (Section 5.1).

SSTH(‡) The Semantic Script Theory of Humour. (Section 7.7).

stage(†) The process of joke comprehension goes through various 'stages' as the text is processed. Of these, there are certain significant points which it is useful to refer to. See also INITIAL STAGE, POST-SET-UP STAGE, POST-TEXT STAGE. (Section 8.2).

startle response/reaction(‡) An involuntary reaction to a sudden intense stimulus such as a loud noise. (Section 8.2).

storyworld(‡) An abstract representation of some set of objects and relations embodying an alternative reality to, though sometimes very similar to, the real world. Similar to a 'mental model'. (Section 4.3).

superiority(‡) An informal term used to describe a feeling experienced by the AUDIENCE or the joke teller, used as the basis for various proposals regarding humour mechanisms. (Chapter 11).

support(†) The 'support' in a VIEWPOINT for a PROPOSITION (or SITUATION) is a set of RULES and PROPOSITIONS in the same VIEWPOINT which, taken together, lead to that PROPOSITION. (Section 4.5).

supported(†) An PROPOSITION or SITUATION *S* for which AUDIENCE INFERENCE has found SUPPORT in the VIEWPOINT containing *S* is said to be 'supported'; otherwise, *S* is 'unsupported'. (Section 4.5).

surprise, cognitive (‡) 'Cognitive surprise' is the second, slower, stage of reacting to an unexpected stimulus. (Section 8.2).

surprise, emotional (‡) 'Emotional surprise' is the third stage of reacting to an unexpected stimulus. (Section 8.2).

surprise, incidental(∗) 'Incidental surprise' is any surprise which occurs during joke comprehension but which makes no contribution to the humorous effect at the conclusion of a joke. (Section 8.3).

surprise, visceral(‡) 'Visceral surprise' is the first, instantaneous stage of reacting to an unexpected stimulus. (Section 8.2).

Teller-benefit(*) One of the attributes of the comprehension of a joke which could be relevant to an analysis based on some form of SUPERIORITY, in which the aim of the telling of a joke may be to provide amusement more to the teller than to the AUDIENCE. (Section 11.9).

temporary gap(*) This describes one of the circumstances where the AUDIENCE becomes AWARE of the need for COGNITIVE EFFORT in order to absorb the most recently encountered segment of text. If the information in question can be integrated into the audience's knowledge after further information has been supplied by the input text, this is a 'temporary gap'. See also ASSIMILATION DIFFICULTY, UNEXPLAINED GAP. (Section 4.7).

unexplained gap(*) This describes one of the circumstances where the AUDIENCE becomes AWARE of the need for COGNITIVE EFFORT in order to absorb the most recently encountered segment of text. If the content in question cannot be integrated into the audience's knowledge even after the information in the complete text has been supplied, this is an 'unexplained gap'. See also ASSIMILATION DIFFICULTY, TEMPORARY GAP. (Section 4.7).

unmentionable directly/indirectly(†) There may be SOCIAL STANDARDS which deprecate the MENTION of certain concepts: a concept which should not be directly mentioned is 'unmentionable directly'; a concept which should not be mentioned even indirectly is 'unmentionable indirectly'. (Section 10.6).

unmentionable with levity(†) This applies to a concept which should not be MENTIONED (either directly or indirectly) in a joking or light-hearted context. (Section 10.6).

viewpoint(†) A knowledge structure containing a BELIEF BASE, and (usually) associated with a STORYWORLD or with some real or fictional character. Viewpoints are linked into a hierarchical structure, so that a viewpoint may have a superordinate viewpoint and possibly subordinate viewpoints. (Section 4.3).

word play(‡) Taken to mean any device within a text which relies on similarity of sound or spelling, between words or phrases. Unlike a PUN, it is not necessarily humorous in intent or in effect. (Section 9.3).

worth scale(*) A form of rating which represents some form of social or cultural status, so that low values correspond to deprecated or inferior ranking, high values are more esteemed. (Section 11.9).

References

Adler, J. E. (2008). Surprise. *Educational Theory, 58*(2), 149–173.

Alonso, P. (2014). The role of cognitive coherence in non-expert processes of literary discourse reception. *Journal of Literary Semantics, 43*(1), 1–23.

Altmann, G. T. M., & Mirković, J. (2009). Incrementality and prediction in human sentence processing. *Cognitive Science, 33*, 583–609.

Apter, M. J. (1982). *The experience of motivation: The theory of psychological reversals*. London: Academic Press.

Apter, M. J. (1989). *Reversal theory: Motivation, emotion and personality*. London: Routledge.

Apter, M. J., & Desselles, M. (2012). Disclosure humor and distortion humor: A reversal theory analysis. *Humor: International Journal of Humor Research, 25*(4), 417–435.

Aristotle. (1920). *On the art of poetry* (I. Bywater, Trans.). Oxford: Clarendon Press.

Attardo, S. (1994). *Linguistic theories of humour*. Berlin: Mouton de Gruyter.

Attardo, S. (1997). The semantic foundations of cognitive theories of humor. *Humor: International Journal of Humor Research, 4*(10), 395–420.

Attardo, S. (2001). *Humorous texts: A semantic and pragmatic analysis*. Berlin: Mouton de Gruyter.

Attardo, S. (Ed.). (2014a). *Encyclopedia of humor studies*. Los Angeles, CA: Sage.

Attardo, S. (2014b). Incongruity and resolution. In S. Attardo (Ed.), *Encyclopedia of humor studies* (pp. 383–384). Los Angeles, CA: Sage.

Attardo, S. (2017). The general theory of verbal humor. In S. Attardo (Ed.), *The Routledge handbook of language and humor* [VitalSource Bookshelf version]. London: Routledge.

Attardo, S., Hempelmann, C., & Di Maio, S. (2002). Script oppositions and logical mechanisms: modeling incongruities and their resolutions. *Humor: International Journal of Humor Research, 15*(1), 3–46.

Attardo, S., & Raskin, V. (1991). Script theory revis(it)ed: Joke similarity and joke representation model. *Humor: International Journal of Humor Research, 4*(3), 293–347.

Baader, F., Calvanese, D., McGuinness, D. L., Nardi, D., & Patel-Schneider, P. F. (Eds.). (2003). *The description logic handbook: Theory, implementation and applications*. Cambridge, UK: Cambridge University Press.

Bailey, P. (1999a). A reader-based model of story generation; or "stories: they're not what you expected". In K. Binsted & G. Ritchie (Eds.), *Proceeedings of the AISB'99 symposium on creative language: Humour & stories* (pp. 36–45). Society for the Study of Artificial Intelligence and Simulation of Behaviour.

Bailey, P. (1999b). Searching for storiness: Story-generation from a reader's perspective. In M. Mateas & P. Sengers (Eds.), *AAAI 1999 fall symposium on narrative intelligence*. Palo Alto, CA: AAAI Press.

Baldi, P. F., & Itti, L. (2010). Of bits and wows: A Bayesian theory of surprise with applications to attention. *Neural Networks, 23*(5), 649–666.

Ballim, A., & Wilks, Y. (1991). *Artificial believers: The ascription of belief.* Hillsdale, NJ: Lawrence Erlbaum.

Beattie, J. (1776). An essay on laughter, and ludicrous composition. In *Essays.* Edinburgh: William Creech.

Berger, A. A. (1998). *An anatomy of humor.* Brunswick, NJ: Transaction Publishers. (First published 1993)

Bever, T. G. (1970). The cognitive basis for linguistic structures. In J. R. Hayes (Ed.), *Cognition and the development of language* (pp. 279–362). New York, NY: John Wiley.

Binsted, K. (1996). *Machine humour: An implemented model of puns* (Unpublished doctoral dissertation). University of Edinburgh, Edinburgh, UK.

Binsted, K., & Ritchie, G. (2001). Towards a model of story puns. *Humor: International Journal of Humor Research, 14*(3), 275–292.

Black, J. B., & Bern, H. (1981). Causal coherence and memory for events in narrative. *Journal of Verbal Learning and Verbal Behaviour, 20*, 267–275.

Black, J. B., Turner, T. J., & Bower, G. H. (1979). Point of view in narrative comprehension, memory and production. *Journal of Verbal Learning and Verbal Behaviour, 18*, 187–198.

Branigan, H. P., Pickering, M. J., McLean, J. F., & Cleland, A. A. (2007). Syntactic alignment and participant role in dialogue. *Cognition, 104*, 163–197.

Brône, G., & Feyaerts, K. (2004). Assessing the SSTH and GTVH: A view from cognitive linguistics. *Humor: International Journal of Humor Research, 17*(4), 361–372.

Brownell, H. H., Michel, D., Powelson, J., & Gardner, H. (1983). Surprise but not coherence: sensitivity to verbal humor in right-hemisphere patients. *Brain and Language, 18*, 20–27.

Carey, P. W., Mehler, J., & Bever, T. G. (1970). When do we compute all the interpretations of an ambiguous sentence? In G. B. Flores d'Arcais & W. J. Levelt (Eds.), *Advances in psycholinguistics* (pp. 61–75). Amsterdam: North-Holland.

Carston, R. (2012). Metaphor and the literal/non-literal distinction. In K. Allan & K. M. Jaszczolt (Eds.), *Cambridge handbook of pragmatics* (pp. 469–492). Cambridge, UK: Cambridge University Press.

Chapman, A. J., & Foot, H. C. (Eds.). (1977). *It's a funny thing, humour.* Oxford: Pergamon Press.

Charniak, E., & McDermott, D. (1985). *Introduction to artificial intelligence.* Reading, MA: Addison-Wesley.

Cherry, C. (1970). *On human communication.* Cambridge, MA: MIT Press. (First published 1957)

Chiaro, D. (1992). *The language of jokes.* London: Routledge.

Cohen, T. (1999). *Jokes: philosophical thoughts on joking matters.* London: University of Chicago Press.

Collins, A. M., & Loftus, E. F. (1975). A spreading-activation theory of semantic processing. *Psychological Review, 82*(6), 407–428.

Coulson, S., & Matlock, T. (2003). Cognitive science. In J. Verschueren, J.-O. Östman, J. Blommaert, & C. Bulcaen (Eds.), *Handbook of pragmatics online* (Vol. 9). John Benjamins. (https://benjamins.com/online/hop/articles/cog5, accessed 11 September 2017)

Critchley, S. (2002). *On humour.* London: Routledge.

Darwin, C. (1872). *The expression of the emotions in man and animals.* London: John Murray.

Davies, C. (1990). *Ethnic humour around the world*. Bloomington, IN: Indiana University Press.

Davies, C. (2004). Victor Raskin on jokes. *Humor: International Journal of Humor Research*, *17*(4), 373–380.

Davies, C. (2010). Translating English into English in jokes and humour. In D. Chiaro (Ed.), *Translation, humour and literature* (Vol. 1, pp. 49–73). London: Continuum.

Demberg, V., & Keller, F. (2008). Data from eye-tracking corpora as evidence for theories of syntactic processing complexity. *Cognition*, *109*, 193–210.

Dibell, A. (1995). Plot. In *How to write a million*. London: Robinson Publications.

Dynel, M. (2012). Garden paths, red lights and crossroads: On finding our way to understanding the cognitive mechanisms underlying jokes. *Israeli Journal of Humor Research*, *1*(1), 6–28.

Eco, U. (1984). The frames of comic 'freedom'. In T. A. Sebeok & M. E. Erickson (Eds.), *Carnival!* (pp. 1–9). Berlin: Mouton.

Ekman, P., Friesen, W. V., & Simons, R. C. (1985). Is the startle reaction an emotion? *Journal of Personality and Social Psychology*, *49*(5), 1416–1426.

Emmott, C. (1997). *Narrative comprehension: A discourse perspective*. Oxford: Oxford University Press.

Encyclopædia Britannica. (2017). Taboo. www.britannica.com/topic/taboo-sociology, accessed 18 September 2017.

Engell, J., & Bate, W. (Eds.). (1983). *Biographia literaria II* (Vol. 7). London: Routledge & Kegan Paul.

Fann, K. T. (1970). *Peirce's theory of abduction*. The Hague, The Netherlands: Martinus Nijhoff.

Fauconnier, G. (1994). *Mental spaces: Aspects of meaning construction in natural language*. Cambridge, UK: Cambridge University Press.

Fetzer, A. (2012). Textual coherence as a pragmatic phenomenon. In K. Allan & K. M. Jaszczolt (Eds.), *Cambridge handbook of pragmatics* (pp. 447–467). Cambridge, UK: Cambridge University Press.

Forabosco, G. (1992). Cognitive aspects of the humor process: the concept of incongruity. *Humor: International Journal of Humor Research*, *5*(1/2), 45–68.

Forster, E. M. (1927). *Aspects of the novel*. London: Edward Arnold.

Foss, D. J., & Hakes, D. T. (1978). *Psycholinguistics: An introduction to the psychology of language*. Englewood Cliffs, NJ: Prentice-Hall.

Foster, M. I., Keane, M., Loewenstein, J , Maguire, P., Maguire, R., May, R. W., ... Ranney, M. A. (2014). Triangulating surprise: Expectations, uncertainty, and making sense. In P. Bello, M. Guarini, M. McShane, & B. Scassellati (Eds.), *Proceedings of the 36th annual conference of the cognitive science society* (pp. 70–71). Austin, TX.

Foster, M. I., & Keane, M. T. (2015). Why some surprises are more surprising than others: Surprise as a metacognitive sense of explanatory difficulty. *Cognitive Psychology*, *81*, 74–116.

Frazer, J. G. (1922). *The golden bough: a study of magic and religion* (Abridged ed.). New York, NY: Macmillan. (First edition, unabridged, 1890)

Freud, S. (1916). *Wit and its relation to the unconscious* (A. A. Brill, Trans.). London: Fisher Unwin.

Freud, S. (1940). *Der witz und seine beziehung zum unbewussten*. London: Imago Publishing. (Original work published 1905)

Freud, S. (1966). *Jokes and their relation to the unconscious* (J. Strachey, Trans.). London: Routledge & Kegan Paul. (Original work published 1912)
Freud, S. (2012). *Totem and taboo* (A. A. Brill, Trans.). [epub]. Retrieved from www.gutenberg.org/ebooks/41214, 18 September 2017. (Original work published 1919)
Gärdenfors, P. (1988). *Knowledge in flux: Modeling the dynamics of epistemic states*. Cambridge, MA: MIT Press.
Garrett, M. F. (1970). Does ambiguity complicate the perception of sentences? In G. B. Flores d'Arcais & W. J. Levelt (Eds.), *Advances in psycholinguistics* (pp. 48–60). Amsterdam: North-Holland.
Garrod, S., & Pickering, M. J. (2004). Why is conversation so easy? *TRENDS in Cognitive Science*, *8*(1), 8–11.
Gavins, J. (2007). *Text world theory: An introduction*. Edinburgh: Edinburgh University Press.
Gazdar, G., Klein, E., Pullum, G., & Sag, I. (1985). *Generalized phrase structure grammar*. Oxford: Blackwell.
Gazdar, G., & Mellish, C. (1989). *Natural language processing in Prolog*. Wokingham: Addison-Wesley.
Genette, G. (1988). *Narrative discourse revisited* (J. E. Lewin, Trans.). Ithaca, NY: Cornell University Press.
Grice, H. P. (1975). Logic and conversation. In P. Cole & J. Morgan (Eds.), *Syntax and semantics* (Vol. 3, pp. 41–58). New York, NY: Academic Press.
Grice, H. P. (1978). Further notes on logic and conversation. In P. Cole (Ed.), *Syntax and semantics* (Vol. 9, pp. 113–127). New York, NY: Academic Press.
Grice, H. P. (1981). Presupposition and conversational implicature. In P. Cole (Ed.), *Radical pragmatics* (pp. 183–197). New York, NY: Academic Press.
Grosz, B. J., Joshi, A. K., & Weinstein, S. (1995). Centering: A framework for modeling the local coherence of discourse. *Computational Linguistics*, *21*(2), 203–225.
Gruner, C. (1978). *Understanding laughter: the workings of wit and humor*. Chicago, IL: Nelson-Hall.
Gruner, C. (1997). *The game of humor: a comprehensive theory of why we laugh*. New Brunswick, NJ: Transaction Publishers.
Hartshorne, C., & Weiss, P. (Eds.). (1935). *Collected papers of Charles Sanders Peirce* (Vol. VI). Cambridge, MA: Harvard University Press.
Haskins, M., & Arnott, S. (Eds.). (2017). *3000 jokes, 2997 laughs*. London: Portico.
Hayes, P. J. (1979). The logic of frames. In D. Metzing (Ed.), *Frame conceptions and text understanding* (pp. 46–61). Berlin: Walter de Gruyter.
Heintz, J. (1979). Reference and inference in fiction. *Poetics*, *8*, 85–99.
Hempelmann, C. F. (2003). *Paronomasic puns: Target recoverability towards automatic generation* (Unpublished doctoral dissertation). Purdue University, West Lafayette, IN.
Hempelmann, C. F. (2004). Script opposition and logical mechanism in punning. *Humor: International Journal of Humor Research*, *17*(4), 381–392.
Hempelmann, C. F. (2014). Reception of humor. In S. Attardo (Ed.), *Encyclopedia of humor studies* (pp. 629–630). Los Angeles, CA: Sage.
Hempelmann, C. F., & Attardo, S. (2011). Resolutions and their incongruities: further thoughts on logical mechanisms. *Humor: International Journal of Humor Research*, *24*(2), 125–149.
Hempelmann, C. F., & Ruch, W. (2005). 3WD meets GTVH: Breaking the ground for interdisciplinary research. *Humor: International Journal of Humor Research*, *18*(4), 353–387.

Herman, D. (2009). Cognitive narratology. In P. Hühn, J. Pier, W. Schmid, & J. Schönert (Eds.), *Handbook of narratology* (pp. 30–43). Berlin: Walter de Gruyter.

Hirst, G. (1981). *Anaphora in natural language understanding*. Berlin: Springer-Verlag.

Hobbes, T. (1840). Human nature. In W. Molesworth (Ed.), *The English works of Thomas Hobbes of Malmesbury* (Vol. IV). London: John Bohn. (Original work published 1650)

Hobbs, J., Stickel, M., Appelt, D., & Martin, P. (1993). Interpretation as abduction. *Artificial Intelligence, 63*, 69–142.

Hornby, N. (2010). *Juliet, Naked*. London: Penguin Books.

Howell, R. (1979). Fictional objects: How they are and how they aren't. *Poetics, 8*, 129–177.

Hurley, M. M., Dennett, D. C., & Adams, R. B. (2011). *Inside jokes: Using humor to reverse-engineer the mind*. Cambridge, MA: MIT Press.

Hutcheson, F. (1987). Excerpt from "Reflections Upon Laughter". In J. Morreall (Ed.), *The philosophy of laughter and humor* (pp. 26–40). Albany, NY: SUNY Press. (Original work published 1750)

Itti, L., & Baldi, P. F. (2009). Bayesian surprise attracts human attention. *Vision Research, 49*(10), 1295–1306.

Jackendoff, R. (1987). *Consciousness and the computational mind*. Cambridge, MA: MIT Press.

Jeffrey, R. C. (2004). *Subjective probability: The real thing*. Cambridge, UK: Cambridge University Press.

Johnson-Laird, P. N. (1983). *Mental models*. Cambridge, UK: Cambridge University Press.

Jurafsky, D. (1996). A probabilistic model of lexical and syntactic access and disambiguation. *Cognitive Science, 20*, 137–194.

Jurafsky, D., & Martin, J. H. (2000). *Speech and language processing: an introduction to natural language processing, computational linguistics and speech recognition*. New Jersey: Prentice-Hall.

Kahneman, D. (2012). *Thinking, fast and slow*. London: Penguin.

Kahneman, D., & Miller, D. T. (1986). Norm theory: Comparing reality to its alternatives. *Psychological Review, 93*(2), 136–153.

Karttunen, L. (1973). Presuppositions of compound sentences. *Linguistic Inquiry, 4*(2), 169–193.

Katz, B. (1993). A neural resolution of the incongruity and incongruity-resolution theories of humour. *Connection Science, 5*, 59–75.

Katz, B. (1996). A neural invariant of humour. In J. Hulstijn & A. Nijholt (Eds.), *Proceedings of the international workshop on computational humor* (pp. 103–109). Enschede, Netherlands.

Katz, J., & Langendoen, T. (1976). Pragmatics and presupposition. *Language, 52*(1), 1–17.

Keith-Spiegel, P. (1972). Early conceptions of humor: Varieties and issues. In J. H. Goldstein & P. E. McGhee (Eds.), *The psychology of humor* (pp. 3–39). New York, NY: Academic Press.

Koestler, A. (1970). *The act of creation*. London: Pan Books.

Konolige, K. (1986). *A deduction model of belief*. Los Altos, CA: Morgan Kaufmann.

Krikmann, A., & Laineste, L. (Eds.). (2009). *Permitted laughter: Socialist, post-socialist and never-socialist humour*. Tartu: ELM Scholarly Press.

Kuipers, G. (2002). Media culture and internet disaster jokes: bin Laden and the attack on the World Trade Center. *European Journal of Cultural Studies, 5*(4), 450–470.

Kuipers, G. (2005). "Where was King Kong when we needed him?" public discourse, digital disaster jokes, and the functions of laughter after 9/11. *Journal of American Culture, 28*(1), 70–84.

Kuipers, G. (2006). *Good humor, bad taste*. Berlin: Mouton de Gruyter.

Kuperberg, G. R., & Jaeger, T. F. (2016). What do we mean by prediction in language comprehension? *Language, Cognition and Neuroscience*, *31*(1), 32–59.

Lang, P. J., Bradley, M. M., & Cuthbert, B. N. (1990). Emotion, attention, and the startle reflex. *Psychological Review*, *97*(3), 377–395.

Latta, R. L. (1999). *The basic humor process: A cognitive-shift theory and the case against incongruity*. Berlin: Mouton de Gruyter.

Legman, G. (1972). *The rationale of the dirty joke*. St Albans: Panther Books Limited.

Leslie, A. M. (1987). Pretense and representation: The origins of "theory of mind". *Psychological Review*, *94*(4), 412–426.

Levinson, S. (1983). *Pragmatics*. Cambridge, UK: Cambridge University Press.

Levy, R. (2008). Expectation-based syntactic comprehension. *Cognition*, *106*, 1126–1177.

Lewis, D. (1973). *Counterfactuals*. Oxford: Blackwell.

Lewis, D. (1978). Truth in fiction. *American Philosophical Quarterly*, *15*(1), 37–46.

Lewis, D. (1979). Scorekeeping in a language game. *Journal of Philosophical Logic*, *8*(1), 339–359.

Li, A. (2005). *Wallace & Gromit Curse of the Were-Rabbit Monstrously Scary Joke Book*. London: Puffin.

Linzen, T., & Jaeger, F. (2014). Investigating the role of entropy in sentence processing. In T. O'Donnell & V. Demberg (Eds.), *Proceedings of the fifth workshop on cognitive modeling and computational linguistics* (pp. 10–18). Association for Computational Linguistics.

Lupker, S. J. (1984). Semantic priming without association: A second look. *Journal of Verbal Learning and Verbal Behavior*, *23*, 709–733.

Maguire, P., & Maguire, R. (2009). Investigating the difference between surprise and probability judgments. In N. Taatgen & H. van Rijn (Eds.), *Proceedings of the 31st annual meeting of the cognitive science society* (pp. 2359–2364).

Maguire, P., Maguire, R., & Keane, M. T. (2011). Making sense of surprise: An investigation of the factors influencing surprise judgments. *Journal of Experimental Psychology: Learning, Memory, and Cognition*, *37*(1), 176–186.

Makins, M. (Ed.). (1994). *Collins English dictionary* (3rd ed.). Glasgow: HarperCollins.

Maldonado, M., Chemla, E., & Spector, B. (2017). Priming plural ambiguities. *Journal of Memory and Language*, *95*, 89–101.

Manurung, R., Ritchie, G., Pain, H., Waller, A., O'Mara, D., & Black, R. (2008). The construction of a pun generator for language skills development. *Applied Artificial Intelligence*, *22*(9), 841–869.

Marsh, M. (2014). Practical jokes. In S. Attardo (Ed.), *Encyclopedia of humor studies* (Vol. 2, pp. 592–594). Los Angeles, CA: Sage.

Marsh, M. (2015). *Practically joking*. Logan, UT: Utah State University Press.

Martin, R. A. (2007). *The psychology of humor: an integrative approach*. London: Elsevier Academic Press.

Martin, R. A., & Fearman, R. (2016). *Association between punchline predictability, comprehension speed, and joke funniness: An investigation of incongruity theories.* Presentation at the ISHS Conference, Dublin, Ireland.

Mayerhofer, B., & Schacht, A. (2013). Salience, accessibility and humorous potential in the comprehension of garden path jokes: A probabilistic approach. In M. Dynel (Ed.), *Developments in linguistic humour theory* (pp. 341–366). Amsterdam: John Benjamins.

McGhee, P. E. (1972). On the cognitive origins of incongruity humor: Fantasy assimilation versus reality assimilation. In J. H. Goldstein & P. E. McGhee (Eds.), *The psychology of humor* (pp. 61–80). New York, NY: Academic Press.

McGhee, P. E., Ruch, W., & Hehl, F.-J. (1990). A personality-based model of humor development during adulthood. *Humor: International Journal of Humor Research, 3*(2), 119–146.

McGraw, A. P., & Warren, C. (2010). Benign violations: Making immoral behavior funny. *Psychological Science, 21*(8), 1141–1149.

McKee, R. (1999). *Story: substance, structure, style and the principles of screenwriting*. London: Methuen.

McNerney, M. W., Goodwin, K. A., & Radvansky, G. A. (2011). A novel study: A situation model analysis of reading times. *Discourse Processes, 48*, 453–474.

Mellish, C. (1985). *Computer interpretation of natural language descriptions*. Chichester: Ellis Horwood.

Meyer, D. E., & Schvaneveldt, R. W. (1971). Facilitation in recognizing pairs of words: evidence of a dependence between retrieval operations. *Journal of Experimental Psychology, 90*(2), 227–234.

Miczo, N. (2014). Analyzing structure and function in humor: Preliminary sketch of a message-centered model. *Humor: International Journal of Humor Research, 27*(3), 461–480.

Minsky, M. (1975). A framework for representing knowledge. In P. H. Winston (Ed.), *The Psychology of Computer Vision* (pp. 211–277). New York, NY: McGraw-Hill.

Morreall, J. (1983). *Taking laughter seriously*. Albany, NY: SUNY Press.

Morreall, J. (Ed.). (1987). *The philosophy of laughter and humor*. Albany, NY: SUNY Press.

Morreall, J. (2009). *Comic relief : A comprehensive philosophy of humor*. Hoboken, NJ: Wiley-Blackwell.

Nieuwland, M. S., & Berkum, J. J. A. V. (2008). The neurocognition of referential ambiguity in language comprehension. *Language and Linguistics Compass, 2*(4), 603–630.

Nilsson, N. J. (1986). Probabilistic logic. *Artificial Intelligence, 28*, 71–87.

Oring, E. (1992a). Appropriate incongruity. In *Jokes and their relations* (pp. 1–15). Lexington, KY: University Press of Kentucky.

Oring, E. (1992b). Between jokes and tales. In *Jokes and their relations* (pp. 81–93). Lexington, KY: University Press of Kentucky.

Oring, E. (1992c). Jokes and the discourse on disaster. In *Jokes and their relations* (pp. 29–40). Lexington, KY: University Press of Kentucky.

Oring, E. (1992d). *Jokes and their relations*. Lexington, KY: University Press of Kentucky.

Oring, E. (2003a). Appropriate incongruity redux. In *Engaging humour* (pp. 1–12). Urbana, IL: University of Illinois Press.

Oring, E. (2003b). *Engaging humour*. Urbana, IL: University of Illinois Press.

Oring, E. (2003c). The senses of absurd humour. In *Engaging humour* (pp. 13–26). Urbana, IL: University of Illinois Press.

Oring, E. (2011). Still further thoughts on logical mechanisms: A response to Christian F. Hempelmann and Salvatore Attardo. *Humor: International Journal of Humor Research, 24*(2), 151–158.

Orwell, G. (1950). *1984*. New York, NY: Signet Classics.

O'Shannon, D. (2012). *What are you laughing at? a comprehensive guide to the comedic event*. London: Continuum.

Parsons, D. (Ed.). (1969). *Funny amusing and funny amazing*. London: Pan Books.

Parsons, D. (Ed.). (1971). *Funny convulsing and funny confusing*. London: Pan Books.

Partington, A. (2006). *The linguistics of laughter: A corpus-assisted study of laughter-talk*. Abingdon: Routledge.

Poesio, M. (2000). Semantic analysis. In R. Dale, H. Moisl, & H. Somers (Eds.), *Handbook of natural language processing* (pp. 93–122). New York, NY: Marcel Dekker.

Pollio, H. R., & Mers, R. W. (1974). Predictability and the appreciation of comedy. *Bulletin of the Psychonomic Society, 4*(4A), 229–232.

Popescu, C. (2011). Understanding ethnic humour in Romanian jokes. In M. Dynel (Ed.), *The pragmatics of humour across discourse domains* (pp. 173–190). Amsterdam: John Benjamins.

Premack, D., & Woodruff, G. (1978). Does the chimpanzee have a theory of mind? *The Behavioral and Brain Sciences, 4*, 515–526.

Quillian, M. R. (1968). Semantic memory. In M. Minsky (Ed.), *Semantic information processing* (pp. 227–270). Cambridge, MA: MIT Press.

Rapp, A. (1951). *The origins of wit and humor*. New York, NY: Dutton.

Raskin, V. (1985). *Semantic mechanisms of humor*. Dordrecht: Reidel.

Raskin, V. (1998). From the editor. *Humor: International Journal of Humor Research, 11*(1), 1–4.

Raskin, V. (Ed.). (2008). *The primer of humor research*. Berlin: Mouton de Gruyter.

Raskin, V. (2017). Script-based semantic and ontological semantic theories of humor. In S. Attardo (Ed.), *The Routledge handbook of language and humor* [VitalSource Bookshelf version]. London: Routledge.

Raskin, V., & Attardo, S. (1994). Non-literalness and non-bona-fide in language: Approaches to formal and computational treatments of humor. *Pragmatics and Cognition, 2*(1), 31–69.

Raskin, V., Hempelmann, C. F., & Taylor, J. M. (2009). The evolution of the SSTH into the GTVH and now into the OSTH. *Journal of Literary Theory, 3*(2), 285–312.

Reder, L. M. (1983). What kind of pitcher can a catcher fill? effects of priming in sentence comprehension. *Journal of Verbal Learning and Verbal Behavior, 22*, 189–202.

Reisenzein, R., Bördgen, S., Holtbernd, T., & Matz, D. (2006). Evidence for strong dissociation between emotion and facial displays: The case of surprise. *Journal of Personality and Social Psychology, 91*(2), 295–315.

Reiter, R. (1978). On reasoning by default. In *Theoretical issues in natural language processing 2* (pp. 210–218). University of Illinois at Urbana-Champaign.

Reiter, R. (1980). A logic for default reasoning. *Artificial Intelligence, 13*(1–2), 81–132.

Rescher, N. (2005). *Epistemic logic: a survey of the logic of knowledge*. Pittsburgh, PA: University of Pittsburgh Press.

Ritchie, G. (1983). Semantics in parsing. In M. King (Ed.), *Parsing natural language* (pp. 199–217). North Holland: Academic Press.

Ritchie, G. (1999). Developing the incongruity-resolution theory. In *Proceedings of the AISB symposium on creative language: Stories and humour* (pp. 78–85). Edinburgh, UK.

Ritchie, G. (2000). Describing verbally expressed humour. In *Proceedings of the AISB symposium on creative and cultural aspects and applications of AI and cognitive science* (pp. 71–78). Birmingham, UK.

Ritchie, G. (2002). The structure of forced reinterpretation jokes. In O. Stock, C. Strapparava, & A. Nijholt (Eds.), *Proceedings of the April Fools' Day workshop on computational humor* (pp. 47–56). Enschede, Netherlands.

Ritchie, G. (2004). *The linguistic analysis of jokes*. London: Routledge.

Ritchie, G. (2006). Reinterpretation and viewpoints. *Humor: International Journal of Humor Research, 19*(3), 251–270.

Ritchie, G. (2009). Variants of incongruity resolution. *Journal of Literary Theory, 3*(2), 313–332.

Ritchie, G. (2010). Linguistic factors in humour. In D. Chiaro (Ed.), *Translation, humour and literature* (Vol. 1, pp. 33–48). London: Continuum.

Ritchie, G. (2014). Logic and reasoning in jokes. *European Journal of Humour Research, 2*(1), 50–60.

Ritchie, G., Russell, G., Black, A., & Pulman, S. (1992). *Computational morphology*. Cambridge, MA: MIT Press.

Rivera, J., Talone, A. B., Boesser, C. T., Jentsch, F., & Yeh, M. (2014). Startle and surprise on the flight deck: Similarities, differences, and prevalence. *Proceedings of the Human Factors and Ergonomics Society 58th Annual Meeting, 58*(1), 1047–1051.

Roberts, C. (2015). Accommodation in a language game. In B. Loewer & J. Schaffer (Eds.), *A companion to David Lewis* (chap. 22). Chichester: John Wiley.

Rosch, E. (1973). On the internal structure of perceptual and semantic categories. In T. E. Moore (Ed.), *Cognitive development and the acquisition of language* (pp. 111–144). New York, NY: Academic Press.

Rosch, E., & Mervis, C. (1975). Family resemblances: Studies in the internal structure of categories. *Cognitive Psychology*, 7, 573–605.

Rothbart, M. K. (1977). Psychological approaches to the study of humour. In A. J. Chapman & H. C. Foot (Eds.), *It's a funny thing, humour* (pp. 87–94). Oxford: Pergamon Press.

Rothbart, M. K., & Pien, D. (1977). Elephants and marshmallows: A theoretical synthesis of incongruity-resolution and arousal theories of humour. In A. J. Chapman & H. C. Foot (Eds.), *It's a funny thing, humour* (pp. 37–40). Oxford: Pergamon Press.

Ruch, W. (1992). Assessment of appreciation of humor: Studies with the 3WD humor test. In C. D. Spielberger & J. N. Butcher (Eds.), *Advances in personality assessment* (Vol. 9, chap. 2). Hillsdale, NJ: Lawrence Erlbaum.

Ruch, W., Hofmann, J., & Platt, T. (2015). Individual differences in gelotophobia and responses to laughter-eliciting emotions. *Personality and Individual Differences, 72*, 117–121.

Ryan, M.-L. (1980). Fiction, non-factuals, and the principle of minimal departure. *Poetics, 9*(4), 403–422.

Samson, A. C., & Hempelmann, C. F. (2011). Humor with backgrounded incongruity: Does more required suspension of disbelief affect humor perception? *Humor: International Journal of Humor Research, 24*(2), 167–185.

Samson, A. C., Hempelmann, C. F., Huber, O., & Zysset, S. (2009). Neural substrates of incongruity-resolution and nonsense humour. *Neuropsychologia, 47*, 1023–1033.

Sanford, A. J., & Emmott, C. (2012). *Mind, brain and narrative*. Cambridge, UK: Cambridge University Press.

Schank, R. C., & Abelson, R. P. (1977). *Scripts, plans, goals and understanding*. Hillsdale, NJ: Lawrence Erlbaum.

Schopenhauer, A. (1964). *The World as Will and Idea*. London: Trübner. (Original work published 1883)

Schroeder, S., Richter, T., & Hoever, I. (2008). Getting a picture that is both accurate and stable: Situation models and epistemic validation. *Journal of Memory and Language, 59*, 237–255.

Shafer, G., & Pearl, J. (Eds.). (1990). *Readings in uncertain reasoning*. San Francisco, CA: Morgan Kaufman.

Shultz, T. R. (1996). A Cognitive-Developmental Analysis of Humour. In A. J. Chapman & H. C. Foot (Eds.), *Humour and laughter : Theory, research and applications* (2nd ed., pp. 11–36). New York, NY: Transaction. (First published 1976 by John Wiley)

Sidner, C. L. (1981). Focusing for interpretation of pronouns. *American Journal of Computational Linguistics*, 7(4), 217–231.

Singer, M., & Ferreira, F. (1983). Inferring consequences in story comprehension. *Journal of Verbal Learning and Verbal Behavior, 22*, 437–448.

Smith, M. (2009). Humor, unlaughter, and boundary maintenance. *Journal of American Folklore, 122*(484), 148–171.

Sperber, D., & Wilson, D. (1986). *Relevance: communication and cognition*. Oxford: Blackwell.

Stalnaker, R. (1973). Presuppositions. *Journal of Philosophical Logic, 2*, 447–457.

Steir-Livny, L. (2016). Is it OK to laugh about it yet? *Hitler Rants* YouTube parodies in Hebrew. *European Journal of Humour Research, 4*(4), 105–121.

Strain, M. (2014). Aggressive and harmless humor. In S. Attardo (Ed.), *Encyclopedia of humor studies* (Vol. 1, pp. 15–18). Los Angeles, CA: Sage.

Suls, J. M. (1972). A two-stage model for the appreciation of jokes and cartoons: an information-processing analysis. In J. H. Goldstein & P. E. McGhee (Eds.), *The psychology of humor* (pp. 81–100). New York, NY: Academic Press.

Suls, J. M. (1983). Cognitive processes in humor appreciation. In P. E. McGhee & J. H. Goldstein (Eds.), *Handbook of humor research* (pp. 39–57). New York, NY: Springer-Verlag.

Swinney, D. A., & Hakes, D. T. (1976). Effects of prior context upon lexical access during sentence comprehension. *Journal of Verbal Learning and Verbal Behavior, 15*, 681–689.

Taylor, J. M., Klinov, P., & Mazlack, L. J. (2007). A description logic based approach to computational humour. In D. Popa & S. Attardo (Eds.), *New approaches to the linguistics of humour* (pp. 167–179). Galaţi, Romania: Editura Academica.

Teigen, K. H., & Keren, G. (2003). Surprises: low probabilities or high contrasts? *Cognition, 87*, 55–71.

Thorndyke, P. W. (1976). The role of inferences in discourse comprehension. *Journal of Verbal Learning and Verbal Behavior, 15*, 437–446.

Tibballs, G. (Ed.). (2000). *The mammoth book of jokes*. London: Constable & Robinson.

Toplyn, J. (2014). *Comedy writing for late-night TV*. New York, NY: Twenty Lane Media.

Triezenberg, K. (2004). Humor enhancers in the study of humorous literature. *Humor: International Journal of Humor Research, 17*(4), 411–418.

Tsakona, V. (2013). Okras and the metapragmatic stereotypes of humour: Towards an expansion of the GTVH. In M. Dynel (Ed.), *Developments in linguistic humour theory* (pp. 25–48). Amsterdam: John Benjamins.

Turner, R. (1984). *Logics for artificial intelligence*. Chichester: Ellis Horwood.

Twain, M. (2006). *A Connecticut Yankee in King Arthur's court*. [epub]. Retrieved from www.gutenberg.org/ebooks/86, 9 August 2017. (Original work published 1889)

Vaid, J., Hull, R., Heredia, R., Gerkens, D., & Martinez, F. (2003). Getting a joke: the time course of meaning activation in verbal humour. *Journal of Pragmatics, 35*, 1431–1449.

van der Sandt, R. (1988). *Context and presupposition*. London: Croom Helm.

van der Sandt, R. (2012). Presupposition and accommodation in discourse. In K. Allan & K. M. Jaszczolt (Eds.), *Cambridge handbook of pragmatics* (pp. 329–350). Cambridge, UK: Cambridge University Press.

Veale, T. (2004). Incongruity in humor: Root cause or epiphenomenon. *Humor: International Journal of Humor Research*, *17*(4), 419–428.

Veatch, T. (1998). A theory of humour. *Humor: International Journal of Humor Research*, *11*(2), 161–215.

Venour, C. (2013). *A computational model of lexical incongruity in humorous text* (Unpublished doctoral dissertation). University of Aberdeen, Aberdeen, UK.

Venour, C., Ritchie, G., & Mellish, C. (2011). Dimensions of incongruity in register humour. In M. Dynel (Ed.), *The pragmatics of humour across discourse domains* (pp. 125–144). Amsterdam: John Benjamins.

Ventis, L. (2015). Thinking fast and slow in the experience of humor. *Humor: International Journal of Humor Research*, *28*(3), 351–373.

Walton, K. L. (1978). Fearing fictions. *The Journal of Philosophy*, *LXXV*(1), 5–27.

Warren, C., & McGraw, A. P. (2016). Differentiating what is humorous from what is not. *Journal of Personality and Social Psychology*, *110*(3), 407–430.

Werth, P. (1999). *Text worlds: Representing conceptual space in discourse*. Harlow: Longman.

Wilson, C. P. (1979). *Jokes: Form, Content, Use and Function*. London: Academic Press.

Wyer, R. S., & Collins, J. E. (1992). A theory of humor elicitation. *Psychological Review*, *99*(4), 663–688.

Xiang, M., & Kuperberg, G. (2015). Reversing expectations during discourse comprehension. *Language, Cognition and Neuroscience*, *30*(6), 648–672.

Young, A. W., Rowland, D., Calder, A. J., Etcoff, N. L., Seth, A., & Perrett, D. I. (1997). Facial expression megamix: Tests of dimensional and category accounts of emotion recognition. *Cognition*, *63*, 271–313.

Zadeh, L. (1975a). The concept of a linguistic variable and its application to approximate reasoning I. *Information Sciences*, *8*, 199–249.

Zadeh, L. (1975b). The concept of a linguistic variable and its application to approximate reasoning II. *Information Sciences*, *8*, 301–357.

Zadeh, L. (1975c). The concept of a linguistic variable and its application to approximate reasoning III. *Information Sciences*, *9*, 43–80.

Ziv, A. (1984). *Personality and sense of humor*. New York, NY: Springer.

Zwaan, R. A., Langston, M. C., & Graesser, A. C. (1995, September). The construction of situation models in narrative comprehension: An event-indexing model. *Psychological Science*, *6*(5), 292–297.

Zwaan, R. A., & Radvansky, G. A. (1998). Situation models in language comprehension and memory. *Psychological Bulletin*, *123*(2), 162–185.

Index

MIX

Papier | Fördert gute Waldnutzung

FSC® C083411

Kolibri 360 GmbH
Ferdinand-Jühlke-Straße 7
99095 Erfurt, Deutschland
produktsicherheit@kolibri360.de